POLICING THE FRONTIER

A volume in the series
Police/Worlds: Studies in Security, Crime, and Governance
Edited by Kevin Karpiak, Sameena Mulla, William Garriott, and Ilana Feldman

A list of titles in this series is available at
cornellpress.cornell.edu

POLICING THE FRONTIER

An Ethnography of Two
Worlds in Niger

Mirco Göpfert

CORNELL UNIVERSITY PRESS   **ITHACA AND LONDON**

First published 2020 by Cornell University Press

Library of Congress Cataloging-in-Publication Data

Names: Göpfert, Mirco, 1984– author.
Title: Policing the frontier : an ethnography of two worlds in Niger / Mirco Göpfert.
Description: Ithaca : Cornell University Press, 2020. | Series: Police/worlds : studies in security, crime, and governance | Includes bibliographical references and index.
Identifiers: LCCN 2019026056 (print) | LCCN 2019026057 (ebook) | ISBN 9781501747212 (cloth) | ISBN 9781501747229 (paperback) | ISBN 9781501747236 (pdf) | ISBN 9781501747243 (ebook)
Subjects: LCSH: Police, Rural—Niger. | Ethnology—Niger. | Niger—Rural conditions.
Classification: LCC HV8276.7.A2 G66 2020 (print) | LCC HV8276.7.A2 (ebook) | DDC 363.2/3096626091734—dc23
LC record available at https://lccn.loc.gov/2019026056
LC ebook record available at https://lccn.loc.gov/2019026057

To Julia

Contents

Acknowledgments

What a beautiful memory, thinking of all those friends and colleagues who helped me in one way or the other over the past ten years that eventually led to this book. What a terrible job, impossible task, trying to thank them all. I will mention just two by name.

Carola Lentz, my teacher.
Jan Beek, my friend and "sergeant."

The rest, I think you know who you are and how much you mean to me. Thank you.

Then there are all the gendarmes whom I have given names that are not theirs and whom I have placed into a town that does not exist. I cannot mention your names but you too know who you are. I am immensely grateful to you and still humbled by the trust you put in me.

I am also grateful to Jim Lance, Kevin Karpiak, Sameena Mulla, William Garriott, Ilana Feldman, and two anonymous referees. You not only made this book real, you also helped me improve it. Lisa Schrimpf and Pauline Bugler were enormously helpful in preparing the manuscript on its final stages.

The research that led to this book was supported by the German Academic Scholarship Foundation (*Studienstiftung*), the German Research Foundation (DFG), the Volkswagen Foundation, the Centre de recherches Sociologiques sur le Droit et les Institutions Pénales (Cesdip), the Institute for Advanced Study Konstanz and, importantly, the Laboratoire d'Etudes et de Recherche sur les Dynamiques Sociales et le Développement Local (Lasdel) in Niamey.

Parts of chapter 5 were previously published in 2016 as "Surveillance in Niger: Gendarmes and the Problem of 'Seeing Things,'" *African Studies Review* 59 (2): 39–57. Parts of chapter 6 were previously published in 2013 as "Bureaucratic Aesthetics: Report Writing in the Nigerien Gendarmerie," *American Ethnologist* 40 (2): 324–34. Parts of chapter 8 were previously published in 2016 as "Repairing the Law: The Search for Justice in the Nigerien Gendarmerie," *Theoretical Criminology* 20 (4): 446–61.

POLICING THE FRONTIER

Part I
INTRODUCTION

INTRODUCTION

A HANDFUL OF GENDARMES, TWO WORLDS, AND THE FRONTIER BETWEEN

You could see it from quite a distance, standing on a small hill beside the prefect's residence and within eyeshot of the courthouse and prison, just outside a small town in Niger. Its two buildings, both of which had been built by a colonial police force under French command, stood there braving time and the sun with its peeling paint. The one on the left served as the brigade commander's accommodation, the one on the right as offices, cells, and a storeroom. Between them lay a courtyard that was at times gapingly empty, at times packed with complainants and suspects, and it was separated from the bush behind the brigade by only a mud wall and two small stables, one of which was used as a chicken coop and the other as a shelter for firewood and canisters with gas from nearby Nigeria. In the corner of the courtyard, right next to the office door and under a thatched roof that was held up with a makeshift construction of tree trunks and branches, stood a couple of plastic chairs, four wooden benches and what looked like an old living room table. This was where the gendarmes spent most of their working days. Sitting on the benches, sipping tea, chatting about all and nothing, looking past the little open-air mosque and over the parking space in front of the brigade, they could easily spot the civilians slowly walking or driving up the hill toward the brigade. Apart from sitting over their worn-out Scrabble board for hours on end, the gendarmes had acquired the habit of playing a cynical guessing game about what stories these civilians were going to tell them: a brawl between herders and farmers? Theft of sheep? Fraud? Rape? Slander? As the civilians came closer, they laid their long sticks, swords or daggers beside the tree some fifteen meters in front of the brigade. Men took off their turbans, slackened their pace, took off their shoes, and then stopped a couple of meters in front of the gendarmes and greeted them timidly with "As-salamu alaykum." The gendarmes interrupted their conversation, replied respectfully, "Wa alaykum as-salam," and then generally continued their discussion. The complainants either stood there and waited or sat down on a mat away from the gendarmes, next to the stables, where other complainants, suspects, witnesses, and detainees were sitting or lying in the shade, waiting for their turn.

One of the gendarmes working there, and probably the best Scrabble player in the unit, was Amadou. He was in his early thirties and few years older than me. Seven years before I first met him in 2010, he had chosen a stable income and family over academic ambition. After two years of economic studies, he applied for recruitment into the gendarmerie, allowing him to get married, cater for his soon to-be-born child, and make sure his wife could continue her studies in sociology. After recruitment, including eighteen months of training, and the usual two years in public order units, Amadou had been posted to regional headquarters as a clerk due to his education. This was now his first posting to a brigade, the gendarmerie's street-level units tasked primarily with criminal investigations. He liked working in the brigade, being in touch with people and helping them. But one day he was deeply troubled. Late one evening, after a rough workday when Amadou was on night duty, there were just the two of us sitting on one of the wooden benches over a glass of tea and he told me: "Those our bosses in their air-conditioned offices, first they want us to make ourselves familiar with the people, to get to know them, understand them, their problems and all that. And it's true, if you're here for some time, you do get to know them." He paused. "And then they tell us to whack them! To enforce the law in all its rigor!"[1] He paused again. "Build up trust and then betray it!" Amadou shook his head, took a sip of his tea, and left me wondering.

Two days later, after dinner and over a cigarette under a bright night sky in front of his house, Amadou said that he had been thinking about what he had told me earlier and that he wanted to add something to it. As a gendarme you had only two things to work with, he said: *les textes* and *le social*. And to do your job well meant to know when to focus on the one and on the other, that is, when to work by the book and when to make a "detour," as he called it, an *arrangement*. Now his job as a young gendarme was to learn how to do that without getting into trouble, he said, all the while being caught between different and often conflicting expectations from the public, the prosecutors, and their superiors. The way to do it was by watching closely his senior colleagues, particularly Adjudant-Chef Souley.

Adjudant-Chef Souley was the only one who spent more time in the office than in the courtyard—drinking less tea and more time working, as he'd call it.

He was the head of the brigade in Godiya, the *commandant de brigade*. He was
in his early fifties, had been a gendarme for more than thirty years, had worked
in nine different units, once as a commander, twice as deputy commander, and
he had spent more than a year in foxholes on the frontlines during the 1990s so-
called Tuareg rebellion and one year abroad as part of the Nigerien contingent
to the United Nation's blue helmets in Côte d'Ivoire. He was what the younger
gendarmes respectfully called *un ancient*.

In Amadou's eyes, Adjudant-Chef Souley was a good example, an all but perfect gendarme: the way he talked to civilians, both complainants and suspects;
the respect he showed for the local village population; how he connected with
superior officers, the prosecutor, and traditional authorities; the way he settled
disputes, but also by the rigor he showed and his lack of empathy when investigating crimes and enforcing the law. The key skill Amadou admired in him was
knowing how to work with les textes and le social. All of this had to be done in an
area that had barely been penetrated by state institutions, where Adjudant-Chef
Souley and his twenty-something gendarmes were responsible for a population
of about 350,000 in an area larger than Switzerland. He was confronted with a
local population he hardly knew, all the while was supposed to hold the moral
high ground against people he and his colleagues often called "savages."

That was not what I had expected when I started the research for this book: a
critical reflexivity about the contradictions of police work, a heightened aware-
ness of the intricacies of bureaucracy, a profound skepticism about the grasp of
the state, and all of this on the part of people whom earlier I might have described
merely as the long and thorny repressive arm of a disciplinary apparatus of dehu-
manizing governance.

Thus, this book is a about police work, bureaucracy, and the frontier between
forms and lives. On one level, the book explores what it means to be a gendarme
investigating cases, writing reports, and settling disputes in a rural community in
Niger. Unlike other approaches to police work and bureaucracy, this book does
not focus on policing as a mode of governance from the outset, and certainly not
as a means of enforcing an unequal social order in the name of public security
and bureaucratic government. Rather, it examines policing primarily as *work*,
notably bureaucratic work.

Beyond that, this book is an exploration into bureaucracy at large. Egon
Bittner, one of the first and most relevant scholars of policing, argues that police
officers actually do enforce criminal law "with the frequency located somewhere
between virtually never and very rarely" (1974, 23). This was also true for the
gendarmes in Niger. But sometimes they did enforce the law. The question the
gendarmes faced was when to do the one or the other. According to Amadou,
this was a matter of bearing and dealing with the irresolvable tension between les

textes and le social: the world of fact, files, and purity on the one hand, and the chaotic and messy outside world of human predicaments on the other. This book is an investigation into this very tension, and I will argue that it lies not only at the heart of the Nigerien gendarmes' daily work, but of bureaucracy in general.

Ultimately, this raises a number of questions about "the state," this host of public bureaucracy, spun up between forms to be filled and lives to be lived. Most scholars of public bureaucracies, many of them along the lines set out by Akhil Gupta in his classic article *Blurred Boundaries* (1995), imply that there is a more or less clear division between state and society—a symbolic boundary. In this book, I suggest, as the gendarmes have taught me, that the state does not have such a dividing line at its outer fringes; fringe is all there is. The state is enacted—and only becomes tangible—in the form of a frontier. In its concrete and territorial sense and according to Gus Deveneaux, the frontier "represents a meeting point, and area of interaction between different and sometimes conflicting concrete realities and philosophies" (1978, 68). As I use it here, the frontier represents a space where diverse worlds collide and merge at the same time—les textes and le social, forms and lives, but also the known and the unknown, the right and the wrong, the general and the particular: in short, differing normative orders and systems of meaning. In rural Niger, a former French colony and mostly desert West African country that is consistently placed at the bottom of the UN Human Development Index, where the penetration by state institutions is still rather weak, this frontier is perhaps more pronounced, more tangible than in cities in Europe and North America. It may be more visible, which gives us all the more reason to take the gendarmes in Niger seriously; but its essence is the same. The late-modern bureaucratic state is not something that has boundaries; it is the moment where the known meets the unknown, the right meets the wrong, and abstract bureaucratic norms and forms meet the messy concreteness of practical reality. It means looking at one side of the coin while feeling the other with the palm of your hand. This kind of frontier moment is probably nothing short of the gendarmes' and all other state agents' daily existential, if not ontological conundrum.

Nigerien Gendarmes Talking Back

This book is a story about a handful of gendarmes in a single post in a small town in Niger, about what happened and how in the offices, and under the thatched roof in a single brigade's courtyard; but there is far more to it.

For one, it contributes to the study of policing and what Thomas Bierschenk and Jean-Pierre Olivier de Sardan (2014) coined "states at work" in contemporary Africa. The Nigerien gendarmerie's unique characteristics notwithstanding, it shares many features with other police and gendarmerie forces in Africa: their colonial and postcolonial experiences; the weak penetration of state institutions in rural areas; their low police per head ratio and the large areas rural units are responsible for; competing public notions of fairness and justice; low levels of popular trust and legitimacy; formal underregulation; minimal resources and improvised equipment. Thus, as detailed and particular as this case study may be, the story of Amadou and Adjudant-Chef Souley resonates widely with the experiences of police and gendarmerie officers throughout the continent (see Beek et al. 2017).

Second, many issues that appear particularly striking in the police and gendarmerie in Africa are central to the understanding of the police and the state everywhere (Beek et al. 2017, 10). The particular case of the Nigerien gendarmerie sheds light on what may be in the dark but is nonetheless essential to any police and bureaucratic organization: fragile police legitimacy, the lag between les textes and le social, between official norms and human practices, bureaucratic formats and the complexity of lived life, and all of this in the context of multiple conflicting, often incompatible expectations and demands from within and without one's own organization. This resonates very well with classical accounts such as Michael Lipsky's of street-level bureaucrats in American public services (1980). Yet the tension between these two worlds is by far more tangible and needs to be continuously and explicitly negotiated by state actors in areas that are characterized by the sheer breadth and expanse of its contact zones: where parts of the local population have never had contact with public bureaucracies; where the population has not been profoundly shaped by generations living through the disciplinary dispositive of modern governmentality but rather by a profound skepticism about uniformed state personnel; where people like Amadou and Adjudant-Chef Souley are the representatives of a distant something that many people think has hardly any significance for their lives and any effect whatsoever. This also forms part of the frontier. Therefore, I think that Amadou and Adjudant-Chef Souley's story merits to be treated as a source rather than a mere object for theory, and that a close reading of their story will be a valuable contribution to police research at large, as well as to broader debates on crime, law, and bureaucratic government in contemporary societies.

Two Worlds, the Stories between Them, and the Drama Within

Sometimes Adjudant-Chef Souley and his gendarmes in Godiya worked by the book, sometimes they did not, but most of what they did was a combination of the two. Some call this the incomplete application or the under-enforcement of the law, which, according to Waddington (1999) is the characteristic feature of all policing; others, like Gupta (1995), describe it as the blurring of boundaries between "state" and "civil society"; again others, following Jean-Pierre Olivier de Sardan's approach to African bureaucracies (2015), call this the use of practical instead of official norms. They all refer to a slightly shady middle world, one in which things are not done in quite the right way. These are insightful depictions, but they gave me little guidance when I came to thinking about the sometimes pure and utterly correct bureaucratic practice of the gendarmes.[2] How could I make sense of moments, even if they were extremely rare and elusive, in which they happened to do exactly what they were supposed to?

Trying to understand what happened when the gendarmes worked by the book, when they enforced the law, without carrying the presumption of any overwhelming gray areas, I found it profoundly helpful to think of the gendarmes' work through the metaphors of translation and story processing. When the gendarmes enforced the law, it always started with what they called a "narrative." Somebody came up the hill and told them about something he or she felt should be dealt with by the gendarmes. If the gendarmes decided to deal with it, they called it a "case," investigated it, and established the facts. Eventually they put it into a literary legal format by writing a *procès-verbal*, or case file. This is a series of translations: from an event into a complaint, a case, a fact, and finally into a bureaucratic file. The "things" that moved along this chain of translation were stories, beginning with those complicated narratives the gendarmes heard and collected from civilians, ending with the story they themselves composed in the form of the bureaucratic narrative of the case file. The further the translation proceeded from one step to another, the less particular, material, and ambivalent the story was and the more standardized it became—the more it left the world of le social and belonged to the world of les textes. What was part of life became part of the bureaucratic form. According to Martin Fuchs (2009), translation is something that takes the translator—here, the gendarmes—back and forth between the source and target contexts and is thus responsible for both the experience *and* creation of difference. So while Sally Engle Merry (2006) describes translation as a negotiation between different systems of meaning, I would add that it is through translation that different systems of meaning—different worlds—emerge as a lived experience in the first place. In the gendarmes' case, they not only negotiated the relationship between les textes and le social, they also produced this very distinction.

When Adjudant-Chef Souley did not enforce the law, he made settlements, *arrangements à l'amiable*: he produced a consensus among the parties of a conflict, whether a law had been broken or not. These arrangements were built on what appears to be a contradiction: all are illegal, but everybody, including the

prosecutor, the gendarmes' superior in all of their criminal investigations, preferred them (because of the extremely drawn-out nature of court cases in Niger
with huge costs and highly uncertain outcomes for everybody). As a result of this
tension, all arrangements followed roughly the same dramaturgy, and to make
sense of this, I am particularly intrigued by Victor Turner's ritual theory and
drama metaphor (1979, 83; 1980, 149). In the gendarmes' arrangements, just as
in Turner's "social drama," after the breach of a norm and the resulting crisis,
the ritualized search for redress began and was key to resolving the conflict. This
"redressive phase" was a gendarme-made liminal time, a betwixt-and-between
with deep, sometimes existential uncertainties for all parties: neither knew if and
when and how the conflict would be resolved; and the gendarmes found themselves torn between the law, rigorous bureaucratic norms and forms, the conflicting expectations of superiors, the prosecutor, the civilian parties, as well as
their own sense of justice. As I will show, through the dramaturgical production
of a compromise in a space within and between les textes and le social (and thus
beyond each one of them), the gendarmes allowed for the distinction between
these two worlds to be suspended, at least for some time, by not bringing them
into direct contact with each other. They let these two worlds merge, all the while
being caught in the exigencies of both.

Forms, Lives, and the Frontier

While enforcing the law, the gendarmes formatted stories about peoples' lives to
fit the needs of the bureaucratic form. While producing arrangements, they kept
these forms and lives apart, thereby allowing for mutually compatible forms of
sociality and morality. The one produced separation through connection, the
other connection through separation. This ambivalent coexistence of connection
and separation is what I want to grasp with the notion of the frontier. Let me
explain what I mean by that.

First of all, the frontier is a *space*, both in its concrete geographical and in a
more abstract sense. The frontier-space is the borderland between life governed
by public institutions and life outside of the state's grasp. This can be due to the
territorial remoteness of some areas, such as the ones the gendarmes worked in,
or it can be due to the fact that, as Veena Das argues, "it is part of the logic of the
state that it constructs itself as an incomplete project" (2004, 249). In Niger, this
frontier is also the shifting line on which the violent work of French colonial rule
was carried out by the hands of the gendarmes' immediate historical predecessors. Beyond that, the frontier is the site where bureaucracy and the world, which
it manages, meet and the tension between the two becomes tangible. It is the

space between bureaucratic form and lived life. This frontier-space can thus be found in the Nigerien desert at the last outpost of the gendarmerie; but like the "margins of the state" it also runs "through the very heart of those offices, institutions, and individuals who seem to embody the very center of the central state" (ibid., 43). In brief, the frontier is the site where people, domains, and histories are kept apart by bringing them in contact with one another.

Out of this space arises a particular condition of doing and being, a *frontier-condition* so to speak. The people caught in this betwixt-and-between, like those who find themselves in the borderlands described by Gloria Anzaldúa (1987) and Gilberto Rosas (2007; 2010; 2016), are confronted with tensions, frictions, and fluctuations: in other words, with profound uncertainties. In this open space lies the permanent tension between threat and guarantee—the permanent, if only latent, presence of the Agambian state of exception. Brenda Chalfin is correct when she refers to the frontier as "a site for expression of excessive state power" (2010, 11). This keeps people on their toes. Yet it also offers them immense possibilities and can be profoundly empowering; it can turn the frontier into a site of creative cultural production, for example, by overcoming the simplistic binaries out of which this frontier or borderland came into being in the first place (see Alvarez 1995; Anzaldúa 1987; Rosas 2010). The ironic effect may nonetheless be, as Cherríe Moraga and Gloria Anzaldúa noted (2001, 63), that what might be intended as a connection can feel like, and thus reproduce, a separation. A confrontation with complexity often produces narratives of simplicity (see Kashani-Sabet 1999), one of these narratives being the clear divide of bureaucratic form and lived life.

The frontier is also a *project*. This is where it contrasts with related notions such as border, boundary, periphery, and margin. The frontier has a direction, a vector, and it represents a constant attempt to push forward, to extend one's reach beyond one's own borders and boundaries, to intrude into a territory that the frontier men and women perceive not necessarily as empty but as open to legitimate intrusion (see Kopytoff 1987; Cole and Wolf 1974).

And, finally, there are particular *stakes* attached to the frontier. The frontier allows for sometimes brutal, sometimes empowering intermingling and flows. Yet in the logic of bureaucratic government, which is a logic of segmentation and separation, such flow is impure and needs to be strictly controlled—for the sake of the law (see Valier 2002; also Kristeva 1982). In the logic of the frontier, also the grip of the law needs to be controlled. True, the gendarmes have the power to declare the state of exception and act outside the law in defense of law itself (see Rosas 2016, 337). But they also have the power to declare an "exception to the state." The gendarmes can decide when to reduce people to bare life, and they can decide when to reduce the law to "bare text." The state of exception is supposed to defend the law, the exception to the state to defend *from* the law. And the result of their actions is not a mere aberration of the central model, an incomplete implementation; it is right here at the frontier where what is considered central is made and remade over and over again (see Das and Poole 2004, 8; Kopytoff 1987, 14; Turner 1921). It is right here where the prevailing moral standards become palpable. Thus, it is here at the frontier that the value of the modern state, bureaucracy, and the gendarme Amadou's work must be judged.

Encountering Police Work, the Gendarmes, and the Brigade in Godiya

When I started the research for this book, I thought I had a rather clear idea of what all these meant: "police," "bureaucracy," "state." Well, time and the gendarmes taught me otherwise. It all started with the presumably straightforward category of "police." My initial plan was to explore "policing in Niger." As it turned out rather quickly, this field of practice and actors appeared too large and complex for me to study ethnographically in a way that would move beyond rather superficial descriptions (see Göpfert 2012). So I decided not to study "policing" but "the police" in Niger. Admittedly, this was also naïve. I had no idea that what I called "the police" actually consisted of at least three different state organizations with policing functions, namely the Police Nationale, the Garde Nationale, and the Gendarmerie Nationale. So I discovered in 2008, during my first stay in Niger, that what I called "the police" was in fact the whole police sector. Although the three overlapped somewhat in terms of their territorial and functional competencies, in principle there was a clear division of labor: the National Police lead criminal investigations, maintain public order, and control traffic in cities; the National Guard is charged primarily with securing prisons and public buildings and patrolling remote desert areas; gendarmes have the same functions as the police, but in rural areas, they are military police with military status. In other words, there was nothing like "the police" that I had naively imagined, but rather a complex ensemble of state-sanctioned and uniformed violence specialists (see Beek and Göpfert 2013b).

In my first fieldwork attempt, I decided to focus on the National Police, which turned out to be a pretty arduous task (see Beek and Göpfert 2011).[3] My request was rejected after I spent months trying to obtain a research permit from the Minister of the Interior and the Director General of the National Police. Friends and colleagues at the LASDEL Niamey,[4] a research center where I was amicably accepted as a visiting researcher, urged me to at least try the National Gendarmerie. I was not very optimistic given the gendarmes' military status; I expected them to be even more unapproachable than the police. Yet my colleagues convinced me that if there was any truth to the gendarmes' reputation as a corps of intellectuals, they might perhaps be more open to researchers than the police. And indeed, while it took me months to be sent away by the police, it took me one day to be accepted by the gendarmes. I presented my project and myself to the secretary-general at the Ministry of Defense, who immediately rang the high commander of the National Gendarmerie. The then high commander, Colonel Harouna Djibo Hamani, received me the same day and promised all the necessary support. He asked me where I wanted to go and immediately rang the regional commander responsible for that unit to inform him about my pending arrival and plans. He hung up, apologized for having run out of business cards, and handed me a post-it note with his mobile number written on it. I was to call him, if there was anything he could do for me. So with both his approval and that of his successor, Brigadier General Mounkaïla Issa, between 2009 and 2014 I spent about eighteen months in different units spread throughout the country: specialized criminal investigation departments, traffic control units, administrative units, and mostly, in regular gendarmerie stations, so-called *brigades territoriales*. The work in these brigades is central to this book.

I still do not know exactly why the gendarmes unlike the police accepted me among them. A journalist in Niamey gave me one possible explanation: "They don't trust themselves. You know, when you meet a policeman, in five minutes he tells you everything. Everything you want to know. But the gendarme is very discrete. You can spend the whole day with him talking; he won't say a word about his work. Nothing, nothing." About a year later, the gendarmes told me the very same thing, and they ironically called this the "welcome charter": they make you feel welcome, offer you a seat and a glass of tea, but they won't give you what you want. This applied to both civilians and the researcher who approached them. And it worked. I spent the first six months sitting in a gendarmerie post for eight to twelve hours a day, most gendarmes were friendly, a few became my friends, but I felt like I had no clue of what was actually going on in the station. In answer to my questions, the gendarmes would politely recite the laws and regulations that governed their work, or they would smile and tell me to ask their superiors. And they would hand me another glass of tea.

Luckily, in Godiya things were different. The brigade in Godiya was in a departmental, not a regional capital, remote and close to the desert; superior officers were more than a hundred kilometers away; radio communication with the regional and national headquarters was patchy; some of the gendarmes there felt like they had been punished by having to work here "in the bush," as they said; others felt privileged to be off their superiors' radar. There, many gendarmes like Amadou and Adjudant-Chef Souley confided in me and shared their thoughts

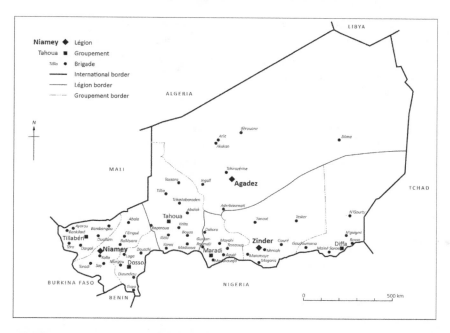

FIGURE 1   Map of Niger and the territorial organization of the Nigerien gendarmerie

and stories. I sat with them through most of their working hours discussing their work. I also accompanied them on criminal investigations, spent evenings chatting with those on night duty. Sometimes I helped them write case files on the computer or count the money collected from fines at the end of the month, and occasionally we invited each other for dinner, breakfast, or drinks. I also held interviews with superior officers in their air-conditioned offices, and I had long conversations with prosecutors, judges, traditional authorities, private security agents, and local bus drivers to get a feel for perspectives beyond the gendarmerie. However, the most important sources are my participant observations of the everyday routines and events at the brigades and friendly conversations with the gendarmes in and outside their offices.

Introducing the Brigade in Godiya

The persons and events I refer to throughout this book are all set in the gendarmerie brigade in Godiya. It was one of Niger's almost sixty so-called brigades territoriales, the gendarmerie's street-level units tasked primarily with criminal investigations.[5] The brigade compound was located just outside Godiya town, the capital with around fifteen thousand inhabitants of a department with predominantly agricultural and pastoralist population, not far from the Nigerian border. Adjudant-Chef Souley was the head of the brigade, and on paper, he had twenty-three gendarmes under him, all men,[6] of whom four were noncommissioned officers and eighteen rank and file; but there was always a lot of movement among them. Every three to four years, each gendarme has to be transferred to a different unit, so that a third of his men were always either just settling in or preparing to leave. Also, half of his gendarmes were either on UN missions, on advanced training seminars in the capital, on detachment in other units, or on temporary leave. This left him with twelve gendarmes. Six of them were always at the brigade's three remote outposts. They went there in pairs, mostly on market day to find a vehicle that would take them along, and spent the week there until the next pair relieved them. This left Adjudant-Chef Souley with six gendarmes at the brigade. One of them was always on a twenty-four-hour orderly shift, one—who had just spent his twenty-four-hour shift—on his rest day.

Adjudant-Chef Souley, himself a noncommissioned officer, had three noncommissioned officers under him. Chef Tahirou and Chef Boubacar, both *maréchal des logis-chef* and in their early forties, and Chef Hamza, a *maréchal des logis* in his mid-fifties and thus the most senior gendarme at the brigade, who had been exceptionally promoted noncommissioned officer due to his seniority.[7] Chef Tahirou and Chef Boubacar had both successfully taken the usual path of advancement, namely through competitive exams and following advanced training. When I was at the brigade, they were just about to leave for another period of advanced training to become *adjudants*. Then there were nine rank-and-file gendarmes: Yacouba, Bassirou, Harouna, Moussa, Amadou were *gendarmes de 1ère classe*; Nouhou, Ali, Omar, and Chaibou who was in his mid-twenties making him the youngest, were *gendarmes de 2ème classe*, the first grade after gendarme-in-training, or *élève-gendarme*.[8]

The daily work at the brigade in Godiya consisted of receiving complaints, summoning alleged offenders, investigating criminal offences, and settling disputes. Most of the cases were conflicts between herders and farmers; brawls between young men; theft, fraud, and slander. As a result of their activities, the gendarmes imposed and collected fines of about 350,000 francs CFA per month, equaling about 530 euros, or 3.5 times the salary of a young rank-and-file gendarme like Chaibou. In more serious cases, they wrote a procès-verbal and forwarded the case to the prosecutor for him to launch legal proceedings. So again, they either worked by the book or they produced arrangements.

Before the story of this book truly begins, I owe the reader a few words on my narrative strategy. Many of the gendarmes, who shared their stories with me, told me that once this book is written and published and if I have not taken sufficient precautions to protect them, they might lose their jobs or worse. Therefore, the brigade in Godiya is somewhat special: it doesn't exist. I want to present my descriptions and reflections so that all my interlocutors are protected. Hence, all names used in this book are pseudonyms, and to further ensure the anonymity of the persons speaking and acting in this book, yet without relegating them to nameless places and times, I invented a fictional brigade in the fictional town of Godiya. The descriptions all stem from my own observations in a dozen brigades and administrative units, the quotations are all from interview transcripts or notes from conversations with more than eighty gendarmes. Yet I present all events, as if they had taken place in one brigade, and all quotations as uttered by the gendarmes working in this brigade. My approach is inspired by Richard Rottenburg's attempt of ethnographic "fictionalization" (2009, xx); however, and here I differ from him, the gendarmes mentioned do not represent any "cumulative characteristics" of all the gendarmes I met, and they do not represent particular types of gendarmes; they are real and their characteristics belong to real gendarmes, only from different brigades. So yes, this ethnographic account is a fiction; but no, it is not a thought experiment.[9]

Structure of the Book

This book is a story of tensions, and it is told through the lens of a handful of gendarmes in a single post in rural Niger. It is about the gendarmes' historicity and practical presence (part I), the sensuous production of bureaucratic form (part II), and the bureaucratic tragedy of policing life (part III).

Chapter 2 retraces the history of the Nigerien gendarmerie. The gendarmes and their colonial predecessors—the *tirailleurs, méharistes, gardes de cercle*, and colonial gendarmes—have always worked in vast rural Niger, populated almost exclusively by subsistence farmers and pastoralists. Since the early twentieth century, these "strangers" have disciplined the rural population, managed the French colonial, later Nigerien national territory, spread French as the national language, established bureaucratic procedures, and imposed French colonial, then Nigerien national law. They have been advancing into a sphere they perceived as an "institutional vacuum" open to legitimate intrusion and in need of a new social order. Working between the known and the unknown, the familiar and the unfamiliar, rural police forces tried to make society legible to govern it and turn a social hieroglyph into an administratively more convenient format of numbers and texts. At the same time, they attempted to impose a normative order on what they perceive as a savage and chaotic, illegitimate sphere. The gendarmes have been pushing this frontier ever since; yet it cannot be crossed—it is the bureaucratic horizon that moves with them.

Chapter 3 offers a detailed narrative of how the gendarmes in Godiya dealt with a criminal case that made the gendarmes hold their breath for two full days. The case was about an investigation into a murder case—the only one I observed during my research. It concerned the murder of two little girls—a case that the gendarmes had never seen before. The exceptional quality of this case will push aspects of the gendarmes' work to the fore that were central to everything they did but would certainly get lost in the description of the trivial everydayness of their usual workdays.

Chapter 4 deals with the gendarmes' sense of hearing. Usually, the gendarmes' work began with what they heard people say, how these people told them what they had to say, how the gendarmes listened to them and tried to make sense of what they had just heard. Technically, the gendarmes were supposed to "hear" structure in what they were told; to make a distinction between civil and criminal matters, between felonies, misdemeanors, and minor offences. Their bureaucratically attuned ear, in other words, was supposed to "hear" order behind all the noise. Yet what the gendarmes' vocational ear was ultimately attuned to was anything but fixed and clear—among others because the gendarmes had little say in what people told them in the first place. In this frontier-condition, both the world and the senses undergo a process of mutual ordering—or attuning.

The gendarmes' ear or, more precisely, their vocational ear, was profoundly shaped by the moral fluidity and factual uncertainty of the frontier-condition. The gendarmes' eye (chapter 5) was subject to the same condition, but it not only tried to make sense of what it perceived; it also tried to perceive even more. It tried to constantly reach out into the unknown, and this reaching out ideally led to the production of knowledge, facts, and truth. The gendarmes' eye, particularly as a device and metaphor for surveillance, is thus at the heart of the frontier as a project of reaching out, pushing forward, and moving beyond. Gendarmes in Godiya had to grapple with Niger itself, as it was still a very poor "registering machine" and knowledge apparatus. The aim of this chapter is to shed some light on what the daily exercise of state surveillance can mean in a context where the state seems to know very little about its citizens. In this context, surveillance in particular and the frontier-project in general does not so much appear like the calculated action conceived by a powerful state dispositive—a strategy—but rather as a tactical way of operating: the improvised, localized, often spontaneous and makeshift practices of "make do." The strategist conceives the map, controls the map; the tactician has to move through the foreign terrain. And without the map, the supposed strategist, now incapable of "panoptic practice," transforms into a tactician who needs to incessantly capitalize on forces and knowledge that are not his own.

When the gendarmes had established the facts, they produced a new story—the bureaucratic narrative of the case file (chapter 6). These reports tell the "true story" and make the events including those involved, legible in the truest sense. By looking closely at the writing process, I show that bureaucratic work has—beyond institutional, material, and social constraints—plenty to do with aesthetics. This acknowledgement helps fill the gap often perceived between official norms and informal practices, between legal and pragmatic reasoning. Aesthetics of form, style, and content are not mere decor on the legal or pragmatic function of documents; bureaucratic aesthetics embrace them all simultaneously. It is thus no contradiction that bureaucratic aesthetics are at once personal and impersonal, predictable and unpredictable, legal documentation and poetry; it connects people, domains, and worlds through translation while making their separation blatantly obvious. It is the aesthetic of the frontier.

Often the result of the gendarmes' work was not a bureaucratic report but an informal arrangement, mostly between the disputing parties (chapter 7). This was, indeed, the more desirable outcome to their work, both from the gendarmes' and the civilians' perspective. "You should never leave black spots in the community," Adjudant-Chef Souley explained. Except when confronted with severe crimes, they saw their function as establishing consensus, resolving conflicts, and thus restoring social order in the disputants' community. Here the dramaturgical skills of the gendarmes were key. Establishing a consensus meant distributing mutually compatible roles among the parties in such a way that everybody could save face and meaningful interaction was possible. In this "social drama on the stage of law," the gendarmes used the ambivalence and possibilities of the frontier-condition not so much to invoke the state of exception (although at times they did threaten to do so during the early stages of so-called arrangement)—quite the contrary. While their bureaucratic work was based on the translation from le social into les textes, from life to form, in these arrangements, the gendarmes allowed for a clear separation of the two. As such, they did not connect mutually compatible forms and formats by pressing life into a bureaucratically exploitable form; but they created mutually compatible forms of sociality (between the persons embodying and those facing the state) and morality (when legal morality and local morality stand in sharp contrast with each other).

When a law had been visibly broken, the arrangement needed to include, beyond the disputing parties, the law itself. The problem was that for the gendarmes the criminal law was profoundly unjust. The Nigerien penal code (Code Pénal) and code of criminal procedure (Code de Procédure Pénale) both originate from the colonial era and still contain largely unadapted elements of it. According to the gendarmes, these outdated and "foreign" laws were largely inappropriate for policing the life worlds of the people they confronted. From the paradigmatic and law-centered perspective, the gendarmes' arrangements appear as the discretion-led, under-enforcement of the law. In chapter 8, however, I suggest a perspective that is more sensitive to those actors' views and practices and takes seriously local concepts of law enforcement, dispute settlement, and the search for justice, in this case: *gyara*, repair work. Seen in that light, the gendarmes repaired a law that they deemed unjust. Not its application, but the law itself was deficient. What was at stake in such instances was the nature of the law and the state itself. True, the gendarmes had the power to declare the state of exception and act outside the law in defense of law; but they also had the power to declare an "exception to the state." The gendarmes could decide when to reduce people to bare life, and the law to "bare text."

Chapter 9 resolves the narrative of the frontier, of the gendarmes' being caught between les textes and le social, between bureaucratic form and lived life—in a lack of resolution. There is nothing beyond this tension, no safe space where the gendarmes can find certainty and protection; there is no bureaucratic haven. This tension is even accentuated by the different and often conflicting expectations of civilians, prosecutors, and the gendarmes' superiors. The gendarmes' mandate is ultimately unaccomplishable, their task impossible. The bureaucratic drama thus created both *communitas* and isolation at the same time. It created communitas among the gendarmes through their shared sense of frustration. But it also caused a sense of isolation as tragic creatures, with neither catastrophe nor catharsis in sight. The gendarme as a bureaucratic Sisyphus: a frontier figure tasked with the impossible project of closing the frontier.

Chapter 2

A HISTORY OF THE GENDARMERIE IN NIGER

In some respects and from the perspective of many Nigerien gendarmes, the Gendarmerie Nigérienne seems to lack a history of its own. First, historians have never focused on the gendarmerie, not in Niger, rarely anywhere else in Africa.[1] Second, there are almost no archival sources available in Niger. The few available are fragmentary or inaccessible. Third, when talking about the history of their institution, gendarmes refer only to the history of the French gendarmerie, beginning with Napoleon, not to their own Nigerien path. Fourth, the number of gendarmes in Niger has more than tripled in two decades, so that at least two-thirds of all gendarmes have been recruited since 2000. Finally, unlike the army, which has played an important role in Niger's twentieth-century political history with many *militaires politiciens*, that is, army personnel as an important component of Niger's political class (Tidjani Alou 2008), the gendarmerie has virtually been absent from this sphere.

However, a closer look unearths countless traces, both material and immaterial, that hint at the complex, multilayered, fragmented, latent, long-term, and contingent colonial and postcolonial history of the Nigerien gendarmerie. Most of the gendarmerie's buildings were built by and accommodated their predecessors, namely colonial gendarmes, colonial administrators (*commandants de cercle*), and the so-called *gardes de cercle*, the primary colonial police force in French West Africa. Gendarmes vividly recall the powerful and most respected, if not feared, gendarmes of the postindependence era, particularly the military regime under Seyni Kountché, and they tell and retell stories about almost mythical figures of the gendarmerie. As fragmentary as official archives are (see Glasman 2010, 57), and as inaccessible as the archives of the gendarmerie are to gendarmes, as carefully do gendarmes keep their own, personal archives of messages, reports, statements, and textbooks from their own and their predecessors' periods of training, depicting French gendarmes with their traditional kepi.

Similar to the appearance of the history of the Nigerien gendarmerie, this chapter is based on heterogeneous sources that are sometimes inconsistent, and always patchy. First, I consulted legal documents and press articles in Niger's national archive. With the friendly and professional support of the archive personnel, I was able to dig up documents that hint at the evolution of the gendarmerie as an institution, but also at the way the gendarmerie has been represented in the print media for the past sixty years. Second, I draw on academic literature. As elaborate as it is regarding the colonial endeavor in terms of military enterprise and administrative revolution, as dispersed are small fragments that hint at the gendarmerie. Third, I interviewed experienced gendarmes of all ranks, elderly traditional authorities (*chefs de canton* and *chefs de groupement*), and ordinary civilians. Contrary to most textual and official sources, these give a more nuanced picture of what the gendarmes' work consisted of, and particularly how the gendarmes and civilians perceived it over the last thirty years.

In all these sources, it is impossible to distinguish fact from fiction. Laws and decrees at times legalized facts already established on the ground; sometimes they legalized what was to be implemented years later, if at all. Most press reports on criminal incidents merely said, "la gendarmerie a ouvert une enquête" or they read like the preamble to their own investigation reports, as if written by gendarmes themselves. Interviewees referred to idealized or demonized gendarmes and their actions, such as the incorruptible gendarmes in the golden Kountché era, or the brutal gendarmes with their inescapable *chicottes* (small whips)—in the same era. What I present here is thus necessarily my own fragmentary reading of the history of the Nigerien gendarmerie.

Apart from the nagging question of historical fact or fiction, there is also a terminological challenge in studying the history of colonial policing. Scholarly and other literature that mentions colonial corps often use just the term *police*, sometimes with the adjective *colonial*, to describe any of the corps that went on "tournées de police," thus *tirailleurs*, *méharistes*, gardes de cercle, gendarmes, and rarely the *police coloniale*. This terminological confusion is certainly, among others, due to the fact that colonial policing, or more broadly the production of a colonial order, defies clear categories, in particular the binary distinction between civil and military. Colonial conquest was pressed ahead by military forces, mainly the tirailleurs, African recruits in the French colonial army; these tirailleurs were the first to take over what was often called policing tasks—they regularly went out on their notorious *tournées de police*; the "desert police" was the camel cavalry of the méharistes sections of the tirailleurs. Soon there were the gardes de cercle, the first nonmilitary police, which consisted mainly of former tirailleurs. When the gendarmes came, they too recruited former tirailleurs and gardes de cercle. Formally different corps, but all under the sole authority of the French colonial administrator on the ground, the commandant de cercle, they usually worked closely together, particularly in these tournées de police. Furthermore the gendarmes recruited so-called *auxiliaires*, later also called *appelés*, who served as interpreters or generally assisted them in their daily work. These were civilians who were given berets, uniforms, and *chicottes*; sometimes they received a salary or a percentage of the fines they collected for the gendarmes. In short, it is literally impossible to reconstruct who was what and who did what exactly.

Today, quite a wealth of research exists on what the proper police did in French colonies.[2] They were first introduced in French West Africa in 1930 and located exclusively in urban centers. Their tasks were not so much the detection and prevention of social deviance or criminal offences; rather they served the colonial administration as a political police. Their main responsibilities were to maintain hygiene in the colonial capitals, control movements into the urban centers, prevent any anticolonial demonstrations and propaganda, and eliminate political opponents of the colonial regime. In most independent African states, this political function was transferred to what are now national police forces, such as the Police Nationale in Niger, and to a lesser extent also to the gendarmerie (Blanchard and Glasman 2012, 33, 37; Fourchard 2003a, 113). If the police's task was to discipline local populations, their numbers were grossly insufficient; the only police station in town usually had ten inspectors at the most. Their role seems inconsequential when compared to those working outside the colonial capitals, that is, tirailleurs, French commandants de cercle with their gardes de cercle and their local collaborators, and, finally, gendarmes. As Brunet-la-Ruche (2012, 33–34) shows, the latter were far more involved in the everyday management of disputes, the fight against criminal offenders, and the production of colonial order.

These rural forces have always been engaged in frontier policing. According to Igor Kopytoff (1987), the frontier designates a sphere that frontiersmen and women see as open to legitimate intrusion and the construction of a desirable social order. Kopytoff had mainly migrations in precolonial Africa in mind, but I suggest that this notion can also be applied to the colonial conquest and rule in Niger. The colonizers not only (thought they) had to fill an "institutional vacuum" (ibid., 10–12, 25); they also had to make society legible, meaning to extend the reach of the known and familiar into what was still unknown and alien. The pragmatic aim of this was, in James Scott's words, "to arrange the population in ways that simplified the classic state functions of taxation, conscription, and prevention of rebellion" (1998, 2). The larger aim was to impose a moral order on the borderland between those spheres perceived as civilized and those considered savage and chaotic, between the legal and illegal, the legitimate and illegitimate, "us" and "them."

It seems that the one corps at the heart of this frontier-project that has not found any particular attention yet is the gendarmerie (see Bat and Courtin 2012b, 211).[3] Here, I retrace the origins of the Nigerien gendarmerie, also in Napoleon's France, but mainly by focusing on the institutions and actors that were the direct predecessors of the gendarmerie in Niger. The French gendarmerie may be the institutional ancestor and eponym of the Nigerien gendarmerie, but by the time the gendarmerie arrived in Niger, apart from so-called traditional modes of policing, there were other colonial corps that fulfilled functions and employed personnel who were later taken over by the gendarmerie. I will start with two histories: first, the local history of colonial policing in Niger, and second, the history of the proper gendarmerie force (beginning in France and via the colonial gendarmerie in French West Africa). Where these two histories meet is not only the birthplace of the Nigerien gendarmerie as an institution, but also where the gendarmes' narratives of identification set in—and where the latter part of this chapter sets out to sketch key events and periods on the national gendarmerie's path since Niger's independence in 1960. In the conclusion, I return to the gendarmes' overall frontier-project. They have been pushing the frontier forward ever since its inception, but they have never truly closed it and probably never will.

The Predecessors of the Gendarmerie in Niger

In 1900, Niger became a formal entity, at least on paper, namely the Territoire Militaire du Niger with its capital in Zinder. The colonial administration was primarily a military one, with 1,000 regular forces in 1910, and roughly 1,700 in the 1920s, of which roughly 220 were French. In a territory more than twice the size of France this is "not a very impressive or intimidating number," as Fuglestad (1983, 112) put it.[4] The African personnel were mainly the rank and file of the different military and police corps, namely méharistes, gardes de cercle, and the notorious tirailleurs, so essential for the colonial conquest (ibid., 79).

Tirailleurs and Méharistes

French colonization of what was to become Niger started with the first official French military mission under Captain P. L. Monteil with a handful of *tirailleurs sénégalais* in 1880. A second mission, of seven hundred soldiers under Major Destenave, followed in 1886; first protectorate treaties were negotiated in Say in western Niger. This established the first permanent post. Another mission was sent out in 1897 to negotiate a protectorate treaty with the *sarkin damagaram*, the sultan of Zinder. The sultan's forces executed the head of the mission, Captain Cazémajou, on the mission's arrival in Zinder 1898, and the small garrison fled. The following year a mission was sent out with the task of avenging Cazémajou's assassination: the infamous Voulet-Chanoine mission. This seven-hundred-man military column set out eastward from Dosso on what they called a "pacification mission." On their way, they left a trail of devastation and desolation in their wake and their numbers swelled to some three thousand people including cooks, servants, carriers, and a considerable number of captives (including many women). As soon as the French government learned of the atrocities of the Voulet-Chanoine "pacification" mission, Lieutenant Colonel Klobb was sent after them; but he was shot on sight the moment he caught up with the column. Soon afterward, the rank and file revolted and killed Voulet and Chanoine (Fuglestad 1983, 50–60).

These were the first and disastrous military enterprises in Niger. Apart from the French officers in charge, the troops consisted exclusively of tirailleurs sénégalais, regular African soldiers in the French colonial army who formed the essence of the troops of colonial conquest and occupation in French West Africa (Dramé 2007; Echenberg 1991). Until World War I, apart from some forty French commanding officers, the corps of the tirailleurs in Niger was composed exclusively of African soldiers from the French Sudan and the Upper Volta. Systematic conscription in Niger began only in 1918, particularly to satisfy the need for war recruits in Europe. The tirailleurs were recruited, mostly with the help of local authorities from royal slaves, war captives, and people of low social status, but also through voluntary enlistment. Members of ruling families were recruited as noncommissioned officers and served as intermediaries between the French commanders and the African rank and file. Like other parts of French West Africa, in order to motivate the offspring of chiefs' families to enroll in the colonial army, they were promised positions as noncommissioned or native officers. In the cercle of Niamey alone, forty-three out of a total of seventy-two recruits were sons or close relatives of chiefs in 1918 (Aliou Mahamane 2008, 51). Serving in the French colonial army also offered several important rewards for tirailleurs, which enhanced both their economic and social standing: steady employment, medical care, pensions, uniforms and decorations. Contemporary European commentators often described the tirailleurs as "the finest fighting material" the French disposed of (Harris 1911, 372). However, those who had witnessed and lived through the atrocities the tirailleurs committed under French command (as in the Voulet-Chanoine mission), villages razed to the ground, the slaughter of innocents, and the capture and quasi-enslavement of women, did not hold them in high esteem.

When the colonial conquest was officially pronounced ended around 1900, the former tirailleurs turned from conquest into occupation troops and thus a sedentary force. In 1901, a battalion of tirailleurs became the first to be permanently installed in Niger with its headquarters in Zinder (Tidjani Alou 2001, 101). When the Territoire Militaire became the Colonie du Niger in 1922, the battalion was subdivided into seven *compagnies*, which were implanted in Zinder, Tanout, Gouré, N'Guigmi, Tahoua, Bilma, and Agadez. In 1925, the second company was transferred from Tanout to Niamey, which became the new capital in 1926 (Abadie 1927, 343–45).

In their role as occupation troops, the tirailleurs' task was to protect the French administration and police and administer the vast territories of the Niger colony, that is, accompany military columns, protect convoys, and collect taxes, at that time mostly millet and cattle (Echenberg 1991, 25–26). If a village refused to pay taxes or to support columns or convoys, a five- to seven-strong detachment of tirailleurs, commanded by a noncommissioned officer and accompanied by an interpreter, would go on tournées de police. According to Rothiot (1988, 119–24), they would take the chief and notables "hostage" and detain them until the taxes were paid. In short, the tirailleurs were thus the first corps formally tasked with the policing of the Nigerien population. Throughout the period of colonial domination, they played a key role in the relationship between the colonized and the colonizers.

A special section of the tirailleurs, and thus of the regular French colonial troops, were the méharistes, or *groupes nomades*, a "police saharienne" (Tidjani Alou 2001, 101). As camel cavalry units, they were tasked with protecting the trans-Saharan trade and remote villages from raids by Tuareg and Toubou nomad groups, and thus defend the French claim of control over these vast desert areas (Bouchez 1910, 16–17; Evrard 2012a; Harris 1911). The first méhariste section in Niger was created in Guidam-Bado near Tahoua in 1901; this unit began with twenty-five men, and a year later was up to sixty men (Duboc 1946, 93). Until 1907, there was officially only one méhariste section in Niger. Yet *officieusement*, every company of tirailleurs that had seized camels from Tuaregs in raids had already created their own méhariste section. This state of affairs was legally ratified in 1907 (ibid., 93–94). The most prominent sections were based in Tahoua, Zinder, and Gouré, later also in Agadez and N'Guigmi (Dramé 2007, 48, 160).

One French army officer and two noncommissioned officers headed each méhariste unit. They were supposed to oversee about sixty tirailleurs and two hundred camels (of which 120 were saddled) (Bouchez 1910, 65).[5] At first, most of the tirailleurs from the méhariste sections came from sedentary societies in nondesert regions; each section recruited just one or two locals, so-called *goums*, who served mainly as guides in the vast desert areas (Dramé 2007, 48). Bouchez, at that time captain of the French colonial infantry, argued: "Our indigenous soldiers will only be perfect Saharans and méharistes when we take them from the Tuareg" (Bouchez 1910, 36; my translation). This strategy was gradually implemented. Thus, by the early 1930s, local recruits made up about one-third of all méharistes (Dramé 2007, 156).

According to Bouchez (1910, preface without pagination), in 1910 there were about five hundred méharistes in the whole of Upper Senegal and Niger. Given the relatively low number of the méharistes in this large territory, there was by no means an effective French presence, but rather a series of sometimes successful, sometimes unsuccessful demonstrations of strength (Dramé 2007, 173, 189). Similar to regular tirailleurs, the *mode opératoire* of méhariste units were "police operations," namely missions of pursuit and retaliation, also called "counter-raids" (*contre-rezzou*), during which they captured dozens of prisoners, weapons, camels, horses, and sacs of millet if successful (ibid., 183–86).[6]

Tirailleurs and méharistes were true frontiersmen (and they were truly all men) in that they were supposed to fill an institutional vacuum. Through punctual demonstrations of territorial control and physical violence, they tried to demarcate the external border of the colonial empire and impose colonial authority over these parts and the people living in the colonial territory that were usually beyond the reach of colonial institutions—and there were many such parts (see Spittler 1978, 50; 1982, 67). By the 1930s, the desert had been officially "pacified" as a result of French military action. But the frontier had not been closed. The frontier was the shifting line on which the violent work of the French colonial conquest was done.

By the mid-1940s, there were only two méhariste units left: the *groupes nomades* of Agadez and Bilma (Duboc 1946, 100). After Niger's independence in early August 1960, the tirailleurs and méharistes turned into the Garde Républicaine du Niger and the dependent *garde nomade* and put under the authority of the Minister of the Interior.[7] Then again, the Garde Républicaine served as the first recruitment reservoir for the newly founded Armée Nationale de la République du Niger.[8] Yet others had already left the corps of the tirailleurs to become gardes de cercle, regional police units under the control of the commandant de cercle, later also gendarmes auxiliaires.

The Commandant de Cercle and His Gardes de Cercle

Administratively, the Niger colony (and young independent Niger) was divided into at first seven, later ten, circumscriptions, the so-called cercles, each headed by a French commandant de cercle (Abadie 1927, 334–35; Fuglestad 1983, 80).[9]

The commandant de cercle was the key figure in policing the Niger colony: "He alone is responsible for the daily management of exploitation and repression" (Olivier de Sardan 1984, 171, my translation). Mostly recruited from former colonial military officers (Dramé 2007, 33), the commandant was "the local chief administrative officer, law-maker (in the sense that he could interpret local customary law as he wished), judge, police chief, military commander, prison superintendent, tax-collector, chief medical officer and much more" (Fuglestad 1983, 81). In these functions, the commandant was the link between the French administration and the "traditionally invented" colonial administrative units, each headed by a *chef de canton* in the case of sedentary populations, or a *chef de groupement* in the case of nomad populations—all appointed by the colonial government (Miles 1987, 233; Olivier de Sardan 1984, 208–15; Tidjani Alou 2009, 3–11). However, it would have been impossible for the French administrators and their African personnel (that is, some *commis* and one or two dozens of gardes de cercle) to exercise day-to-day control over the chiefs; it was rather about "occasional displays of authority, resorting to heavy-handed methods to demonstrate that they were still in command" (Fuglestad 1983, 86); and it was about requisitions: the forceful seizure via the chefs de canton of food-stuffs, animals, forced labor, and during the World Wars the conscription of soldiers—tirailleurs—to fight for the French.[10]

Similar to anywhere else in French West Africa, the commandant de cercle had all the judiciary powers in his cercle (Abadie 1927, 340). Crimes were judged by cercle courts presided over by the French commandant and two local, assistant notables. Simple offences were met with arbitrary sanctions at the discretion of the French administrator alone. This practice was governed by the *indigénat*, a legislative principle introduced in French West Africa in 1904 and abolished only after World War II (Fuglestad 1983, 81; Mann 2009; Rothiot 2001). It fixed both the inferiority of the local population and the French commandants' power to deliberately impose sanctions on their colonial subjects. The indigénat-decree contained a list of twenty-six offences. Fuglestad lists among others: "The refusal by a *sujet* to carry out, or even to carry out in a careless or reluctant manner, requisitions ordered by the administration. . . . the non-payment of taxes and fines; a disrespectful attitude towards the administrators; disrespectful speeches or even remarks made or uttered in public, together with songs intended to undermine the respect due to the French; and a non-collaborative attitude" (Fuglestad 1983, 81). In brief, the French penalized anything that was perceived as a challenge to the colonial administrator or state. Formally, the commandant de cercle could sentence the sujets to up to fifteen days' imprisonment, fine them fifty francs or alternatively requisition them as forced labor for up to five days a year. More often than not, they went far beyond these limits.[11]

Due to the remoteness of most posts, the French commandants were often cut off from supplies and hardly controlled by their superiors (Fuglestad 1983, 82). Effectively abandoned by the central government, they became more and more acquainted with the local context and population and often spoke the local language. The downside was that they, in Fuglestad's words, "tended increasingly to administer their *cercles* as if they were *chefferies*, and as if the *commandants* were African chiefs" (ibid., 115; see also Roberts 2005, 46). According to Charlick, they adopted "patrimonial organization, alliances based on patronage and the exchange of benefits, and a Machiavellian game of dividing rivals" (1991, 35). Dramé (2007, 33) describes them as despotic "dieux de brousse," and thereby certainly not by coincidence implies their resemblance to Joseph Conrad's Kurtz. As the last outpost on the frontier, they sometimes appear to have lost allegiance to either side.

Both colonial and early postcolonial modes of local government depended to a large extent on the person of the commandant de cercle. His immediate means of authority and force lay in the gardes de cercle (often also called *gardes-cercles*), which was the main colonial police force under his control. Instituted in Niger in 1905, they were recruited from former tirailleurs, not locals, preferably officers (*gradés*) who wanted to return to civilian life and still benefit from their former employment in colonial forces and avail of their right to pensions (Dramé 2007, 52).[12] The first company of gardes de cercle was created in Dosso, after the ephemeral *Milice du Djerma*, and consisted of former tirailleurs who had married and settled down in Dosso (Rothiot 1988, 218–19). A few years later, each cercle in Niger had one platoon, each *subdivision* one detachment; their direct superiors were, until the arrival of the gendarmes, the French commandants de cercle (Cabry 2009, 146; Dramé 2007, 52), and they were regulated by the rules of service of the gendarmerie.[13]

Similar to the tirailleurs, they had the tasks of executing the orders of the commandant de cercle or passing them down to chefs de canton, groupement, or village, carrying out censuses, collecting taxes, transmitting mail, protecting the colonial authority, guarding public buildings, prisons and convoys, maintaining public order (until, in severe cases, the arrival of the tirailleurs), organizing the conscription of tirailleurs and laborers. As a "gendarmerie locale" (Tidjani Alou 2001, 101) they were "an extension of the commandants' power into the countryside" (Mann 2009, 339), the commandants' "homme à tout faire" (Dramé 2007, 53). In contrast to the tirailleurs, the gardes de cercle did not go on tournées de police except in case of general mobilization or a state of emergency; they were a corps charged with the "défense sédentaire" of the colonial acquisitions (ibid., 52). Their job no longer consisted of pushing forward the territorial frontier of the Niger colony, but rather in maintaining control over the existing and more or less stabilized acquisitions. It was not about intruding into an institutional vacuum, but about controlling the villages through which the frontier ran between town and countryside, the known and the unknown, the civilized and the savage. It was thus an internal colonization, and about "the imposition of their particular kind of *pax*" (Kopytoff 1987, 21).

Given the huge distances and the lack of communication infrastructure, most gardes were neither closely controlled nor well equipped by their commandants de cercle. Consequently, just like the early colonial administrators in Niger, they had to "muddle through" and live off the land, and often they overused their right to collect taxes, be it in the form of millet, cattle, or forced labor (Dramé 2007, 116; Fuglestad 1983, 64, 84). However, they could not overstretch their prerogatives arbitrarily. As they were often not from the locality and did neither speak the local tongue nor know the areas and the people they were supposed to control, they needed the cooperation of local chiefs, guides, or other intermediaries. When, for example, the Dosso company of gardes de cercle went on missions, the cavalry of Aouta, a local authority that had collaborated with the French since 1899 usually accompanied them (Rothiot 1988, 86, 218–19).

In most villages, the gardes de cercle were altogether absent. Here the chiefs had their own policelike forces, called *dogari* in Hausa. They often rode on horseback, were uniformed, and armed with small leather whips, or *chicottes* (Rash 1972, 166; Spittler 1978, 146). They received basic pay from their chiefs and their tasks were quite similar to those of the guards, namely to collect taxes and other dues, and help settle disputes in the chiefs' courts. They earned the larger part of their income from village chiefs' gifts, the creative invention of new fees (such as for tax payment receipts), and sometimes through outright extortion (Spittler 1978, 46–47)

In 1927, Colonel Abadie (1927, 340) wrote that the number of gardes de cercle amounted to only 318 for the whole Colonie du Niger. About half of them were foot guards while the other half were horse guards. Each cercle or subdivision had a detachment of gardes, of between fifteen (e.g., in Tanout) and forty-eight police (in Zinder). Due to their small numbers, the gardes de cercle, let alone the colonial administrator, rarely visited villages strewn across the vast colony of Niger (Mann 2009, 339). In the 1950s, the gardes de cercle became one of the main recruitment basins, first for the colonial gendarmerie and police, later for the newly founded Garde Républicaine (Tidjani Alou 2001, 101–2).

The French and Colonial Gendarmeries

While the Nigerien gendarmerie seems to lack a history of its own in some respects, the history of the French gendarmerie is often said to extend back eight hundred years to the early twelfth century with the *sergeants d'armes*, personal guards of the crusader King Philippe II in Palestine (Dieu 2002, 52; Emsley 1999, 13–14). To perceive a historical continuity between these crusader bodyguards and today's French gendarmerie is, to say the least, a bit of a stretch (see Zauberman 2001, 149). The next predecessor of the French gendarmerie is said to be the *maréchaussée*, created in the sixteenth century. A military force paid by the king, they were charged with police tasks in rural areas, mainly maintaining public order, supervising the main traffic routes, and enforcing monarchal authority. In the early eighteenth century, the maréchaussée was reformed under Louis XV and Louis XVI: hierarchical control was intensified; about six hundred brigades were created all over the kingdom, with five elements each; a proper uniform for the maréchaussée was introduced (Dieu 2002, 53–54; Fontaine 2007, 33). After the French Revolution, in 1791, the king's maréchaussée from the Ancien Régime was turned, or renamed, into the *gendarmerie nationale*; the force of the king became the force of the law.[14] Like the maréchaussée, the gendarmerie was a semimilitary, semicivil force charged with policing rural France. Since then, the gendarme has been called a "pluriel en uniform": a soldier of order, a village police officer, and a magistrate. Depending on these three basic functions, gendarmes were and still are subordinated to three ministries: concerning their military functions to the Ministry of War (later Defense); concerning the maintenance of public order to the Ministère de le Police Générale (later Ministry of the Interior); concerning their judicial policing (*police judiciaire*) to the Ministry of Justice. Gendarmes were central to the defense of French territory, the maintenance of public order, and the provision of judicial policing. As such, in the nineteenth century the gendarmerie played an essential role in disciplining the rural population, managing French national territory, the diffusion of French as the national language, the proliferation of public service procedures, and the imposition of French national law—in short, in France's internal colonization (Weber 1976). In other words, they appear to have closed the French internal frontier.

The gendarmerie was not only an internal colonizing force; in the first half of the nineteenth century, gendarmes also began participating in the French colonization of overseas territories (Cabry 2009; Touchard and Lacoste 1860).[15] The first gendarmes arrived in what was to become French West Africa in 1843: two brigades were established in Senegal, one in Saint Louis, the capital of the colony, and one on Gorée Island, an important trading post, which later became administratively part of Dakar. At the time, there were eight French gendarmes in total. In 1854, the two brigades were turned into the first *détachement de gendarmerie* with a total of sixteen gendarmes. In 1893, they were disbanded and three years later replaced by a *corps indigene de gendarmerie* consisting of fifteen men. In 1894, the French Ministry of the Colonies was created and in 1895 French West Africa with its capital and governor-general in Dakar was established.[16] In 1900, there were 865 gendarmes in the French colonies worldwide, but only roughly eighty in Africa: sixty-four in Madagascar (where the gendarmerie had played an important role in the colonization) and fifteen in French West Africa, namely Senegal.

From 1904 onward, the colonial gendarmerie in French West Africa—that is to say, in Senegal—recruited local auxiliaries, so-called gendarmes auxiliaires, who had often served as interpreters for the colonial administration. Potential recruits had to be able to speak and write French and know basic arithmetic. Once recruited, they were sent to the Centre d'Instruction in Dakar for training lasting six months; however, it is questionable to what extent these rules were effectively applied (see Faulkingham 1971, 67).[17] Until the early 1920s, French noncommissioned officers commanded them. The first full officer of the French colonial gendarmerie in West Africa was Lieutenant Merlhe (later captain, later *Chef d'escadron*). From 1921 to 1941, he was the commander of the detachment of the gendarmerie of French West Africa (*détachement de gendarmerie de l'Afrique occidentale française*) in Dakar, thus also the chief inspector and commander of all gardes de cercle in French West Africa. He had 34 noncommissioned officers and gendarmes under him. The number of gendarmes in French West Africa increased significantly only when they crossed into French West Africa and farther than Senegal in the early 1930s. In 1932, the first two gendarmes arrived in Côte d'Ivoire, and then more came and were installed along the railway from Abidjan up north to Ouagadougou until the second half of the 1930s. In 1939, there were 142 gendarmes in French West Africa, in 1945 already 237: 11 officers, 226 noncommissioned officers and gendarmes,[18] plus 700 African auxiliaries.[19] By the mid-1950s they counted roughly 50 officers, 600 noncommissioned officers and gendarmes, plus, according to Clayton (1988, 364) roughly 2,500, according to an official *décret* some 1,500 auxiliaries.[20] By then, the gendarmerie encompassed all colonial police and local military services—including the gardes de cercle—in all of French West Africa.[21] Anthony Clayton (ibid., 290) summarizes the colonial gendarmes' functions as follows: "An important part of their work was the display of a French presence, of which in some areas they were the only representatives. In such areas the gendarme would act as a local junior administrator: he would hear minor cases, supervise minor public works and serve in a variety of other capacities including policeman, gaoler, customs officer, weights and measures inspector and post official."

This description is not only reminiscent of nineteenth-century gendarmes in France, but also of the gardes de cercle and commandants de cercle, the "hommes à tout faire" and local representatives of the colonial authority. And just like the commandants and gardes, they had to be particularly adaptable, both to their difficult working conditions and to local customs and languages—"même dans les villages les plus hostiles" (Haberbusch 2003, 297). Often located at great distances from their superiors and administrators, they were on their own in terms of making decisions and taking initiatives (Cabry 2009, 54; Le Rouvreur 1997).

As they were often the sole administrators in the countryside, they had multiple functions. They issued birth certificates, became quasi customs officers inspecting weights and measures, measured rainfall and grain yield, and as a rural police force they controlled the movement of civilians. They collected more and more data about the land and the population in order to make it more legible and easier to rule (see Scott 1998, 3).

With the gendarmes' arrival, the colonial administration became more "mature," more bureaucratized, and peacekeeping per se became an administrative value (Kopytoff 1987, 21). Thus one of their main occupations was to deal with offences and litigations brought before them by gardes de cercle or representatives of local chiefs. Through their actions and judgments, they not only bureaucratically separated the legal from the illegal and acceptable from unacceptable behavior, but they also, and more important, unbureaucratically "solved problems," meaning disputes, and often "amicably" so, as Cabry (2009, 145), perhaps a bit too euphemistically, notes.[22] To this day, this has been part and parcel of the gendarmes' everyday occupation.

The Gendarmerie Nationale du Niger

In Niger, the first gendarmerie unit was put in place in the late 1940s, the *brigade de Niger*; although precise numbers of gendarmes are unknown, with the future composition of typical brigades in mind, they were certainly less than a dozen.[23] Significantly more came in the 1950s; but still, as Cabry (2009, 129, my translation) notes: "Niger, vast expanse with an area equal to twice France, on the border of desert and semi-desert regions, isolated in the middle of the land, lost at the outer fringe of French West Africa, far from Dakar is a forgotten, under-administered, under-equipped and under-policed territory."

In 1954, a groupement de gendarmerie was implanted in Niger and consisted of two *compagnies*, one in Niamey and one in Maradi, twenty brigades territoriales, and three platoons (*pelotons*) of the Mobile Gendarmerie. French gendarmerie cadres commanded all units, and in the beginning not even the auxiliary gendarmes were locals, but had come from other French territories in West Africa (Cabry 2009, 129). A brigade such as the one in Zinder usually comprised two French and four African auxiliary gendarmes; smaller posts such as Magaria or Birni-N'Konni consisted of one French and two auxiliaries (ibid., 153).[24] All in all, there must have been about thirty French gendarmes and some sixty African auxiliaries, thus former gardes de cercle, in the whole of Niger. In other words, the frontier was still gapingly wide open.

Niger became independent in 1960 but the transfer of the gendarmerie to Niger and to Nigeriens was a long-drawn-out process that took until the mid-1980s. Niger's independence was a rupture in the sense that the country's administration was officially handed over to Nigerien officeholders, including the commandants de cercle. The authority over the Nigerien police and military forces was, as in other parts of francophone West Africa (see Blanchard and Glasman 2012, 37), formally transferred to Nigeriens in 1961. Apart from this formal transfer, things changed slowly for the gendarmerie. Those who had served in the French colonial gendarmerie were now integrated in the Nigerien gendarmerie; the French chefs de la brigade or commandants de brigade as the heads of the local gendarmerie units, stayed in charge too. Only they were now detached to the Gendarmerie Nigérienne and thus officially served in the name of the Nigerien government, like most of the other French officers and noncommissioned officers of the colonial gendarmerie (Aliou Mahamane 2008, 54, 58). Now, the heads of the army and the gendarmerie were Nigerien officers for the first time, assisted by French "coopérants" or "conseillers." The first Nigerien commander of the gendarmerie was Lieutenant Badié Garba; his conseiller was the French captain Maurice Daprement (thus one step higher in the military hierarchy) (ibid., 63). At that time, the commandant de cercle of Magaria, near Zinder, summarized this transfer as follows: "La gendarmerie devient nationale, c'est-à-dire nigérienne mais avec des cadres français" ("The gendarmerie becomes national, that is, Nigerien, but with French cadres"; cited in ibid., 58–59). This remained true until the early 1980s when the last French gendarme apart from the conseiller left; he had been the commander of the gendarmerie's Centre d'Instruction.[25]

The First Nigerien Gendarmes

To gendarmes, the history of their institution is first and foremost the story of those whom they remember as "les anciens." They have childhood memories of their seniors or elders roaming through their villages or they met them later when they joined the gendarmerie. These were, at least for gendarmes in their fifties, auxiliary gendarmes and the early Nigerien full gendarmes who were still working with the French.

Right after Niger's independence, auxiliary gendarmes made up two-thirds of all gendarmes in Niger; besides the French brigade commanders they were the only personnel in most brigades. As they consisted mostly of former tirailleurs or gardes de cercle, most of them arrived in Niger with the French. Some supplementary auxiliaries were, as Faulkingham (1971, 67) indicates, recruited among the physically strongest and most impressive young men in Nigerien villages. They were given berets and uniforms, assisted the local gendarmes in summoning defendants and witnesses, and they served as interpreters between the gendarmes (or the commandant de cercle) and the local chiefs. Although as auxiliaires formally entitled to a salary and special allowances (Cabry 2009, 145), they were enrolled as temporary *appelés*, without any of the auxiliaries' rights and responsibilities, and thus paid on the ground.[26] They usually received a percentage of the fines they collected for their superior gendarmes, commanders, or chiefs (Faulkingham 1971, 67).

The first Nigerien full gendarmes, not auxiliaries, were recruited in 1962. In June of that year, the potential candidates were told to present themselves at the gendarmerie in Niamey, Maradi, Zinder, Tahoua, or Agades.[27] They had to be Nigerien nationals between twenty and thirty years old (if they had been in the army before, the age limit increased by three years), at least 1.68 meters tall, and they had to have clean criminal records. If they met these conditions, they had to sit an exam, a *concours*, which consisted of writing a short essay, dictation, and simple arithmetic exercises. Candidates who had a *certificat d'études primaires,* C.E.P., that is, who had completed primary school, were exempt from this exam. A total of forty-five were recruited, of whom twenty-four had passed the exam and twenty-one had completed primary school.[28] They now faced eighteen months of training in Niamey: six months of military training, six months of professional gendarmerie training, notably training on *police judiciaire, administrative* and *militaire* (judicial, administrative and military police work), and six months of practical training as élèves-gendarmes in gendarmerie units.[29] Including these recruits, the Nigerien gendarmerie comprised roughly three hundred gendarmes, all ranks considered. The number of gendarmes, and thus the number of Nigeriens in the gendarmerie, grew steadily, and more and more brigades were created throughout the country resulting in some forty brigades by the end of President Diori's rule.[30]

The auxiliaries were notoriously brutal, according to many elderly gendarmes who told me about their "anciens." "At that time, the gendarme was something else. When you see a gendarme in the countryside, it was like somebody whistled the end of the world," Adjudant-Chef Souley remembered. This is also reflected in the accounts of Jean-Pierre Olivier de Sardan and Gerd Spittler, who conducted extensive fieldwork in Niger in the 1960s and 1970s; they describe the gendarmes as the heavily armed and motorized ultima ratio in case the gardes de cercle met with reluctance or rejection from civilians (Olivier de Sardan 1984, 170–71; Spittler 1978, 50; 1982, 67). This violent behavior rubbed off on the young recruits to some extent. A chef de groupement Fulani remembered that in an interview: "At that time, they didn't joke with you, they didn't talk with you.

They beat you, that was all." More and more full gendarmes were recruited in the 1960s, 1970s, and 1980s as more auxiliaries retired. The number of auxiliaries decreased proportionally and absolutely, until the remaining few retired in the mid-1980s. The corps of the gendarmerie became thus not only increasingly Nigerienized but also intellectualized; and—ironically paralleled by the retreat of the French—the share of the *chicotte* in the gendarmes' daily work, although still conspicuously present, slowly but gradually decreased in favor of paperwork—at least in the gendarmes' memories of their institution. In other words, the frontier the gendarmes worked on was not pushed forward anymore by the lashes of the *chicotte* but by the strokes of the pen.

From Unease with Diori to the Golden Era of Kountché

Apart from their memories of "les anciens," gendarmes remember the history of their institution also as a history of mutual trust in their heads of state and superiors. From the gendarmes' point of view, the period from 1960 until 1974 was not easy. According to gendarmes I talked to, President Diori did not hold the gendarmerie in great esteem. They have never forgiven him for attaching the gendarmerie to the Ministry of the Interior in 1963—home ministry of the National Police, the gendarmes' unloved stepsister—instead of the Ministry of Defense.[31] Diori was obviously careful not to leave too much (military) power under one roof, particularly after an attempted mutiny by army soldiers in 1963. In addition to this, he created a party militia with recruits drawn from his party's youth movement, and he strengthened the Garde Républicaine and turned it into a quasi-private presidential guard. All this led to even greater neglect of the army and the gendarmerie. In 1972, Diori added yet another control mechanism, an Inspection Générale des Armées and an inspection for the national gendarmerie, which were attached directly to the presidency (Addo Mahamane 2008, 36).

The period of the gendarmes' unease ended in 1974, when Lieutenant Colonel Seyni Kountché ousted President Diori Hamani in a military coup. Given the armed forces' discontent with Diori, according to Higgot and Fuglestad, the coup was not very difficult to accomplish: "Not that any opposition was expected, with the possible exception of the Republican Guard. The reports of the actual take-over, and the minimal conflict which occurred, would suggest that it had the total support of the army and the powerful armed *gendarmerie*" (1975, 396–97).

Most gendarmes I talked to had joined the gendarmerie during or shortly after the Kountché period because in hindsight they had witnessed the powerful, neatly dressed gendarmes of that era, "les anciens," strutting through their neighborhoods in their shiny, polished boots, holding their heads proudly and high, they said. According to these gendarmes, the military rule of the Conseil Militaire

Suprême under Kountché marked the dawn of the golden era not only for the country, but also for the gendarmerie. As an institution the gendarmerie grew rather quickly: instead of twenty to twenty-five under Diori, under Kountché one hundred gendarmes were recruited at least every other year. The number of gendarmes thus doubled in about ten years to almost two thousand. By the mid-1980s, there were fifty-one brigades, five pelotons of the Gendarmerie Mobile, all organized in seven groupements, which corresponded to the then seven regions of the country.[32]

Kountché had enormous trust in the gendarmerie, gendarmes said. In an introductory presentation held for me in 2009, a gendarmerie officer explained that Kountché had immediately reattached the gendarmerie to the Ministry of Defense, and thus affirmed its military status; this actually happened eight years after he had taken office, but was interpreted as a proof of his appreciation of the gendarmerie.[33] From 1984, Kountché even used the gendarmerie in his struggle against corruption and inefficient administration to monitor "bureaucratic laxities" in public institutions closely (Amuwo 1986, 294). In that era, the gendarmes' frontier-project gained another dimension. Besides the frontier at the rural fringes of state control, the gendarmerie was now supposed to push forward a bureaucratic frontier that like Das and Poole's margins of the state ran "through the very heart of those offices, institutions, and individuals who seem to embody the very center of the central state" (Poole 2004, 43).

The Kountché period and that of his military government (Conseil Militaires Suprême), which lasted until the late 1980s, often served as a reference to which gendarmes compared their contemporary work and the now "pitiful" state of their institution. Gendarmes (but also a considerable share of the population) tend to idealize Kountché and his rule until his death in 1987: everybody was well equipped and well paid; everybody was disciplined and honest; there was no corruption; all in all, everything and everybody worked the way they should (see also Abdoulkader 2013, 34–35).

Unease, Again: The Early Post-Kountché Period and Democratization

"Tout est foutu avec la mort de Kountché," a lot of gendarmes told me. Everything deteriorated with Kountché's death, they said. Since the late 1980s, Niger has experienced significant political changes, beginning with the crumbling of the military-controlled, one-party system and the downfall of President Seyni Kountché. Under the pressure of structural adjustment programs, Kountché's successor, Ali Saïbou, paved the way for democratization and cut back on social services, student bursaries, and spending on equipment for public services to balance the national budget. Civil servants, teachers, students, and trades unions, who had been badly hit by these cuts, organized and dominated proceedings at the National Conference held in 1991, the key moment in the country's democratization. They managed to mobilize and maintain opposition to negotiations with the International Monetary Fund until 1994, so that Niger was more or less cut off from external financial flows. In addition, it suffered from high inflation and the fall in demand for uranium, the country's main raw material export, particularly after Chernobyl and the end of the Cold War (Gazibo 2005; Gervais 1995; Graybeal and Picard 1991).

This was the context in which a number of changes in Niger's overall security setting took place. Most important, the disintegration of Kountché's military regime coupled with internal financial bankruptcy forced Ali Saïbou, who was obliged to balance the national budget, to cut back on police and military expenses. As a result, Kountché's powerful secret police (La Coordination) was suppressed, police patrols and raids that had previously evacuated homeless laborers and beggars from the cities to their home villages were largely trimmed back, and road blocks by gendarmes throughout the country were removed (Gilliard and Pédenon 1996, 53; Idrissa 2008, 177). In addition, after long years of military rule, the absence of pluralist expression, and the citizens' diffuse fear vis-à-vis "un État extrêmement policier" (ibid., 199), the *corps habillés* were largely discredited and kept a low profile, especially following the National Conference in 1991 (Lund 2001, 859–60). Adjudant-Chef Souley recalled this difficult period in an interview: "When there was the [national] conference, there were moments when we felt uncomfortable wearing the uniform! During the national conference they insulted the military. Our bosses have trembled before thugs. . . . They turned everything into a settlement of scores and this is the damage that we blame our bosses for, they who let it drift up to a point where the image of the Nigerien army and gendarmerie was harmed."

Gendarmes were deeply wounded by these events and their superiors' performances on this occasion. Their pride was badly hurt; they felt they had lost all the civilians' respect. "The army was discredited during the conference," Chef Hamza remembered, "humiliated in such a way that if you put on the uniform, one might say they would spit on us."[34] In addition to that, gendarmes also had to change the way they worked fundamentally. With democratization and the continuous arrival and rising influence of human rights' groups, they were for the first time confronted with the risk of legal prosecution if they used violence against civilians (see Beek and Göpfert 2013a, 483–84); this slowly eroded one of their former, principal sources of authority and means for advancing the frontier.

The Tuareg Rebellion as a Necessary Evil

At about the same time, the Tuareg rebellion in the north, which lasted from 1990/91 until the peace treaty in 1995, left a lasting imprint on the gendarmerie as an institution, and even more so on the gendarmes who fought in it. Territorial integrity was at stake and the frontier needed to be secured. For the first time since 1992 the number of recruits rose from 100 to 250 and stayed at this level until the 2000s.[35] The rebellion also had a huge impact on the gendarme's equipment, as they obtained arms following the disarmament of former rebels. According to some gendarmes' estimates, more than half of all pistols and assault rifles used by gendarmes are former rebels' arms.

Just as lasting was the impact on the personal and collective memory of the many gendarmes who were sent to the frontlines. Young Tuaregs first attacked a gendarmerie post in Tchin Tabaraden in May 1990; it has often been described as the trigger of the rebellion (Brachet 2009, 36n29; Djibo 2002, 136). Gendarmes told me that they lost colleagues who had been shot in broad daylight during banal everyday activities; that they lived through numerous violent exchanges of fire, were ambushed during patrols, and that they had to sleep in foxholes for months, sometimes, with few interruptions, for years. Experienced gendarmes told their younger colleagues about their suffering during the rebellion; they shared memories of friends and colleagues they had lost in battle; they talked about brave and not so brave superiors; and they all stressed that they worked well even though conditions were harsh. "People got welded together! We really ensured security," Adjudant-Chef Souley remembered. Against the backdrop of their humiliation during and after the national conference, gendarmes regained their pride. And as they saw it, they were also able to regain the respect of civilians, but this time not through the *chicottes'* strikes against civilians but through acts of bravery against the enemies of the nation. In this sense, the rebellion was a "mal nécessaire," a "necessary evil," as Chef Hamza told me: "It is only now, right in the middle of the rebellion that they saw the importance of the gendarmes!"

Also the gendarmes' respect for their superiors returned slowly, but not unequivocally. Gendarmerie officers who committed brave acts are not forgotten; neither are those whom gendarmes considered cowards. However, in such crises, most officers on the frontline seemed to have proven themselves worthy of their men's respect. Even those officers not in the field gained the gendarmes' respect because they at least seemed to be aware and acknowledge the hard work gendarmes did on the frontline; they handed down formal commendations, extraordinary promotions, but also gave them less formalized compensations and rewards such as postings to "juicy" traffic control units after having worked on the frontline.

Another more or less direct consequence of the rebellion was the creation of the Forces Nationales d'Intervention et de Sécurité (FNIS) in 1997, and they were to become the gendarmerie's closest competitor. Unlike the gendarmerie, they are under the control of the Minister of the Interior. They comprised the already existing Garde Républicaine and the newly founded Unités Sahariennes de Sécurité (USS). The USS were, as stipulated in the 1995 peace treaty, the main reservoir for former rebel fighters—often without any school education whatsoever, even in higher ranks—and charged with patrolling and securing northern Niger's desert and mountainous regions.[36] Since their creation, the FNIS have also been endowed with competencies in criminal investigation (but they have only recently been trained in this). According to Adjudant-Chef Souley, this was "pure stupidity. A piece of wood will never become a crocodile!" From the gendarmes' point of view, their position—particularly their centrality to the frontier-project—has become increasingly threatened by the FNIS. Some perceived this as Albadé Abouba's personal project. Abouba was minister of the interior under President Mamadou Tandja, who was elected in 1999 after a military coup led by Commandant Daouda Malam Wanké that same year. The FNIS increased rapidly in number and received more professional training. They were militarily trained, worked mainly in rural areas, and were endowed with criminal investigation competencies—which had always been the gendarmes' distinctive features. Combined with President Tandja's lack of respect and trust in the gendarmerie, this led to a period of unease among the gendarmes which ended only in 2010 when Tandja was overthrown in a military coup led by capitaine, shortly thereafter général de corps d'armée, Salou Djibo. The FNIS were soon renamed Garde Nationale, to mark a symbolic rupture to Abouba's and Tandja's use of this corps for their own purposes—as a regime-stabilizing counterforce to a military that had been responsible for two coups since 1996 (led by Baré in 1996 and Wanké in 1999).

Post 9/11 Changes

In the aftermath of 9/11, the overall state security establishment in Niger changed significantly, with considerable impact on the gendarmerie. Niger was counted among the "frontline states" in the global war on terrorism (GWOT), together with Chad, Mali, and Mauritania (Davis 2007, 1) because they were said to have "what it takes to become a terrorist breeding ground" (Palmer 2007, 103).[37] From 2002 onward, Nigerien military and paramilitary forces were targeted by foreign initiatives such as the American-led Pan-Sahel Initiative, which in 2005 turned into the Trans-Sahara Counterterrorism Partnership, mounting joint military operations under US command, financial aid, and training from US Special Forces, particularly in intelligence gathering and analysis and counterterrorism intervention (Ellis 2004, 459).[38] Since 2009, France has taken over the leading security role in the region, particularly in Niger where they aim to secure their country's economic interests in uranium exploitation in the north, as French diplomats told me (see also Keenan 2009a, 17). When I talked to them in 2009 and 2010, they also seemed to have taken over the GWOT rhetoric, terming the Sahara a "second Afghanistan."[39] Nigerien authorities also adopted this anti-terrorism rhetoric, as Keenan (2007, 46–47) argues, to advance national interests such as strengthening their security establishments. Most efforts focus on training and equipping military and paramilitary units; a flagship project was the creation of the Unité Spéciale d'Intervention de la Gendarmerie Nationale (USGN) later renamed Groupement d'Intervention de la Gendarmerie Nationale (GIGN). This unit is charged with interventions against terrorists and organized crime and freeing hostages.[40]

The overall outcome was increased militarization with a remarkable rise in army and gendarmerie personnel: the number of army soldiers rose from 4,000 to 10,000 until 2006 (Keenan 2006b, 281); with biennial recruitments of initially 500, then 1,000, the number of gendarmes doubled from some 2,000 in the early 2000s to around 4,000 in 2008 (ibid., 281; Zangaou 2008, 266) and about 6,000 in 2013. Their numbers have thus almost doubled in only five years, and tripled in ten. According to one superior gendarmerie officer, the ultimate aim is 10,000 within a couple of years.[41] All of this resulted in Niger, and by extension the Nigerien gendarmes, being called on as frontiersmen and women in the "global war on terror"—at the frontier between the so-called civilized world and the world of evil.

The evolution of the Nigerien gendarmerie is a history of frontier policing. The early gendarmes and their predecessors, few in numbers, geographically and socially far removed from the local population, had the task of pushing forward and maintaining the external boundary—first of the colony, later the nation-state. Apart from those civilians living near one of the early twenty-something brigades, the local population only met gendarmes when they were on their oft-violent tournées through villages and remote areas. With the continuous recruitment of Nigerien gendarmes, the increase in personnel up to ten thousand, the spread of brigades throughout the country, the growing influence of human rights associations in Niger, and the gendarmes' involvement in the "global war on terror," the gendarmeries' mode of policing society underwent profound transformations. What had been a punctual, violent, hit-and-run, expedition-based style of policing slowly turned into a more sedentary, judicial, and consent-based style, only recently undermined by the internationally funded efforts to remilitarize the gendarmerie. Thus the nature of the frontier-project changed also: from the conquest and control of the territorial periphery, via the internal colonization and production of discipline and legibility, to the fight against terrorists, that is, the enemies within.

In the frontier it has always been difficult to distinguish between the defense of external borders and the maintenance of internal order, a classical distinction reflected in the equally classical distinction between military and police forces and their division of work. One appears to be outward-oriented, the other inward looking. This divide completely dissolves in the gendarmerie, a police corps with military training and status. The gendarmerie in Niger has always by definition been both a defender of the national territory and a contributor to the internal construction of the nation-state, with the maintenance of public order, the proliferation of national bureaucratic procedures, French as the national working language, symbols of the Nigerien nation, in short, the images and practices of the state.

The frontier is thus not only the external or internal border between those areas and groups penetrated by state agencies and those which are not, but also the space between those spheres perceived as civilized and those spheres gendarmes consider savage and chaotic, between the legal and illegal, the legitimate and illegitimate, the legible and the illegible, the familiar and the unfamiliar, between "us" and "them." The gendarmes have been pushing this frontier ever since; yet it cannot be crossed—it is the horizon that moves with them.

Chapter 3

A STORY OF A MURDER, NO TRACES, AND NOTHING TO REPORT

The brigade was at its most peaceful between 6:00 and 7:00 a.m. There were no complainants, no accusations or heated discussions, no rattling office fan, no squeaky printer. Yacouba was the only gendarme there at that hour. His twenty-four-hour orderly shift began at 6:00 a.m. and the remaining officers would only come around 7:00 a.m. at the start of regular office hours. Apart from him, only two detainees were sitting out in the morning in the open courtyard in front of the building. A young boy working for a coffee vendor a little down the road had just brought them two sandwiches for breakfast. Yacouba had ordered and paid for them while drinking his early morning white coffee with lots of sugar on his way to the brigade.

I arrived at quarter to seven, so a bit earlier than usual. Yacouba had just finished his solid breakfast and the pot with leftovers from yesterday's supper was still on the small, rickety table in front of the brigade's entrance. Sitting on a wooden bench that looked just as rickety, Yacouba was lighting the tiny charcoal stove for today's first green tea. The first and strongest round would usually go to him and the detainees only. That day I was lucky enough to be among the lucky tea drinkers. By the time the rest of the gendarmes came, the second and third rounds would be ready.

That morning, the slow rhythm of the early hours hardly changed at 7:00 a.m. and during the office hours. Only two complainants came; one at nine, one at ten. One was sent to the civil judge immediately, one to his neighborhood chief. At 10.30 a.m. a shoe vendor and cobbler came up the hill and offered his services.

As we got closer to noon, the gendarmes were getting ready for the midday prayer and the three-hour lunch break. In gendarmerie parlance that morning had "N-T-R," nothing to report.[1]

When I came back to the brigade after lunch, I was struck by the contrast. I was again a bit early, but all the gendarmes were already there and were all visibly agitated. They hurried in and out of the office; Chef Tahirou, the interim brigade commander was on his mobile phone talking hectically to what seemed to be a superior; Nouhou adjusted handcuffs hanging from the belt of his uniform; Omar was checking the magazine of his semi-automatic pistol; Moussa carried assault rifles out of the office, two at a time, handed an AK-47 to Chef Tahirou, a G3 to Nouhou, then another G3 to Omar and another AK-47 to Amadou, who was checking the oil level of the brigade's four-wheel-drive Toyota.

Only Yacouba was sitting calmly on the bench outside the building. He was about to prepare more tea, which he and the others usually drank in the early afternoon. I sat down beside him, shook his hand, lit a cigarette, and watched the others go about their hectic business. Yacouba also lit a cigarette from the blaze of the small coal stove on which tea was brewing, and told me that "an event occurred." The chef de canton from Tsaga had called. Yacouba did not know what it was all about, but he knew that his colleagues now had to go there on a mission. I had always been told that the Tsaga canton chief never, ever calls the gendarmerie. "That is true," Yacouba replied and took a puff of his cigarette. "But now he did. So be sure that there are dead bodies."

Chef Tahirou had just gotten off the phone and came toward me. The regional commander had called him ten times already in the last two hours, he said rolling his eyes. He said they had to drive to Tsaga and that they must leave immediately. Two girls had apparently gone missing in Tsaga two and a half days earlier. They had gone into the bush with a small flock of goats and sheep and were surprised by the heavy rain. It had washed away all traces of the girls and all efforts by a search group from their village had been in vain. This morning, a group of young herders had come across their bodies in the bush—the girls were dead and had been severely mutilated.

Before leaving for Tsaga, Chef Tahirou told me that the girls had been killed with a machete and their genitals cut off. Tahirou was certain that the perpetrators were Nigerian organ traffickers who had slipped in over the nearby border. And he was just as certain that they had already slipped back to Nigeria and that it would be impossible to catch them. Plus, the rain had washed away all traces of them. This is also what Chef Tahirou had immediately told the public prosecutor, who then told Tahirou to inform the imam and have him "brandir le Coran" in order to find the perpetrators as quickly as possible. After he had given me this brief update, Chef Tahirou told Nouhou, Moussa, Omar, and Amadou to get into the car. Nouhou and Omar fixed their turbans and got onto the Toyota pickup, Amadou, Moussa, and Tahirou got into the cabin and off they drove. They had a fifty-kilometer drive on a sand and mud trail before them.

At the brigade, the slow rhythm of the early hours reemerged. No more complainants came, merely two visitors for the detainees, who were again sitting in the open courtyard. After the evening prayer, Yacouba's son came up the hill with two pots of rice and stew for supper. Yacouba poured a good portion into the pot he had kept (and washed) from his breakfast and handed it to the detainees.

It had been dark for three hours, shortly after 9:00 p.m. when Chef Tahirou and the others came back from Tsaga. Tahirou and the gendarmes got out of the car and the only thing he said was "N-T-R," nothing to report, and that was that. They all looked exhausted and disappeared into the brigade, locked their weapons into the gun cabinet, came back out again, mounted their motorbikes, silently waved goodbye to us and drove home. Only Chef Tahirou briefly stopped by Yacouba and me, the only ones still at the brigade, and told us that they had found nothing—just as he had expected. No traces, no witnesses, just the two dead girls' bodies. He too was exhausted, wished us a good night and left on his motorbike. Yacouba turned the volume up on the radio again and lit another cigarette. So did I. After the last puff, I wished him good night and left.

When I arrived at the brigade the next morning, it felt like a déjà vu: Chef Tahirou was on the phone, Nouhou and Omar were adjusting their turbans, Moussa was distributing the assault rifles and Amadou was checking the Toyota. They were preparing to go to Tsaga again. Yacouba sat on the bench. Because of the new mission to Tsaga, he could not have his day off, as is usual after a twenty-four-hour shift; he had just gone home to take a shower and fetch some breakfast. Chef Tahirou greeted me as soon as he hung up the phone. He said he had received another call from Tsaga: "The population has caught the perpetrator," he said excitedly. "We'll go and fetch him." Then he described in detail what he was quite sure had happened to the girls: the man, caught and ready to be fetched, had met the two girls in the hills, where they had probably sought shelter from the thunderstorm. He had first encouraged them and gained their trust, talked to them nicely while hiding the machete behind his back. When the two girls approached, he dealt the first girl a fatal machete blow on the left side of her neck (he was right-handed); the second girl ran away, he rushed after her and dealt her a fatal blow, also with his right hand, but now from behind and thus on the right of her neck. Afterward, he mutilated them. He cut their arms and upper bodies and he cut off their genitals. It was impossible to tell whether he had penetrated them before doing so. Not even the nurse from Tsaga that Chef Tahirou had taken with them and asked for medical expertise could determine this.

Chef Tahirou sent this detailed account of the events in a written radio message to the regional commander, and he verbally explained it in the three phone calls he had thereupon received from the commander that morning. According to Yacouba, this was a big mistake. "You need to know what you need to write," he said. Chef Tahirou should have better written in the message "to verify information received" or "according to information received" or "for further investigation," and he should have used the conditional tense. But he should have never given unconfirmed information that had not been thoroughly investigated and established as facts. But when Chef Tahirou told his superior about the dead girls, he first mentioned the gang of Nigerian organ traffickers, who had already left the country. Then he mentioned the solitary man who had since been apprehended and was waiting to be picked up by the gendarmes. According to Yacouba, it was no wonder the commandant de groupement was rather disoriented and had called Tahirou a dozen times already.

They arrived back from Tsaga at around 10:00 p.m., I learned the next morning. When I arrived at the brigade, Chef Tahirou walked toward me cheerfully as I got off my motorbike. "Monsieur Mirco! We got him!" he said as we shook hands. "It's a giant fellow," Chef Tahirou said as he took me by the arm and led me into the office to present his catch to me. He told Omar to open the cell door and I had to step back a little. "He has confessed everything," Tahirou said as the door opened, "but he is a madman." A small chubby man with big eyes and a gentle face sat in the corner of the dark cell. He was the only inmate as the other prisoners were again outside on a mat under the thatched roof.

Chef Tahirou shut the door again and told me what had happened the day before in Tsaga. When they arrived there, they discovered that nobody had actually caught the perpetrator. Some Tsaga residents, via the chef de canton, only indicated his whereabouts in the hills a couple of kilometers west of the village, where the girls' bodies had also been found. The *chef de canton* gave the gendarmes a local guide who rode with them in the Toyota to the indicated area. It did not take them long to find the suspect. He was sitting under a tree with his long stick leaning against the tree trunk, and an axe beside him on the ground. Amadou, driving the Toyota, pulled over right in front of this man, Chef Tahirou opened the door and greeted him three times, but he didn't respond. "As soon as I saw his eyes, this giant madman's eyes, it looked like he was about to attack. This was when I said to the gendarmes, Nouhou and the others on the rack of the car, to unlock and load their weapons. They made *chak-chak* and this madman immediately—even though he is mentally insane—he immediately took flight." But they caught him shortly after. "Immediately he said, 'It wasn't me! It wasn't me!' even though we had not even asked him. So he has already confessed. We took him to the crime scene, and over there I explained to him what had happened. 'The first one, you have attacked her standing in front of her, gave her a blow on the neck with your right hand, the second one from behind while she was running away, again with your right hand.' The only thing he replied was: 'You are very intelligent! This is exactly what happened.'"

When they stopped in Tsaga on their way back to the brigade, Chef Tahirou was told that this man was a native of Tsaga and the victims were his direct cousins. He had lived in Libya for seven years but had been repatriated because of his mental state. His relatives in Tsaga said that he used to have such crises every now and then, but then he often went out of the village and spent a couple of days in the bush or up in the hills. And he had never been violent before. However, the people from Tsaga noticed that he had been absent since the girls disappeared, and this had made them suspicious. As they knew where he usually went when he had one of his crises, they knew where to guide the gendarmes. "Thank God that we caught him," Chef Tahirou said and lit his first cigarette in months.

He asked me if I could help him write up the procès-verbal about the murders in Tsaga on the computer. He was keen to finish the report quickly so that he could present the detainee to the judge and then have him jailed and thus get rid of this supposedly dangerous man. I sat down at the desk. But before we began to write, he explained that he had modified what he thought had happened and what he had already explained to the regional commander in detail. First, the perpetrator was not a Nigerian organ trafficker; second, the weapon was not a machete but an axe; and third, the girls' genitals were not cut off but simply "smashed" with the axe. Then Chef Tahirou began to dictate. He drew some parts from an older procès-verbal of a murder case, and he had already drafted other parts on loose sheets of paper. He dictated yet other parts such as the suspect's statement off the cuff. "It's not necessary to ask him; I know everything he has said." And yet, he did not know everything. Time and again, Chef Tahirou asked the man through the closed cell door details such as his date of birth, names of his mother and father, when he had left the village, which girl he killed first and in which hand he held the axe. Chef Tahirou paused and then asked him again: in which hand? As it turned out, contrary to Chef Tahirou's initial assumption, the man was left-handed. Toward the end of the man's statement, Chef Tahirou added, again off the cuff, a few more questions and answers,[2] then the precise time of the interrogation: 10:02 a.m. until 10:28 a.m.

Chef Tahirou was meticulously searching for the right words to describe the brutal killing and mutilation of the two girls. He decided on the key phrase, "He scalped the neck of the girl."[3] We took a break and went out to smoke cigarettes. He explained how the girls' wounds matched the man's axe perfectly and that we absolutely needed to mention this in the procès-verbal. He put out his cigarette after just a couple of puffs, went into the office and sat down with a French dictionary on his lap. Two minutes later, he called me back in just as I put out my cigarette. He wanted me to change "scalped" into "chopped with an axe."[4] You cannot scalp with an axe, he said.

We finished the procès-verbal, and Chef Tahirou had the suspect immediately sent before the judge and then to prison. The suspense that gripped Chef Tahirou and the other gendarmes eventually gave way to a more cheerful atmosphere. The gendarmes started to make jokes about the "giant madman" and took the rest of the day's work rather easy. Chef Hamza was relaxed and chatted to people sitting in front of the brigade, detainees, complainants, suspects, and an ambulant drug peddler. He did not mention the atrocities committed by the child murderer; he highlighted how bizarre this man was, "You know, every morning he asked for camel milk! Can you imagine?" he said and everybody laughed heartily.

Two days later, Adjudant-Chef Souley returned from temporary leave. Chef Hamza was visibly relieved when he saw Souley driving his Mercedes slowly toward the brigade. As we waited for the approaching car, I realized that nobody had mentioned Adjudant-Chef Souley in the last days and I asked Hamza whether somebody had called Souley to inform him about the murder in Tsaga. "Oh, he knows," Hamza said. "But it was not the brigade that informed him. He has his pigeons everywhere. Nothing can happen in the department without his knowledge." After exchanging friendly greetings with Adjudant-Chef Souley, Chef Hamza told him about Tahirou's radio messages and reports of "organ traffickers" and "picking up the perpetrator who had been caught by the population" made to the commandant de groupement. Adjudant-Chef Souley laughed out loud and Chef Hamza and I joined in. "It's me who told him to return to Tsaga immediately," Souley told me later. "I told him what to do: talk to the family! Talk to the chief! Needle the population! It is impossible that strangers come to this area without anybody seeing them."

As the other gendarmes heard Souley's laughter they poured out of the office with clear signs of relief on their faces. Chef Tahirou was also relieved, he later told me. It is one thing to arrange a case of theft on market day; it is another to investigate a murder and manage a whole unit.

Part II

PRODUCING FORM, OR BUREAUCRATIC SENSES

Chapter 4

THE EAR

Listening to Noise, Hearing Cases

It all depended on the gendarmes' ear. Of course, first somebody needed to see "something-that-ought-not-to-be-happening-and-about-which-somebody-had-better-do-something-now," as Egon Bittner famously put it (1974, 31); and then somebody needed to decide to tell the gendarmes about it. But then, again, it all depended on the gendarmes' ear. What and whom Amadou, Souley, and the others decided to listen to, and what they heard in the stories they were told was key to everything that followed. This chapter is, in a way, about what the gendarmes were told, what they listened to, and what they heard.

Sometimes the gendarmes saw a crime or offence occurring in real time, in flagrante, and in front of their own eyes, but this happened only on rare occasions and mainly when they were on traffic control duty. Out on the streets checking vehicles, drivers, cargo, and passengers, they regularly saw offences to the Highway Code (Code de la Route), and they dealt with them just as quickly as they saw them by handing out tickets and collecting fines. Other than that, their view was rather restricted. Alternatively, Adjudant-Chef Souley could be given hints about possible "events," as he called them, by his informants, but this happened rarely. Informants were more important when it came to investigating cases, not in finding them. Usually the people directly involved informed the gendarmes about such "events."

Yet listening to complaints didn't necessarily mean that anything would follow from that. The gendarmes still needed to accept the complaint and turn it into a case, that is, a bureaucratic form that allowed them to become active. What kind of an offence it was (a felony, misdemeanor, or a minor offence?) and what the gendarmes then did in response depended, again, on the gendarmes' ear—more precisely, their "vocational ear," a phrase I borrow from Bittner (1974, 28), and to what it was attuned.

This has often been discussed as a matter of police discretion, a necessary principle of police work everywhere.[1] But little has been said about the subtleties underlying this practice, at least not beyond the (often well-founded) assumption of ethnic, political, or other biases by the police. Two articles by Jeffrey Martin (2007) and Jan Beek (2011) are remarkable exceptions. They both take a close look at the police officers' decision-making process and reflect on the complex rationalities involved therein. This chapter adopts a similar approach, but it not only begins a couple of steps prior to the gendarmes' decision making, it also describes it as profoundly shaped by the frontier-condition. Sitting in a bureaucratic outpost and confronting a mostly "illegible" and "undisciplined" population (in James Scott and Michel Foucault's sense), their vocational ear had far more (or far more sensitive) hair cells than police officers and public bureaucrats were usually attributed. And this was precisely because Amadou, Souley, and the other gendarmes, although they were bureaucrats, did not live in a "utopia of rules" (see Graeber 2015); if anything, it was a "frontier of rules."

Yes, the frontier is a kind of utopia, although not one of rules but of possibilities. Here, pushing forward is a process, not a result; the law is not deemed an end in itself but a means for a better life; order is in the making, not a given. The ear just like the eye is deeply caught up in the modern project of ordering the world and producing certainty (see Erlmann 2004), and where this order has not been properly established, bureaucrats may find their surroundings confusing—not unlike those nineteenth-century European travelers who found Egypt visually confusing, as Timothy Mitchell describes (1991a, xv). But also, and unlike Mitchell suggests for his travelers' eyes, the bureaucrats' senses have not been totally domesticated; in the frontier, where order is being established, negotiated, and reestablished over and over again, they never are. Amadou, just like any other bureaucrat, never knew what exactly he was supposed to listen to and what he was supposed to hear from that. Both his world and his senses were undergoing a process of mutual ordering. And this process unfolded when the gendarmes were told stories, listened to them, and tried to figure out what they had just heard.

Weighing Up the Options

When "something-that-ought-not-to-be-happening" had happened and the people involved decided that "somebody-had-better-do-something-now," they had several options available to them. The one most frequently used in Godiya and all over (at least rural) Niger was to confront the person or group whose act had caused the grievance in the first place. If this didn't work or was not an option, for example, because the author of the crime was unknown or had simply left, or was too scary to confront directly, the remaining grieving party entered directly, from what Laura Nader and Harry Todd (1978) called the "conflict stage" in the disputing process, into the "dispute stage." This means they made the matter public by involving a third party—which could be the gendarmerie.

In many places, however, the gendarmerie was not an option. Sometimes the next gendarmerie post was just too far away for people to reach; and sometimes people were pressured into not making contact with state officials altogether. In Tsaga, for example, a tiny town north of Godiya, the canton chief, the highest local authority, and his marabout had threatened by the Qur'an that if any of his subjects talked to the gendarmes without consulting them first, they would bring great suffering on themselves and their families.[2] As a result, the gendarmes never received calls from people in Tsaga—except from the chief himself, when he had run out of options. According to Chef Hamza, the canton chief had done this because he wanted absolute control over his subjects and his circumscription and because he wanted to "eat" the money his subjects brought to him.[3] The gendarmes were aware of that, but there was nothing they could do about it, Hamza said. They only knew that when they received a call from Tsaga something terrible must have happened, something to which the canton chief had no response.

In many areas, particularly those a little more urbanized than Godiya, even when the next gendarmerie post was well within reach, people would consider several other options from which to choose. They could talk to private security agents, vigilante groups, circles of young men gathering on the streets, the so-called *fada*, spontaneous gatherings often pejoratively called "the mob," but also traditional authority figures like imams and chiefs, or other influential individuals (see Göpfert 2012; Jensen 2007, 51–52). Who would eventually be called to respond to a given event—in Schapera's (1972, 390) terms, who was "entitled" to do so—depended on the type of transgression perceived, who committed it, and who the victims were.

In short, the world of law and policing in its broadest sense is and has always been, in Niger and anywhere else, a pluralized one.[4] And talking to the gendarmes was at best only one of many options. According to widespread explanations, civilians only report an offence to the gendarmerie or police when alternative responses do not exist or have failed to achieve the desired results. This was to some extent true in Godiya and the area nearby. Usually, people would first go to their chiefs—*chef de quartier* or chef de groupement, depending on their ethnic affiliation—and "arrange" things there. Elhadji Shehu, a Fulani chef de groupement in Godiya explained in an interview, originally in Hausa: "If you have a problem, you come and tell it to me. If the other guy is also a Fulani, we will arrange it here. If he's not a Fulani, we will go and tell his chief. . . . And if it is too big, we bring him to the gendarmerie." The stronger the control the chiefs had over their subjects, the more the gendarmerie turned into a last resort. Yet, at least in Godiya, people could and did easily bypass their chiefs. One day, a man in his sixties came to the brigade to file a complaint, and the gendarmes asked him why he had not brought his neighborhood chief with him. "I am an ancient soldier," he replied in Hausa. "What I do is none of the chief's business!" He and many others simply did not recognize the chief's authority and at least to my knowledge this didn't cause them any harm in Godiya whatsoever. Others came directly to the gendarmes because they were looking for something that their chief did not have on offer. They strategically evaluated the different options available to them—they engaged in the oft-cited "forum shopping" (Benda-Beckmann 1981)—and chose the gendarmes because they were looking not so much for uncertain and often indefinite reconciliation (which civil judges and chiefs were notorious for), but rather for a quick and decisive judgment.[5] They wanted, for example, quick compensation or for the perpetrator to receive an additional punishment for his wrongdoings. This was something the gendarmes, thanks to Adjudant-Chef Souley's rigor and cells, did have in store and the others didn't.

Approaching the Gendarmes

When people did decide to bring their grievances to the gendarmes' attention, they still had different ways of approaching them, which in turn influenced the way the gendarmes listened to them. Some came alone. Those were usually people who lived in Godiya or the surrounding villages. Sharing neighborhoods with the gendarmes and their families, they had no particular qualms about talking to them, as opposed to people from remote villages who only knew the repressive image of patrolling gendarmes and other uniformed state personnel. And yet, most of those who approached the brigade were extremely respectful and reticent, falling back on habits well rehearsed in interaction with chiefs, elders, and other traditional authorities. They took off their shoes, timidly greeted the gendarmes, squatted down in front of them, talking quietly and only when asked to. Those who had at some point already had contact with the gendarmes were a bit more confident and addressed one of the gendarmes directly, aiming at the one they thought must be the highest-ranking of those present. Since most civilians did not know the meaning of the stripes on the gendarmes' shoulders, they often aimed, again in accordance with customary behavior, at Chef Hamza (for his age) or the gendarme Yacouba (for his big belly). After the respectful greetings, they said "Ina son in kai kara" ("I want to bring a complaint"), or "convocation nike so" ("I want a summons"), since they knew the gendarmes usually started a case by handing the complainant a summons for the alleged wrongdoer. As neither Chef Hamza nor Yacouba were the highest-ranking gendarmes present, they politely asked the complainants to be patient and wait for a superior to listen to them.

Others wanted to speak directly to Adjudant-Chef Souley. Having met him before, they knew that he would decide whether to take over a case. When they greeted the gendarmes and asked whether the "commandant" was around, the gendarmes usually told them that Souley was busy and would deal with them shortly. They would offer them a seat on a bench a bit away from the gendarmes, "ka zamna, ka yi hankuri kadan" ("take a seat, have a little patience"). Yet others greeted the gendarmes only in passing and self-confidently entered the brigade building; some merely threw a casual "yana ciki?"—"Is he inside?"—in the gendarmes' direction before stepping in. In this case, one of the gendarmes, most often Chef Hamza, would call them back and rebuke them: they should greet them first, tell them what they wanted; then the gendarmes would inform the brigade commander, if necessary. Hamza made clear that nobody should enter the gendarmes' office just like that. Then he would have them sit and wait on the bench or on the mat like everybody else.

Still others came accompanied by their chief or, which was more often the case, by their chief's representative, the so-called *baruma*. The baruma are, like the gendarmes, a kind of frontiersmen (and only men). They are intermediaries between traditional officeholders and state administrations, such as hospitals, the mayor's office, the prefect's office, forestry and custom services, and the gendarmerie. They supposedly always knew where to go with what kind of problem, were experienced at negotiating with state officials, and knew how to present a story to the gendarmes. Gado, Elhadji Shehu's representative and baruma, was a well-known guest at the gendarmerie brigade in Godiya. He came there almost every other day, greeted all the gendarmes with a handshake, knew everybody by name, and sat down on the gendarmes' benches, where no other civilians were allowed to sit. The reception was similarly warm hearted when other influential supporters such as local politicians, trade union leaders, members of the National Guard, or other public officials accompanied the complainants.

Talking to the Gendarmes

People who decided (or were summoned) to talk to the gendarmes knew that rhetoric was highly valued. I often heard stories about friends of friends hesitating to file a complaint because they felt they could not "speak well" and that "the other can speak better than you" and that whoever is able to express themselves properly in either French or Hausa would be able to argue for and eventually gain their right. And the gendarmes too felt that many people were poor speakers, that many "don't even know how to talk," as Chef Hamza said. "They don't even know what they are going to say. They will talk nonsense. As soon as they see the uniform they start to tremble." And in many cases this was true. Thus beyond the chiefs' and barumas' personal connections and technical know-how also their rhetorical skills and experience in talking to the gendarmes often proved essential for complainants and defendants.

True, eloquence and rhetorical skills were highly regarded by the gendarmes. But this also meant that in many cases rhetoric trumped social status. One day a married man in his late thirties filed a complaint against a seventeen-year-old, illiterate girl, who sold groundnut oil and dried groundnut paste (*kulikuli*) at the market. According to the man, the girl had promised to marry him (as his second wife) but was now having an affair with another man. The complainant was sitting on a bench in front of Chef Hamza; the girl was squatting on the ground. While the man was talking, interspersing French words here and there, she interrupted him several times and was thus harshly reprimanded by Chef Hamza, "Shiru! Yel iska!," "Shut up! Half-wit!" After the man had finished, it was her turn. She was very confident and speaking fluently in Hausa with a firm voice for about ten minutes and without any stuttering, ahems, and the like, she kept eye contact with Chef Hamza and me. She defended herself vehemently. When she finished, and she clearly marked the end of her narration rhetorically, Chef Hamza turned to me and said: "Ouallahi, she knows how to talk." He looked at me with an air of surprise. "This girl? Even a woman, often even a man cannot talk like she can. And what is more, she is right!"

Talking to the gendarmes was always ambivalent. Presenting one's complaint was what Thomas Bierschenk describes as the first step in the legal funnel which, in most people's view, "seems like a vacuum cleaner which functions on the basis of obscure mechanisms and which, once it aims its hose at the target group of a legal norm, threatens to suck it up in a vortex leading to the unknown" (Bierschenk 2008, 119) with the last step being unpredictable convictions and sanctions. This is not something the complainants desired. Not for themselves, nor for their opponents. Complainants wanted the gendarmes to listen to them and become active; and because the gendarmes (as other legal workers) had an interest in limiting their workload, complainants had to make a strong case for themselves. But complainants also didn't want the gendarmes to become active in the legally sanctioned and most rigorous way. They didn't want the opposing party to be sucked into the legal funnel; they merely wanted compensation. In this ambivalent situation, it was an important advantage to have supporters such as the baruma, who were versed in navigating this frontier-space, and thus in reducing the uncertainty regarding what would happen next.

In a few cases, civilians had already reported their complaint to the public prosecutor before coming to the brigade. The prosecutor then sent them to the gendarmes, with a small piece of paper indicating "See Monsieur CB [commandant de brigade] of Godiya for compiling the procedure of . . ."[6] with a red stamp on the back: "Tribunal d'Instances [district court] de Godiya, le Président," no signature. In this case, the gendarmes had little leeway; the case was already established. The prosecutor had already qualified the offence and as their superior in judicial matters, he tasked them with investigating the case and compiling the procès-verbal. In all other complaints, it was up to the gendarmes to decide what to do next. After all, not all complaints turned into cases.

Listening (Is It a Case? Or: Should We Do Something About It?)

First, as banal as it may seem, when people talked to them, the gendarmes needed to listen. The complainants would be either standing or sitting a bit off from the gendarmes waiting to be addressed. When the gendarmes' conversation drew to an end, one of them would turn to the civilian and ask him or her, "Lahiya?" "Are you alright?" "What happened?" "What is it?" or simply "Oui?" Then the civilian would come a few steps closer, often squat down in front of the gendarme who had addressed him and begin explaining what brought him or her there. Rank-and-file gendarmes would then report this to one of the noncommissioned officers, the chefs, who were usually in one of the offices. These would then listen to the complainant again. In cases they considered very serious, they would report directly to the brigade commander, who would then listen to the complainant too and eventually, after consulting the public prosecutor over the phone, decide how to proceed.

But often complainants were simply forgotten on the mat.[7] They would sit there for hours on end without anybody listening to them. Every few hours, Adjudant-Chef Souley would step out of his office to stretch his legs, just to find sometimes a good dozen of complainants waiting to be listened to. Souley would get angry, reprimand his gendarmes for their laziness and then approach these complainants directly. Rather quickly he would sort out those he felt should be sent away, those who should be given a summons to deliver to the alleged wrongdoer, and those who should be listened to more carefully, whom he would either refer to one of his noncommissioned officers or invite into his own office. "You haven't killed somebody, have you?" he often asked those who wanted to talk to him. He knew that a lot of complainants were afraid of going to the gendarmes not to mention talk to them. His jokes often built on joking relationships between ethnic groups, he wanted to break the ice and make complainants feel a bit more at ease, he told me.

When the gendarmes listened to the complainants, the question was whether these complaints were valid and gave them a mandate to become active. Technically, for a complaint to turn into a case, the gendarmes had to identify three elements constituting a criminal offence: the legal, material, and moral elements (see Bauer and Pérez 2009, 97), the breach of a law caused by concrete acts and the authors' intention. If only one of these elements was missing, there was no offence, there was no valid complaint, and the gendarmes had no legal mandate to engage. If all but the legal element were found, it was a civil complaint, most of which were matters of land-conflict, heritage disputes, marriage disputes, adultery, issues of debt, and allegations of sorcery—all of which the gendarmes were supposed to keep their hands off. Complainants with civil issues had to be sent to the civil judge (or to ethnic or religious authorities). Yet the line between civil affairs and criminal cases was thin. Adjudant-Chef Souley noted: "Almost all civil affairs can turn into criminal affairs. For example in an affair about debt: As soon as you penetrate just a little bit—how has he taken on this debt? You will notice that there were some deceptive maneuvers, or he has breached his confidence, or he defrauded him, and so on. So it's a breach of confidence [*abus de confiance*] or fraud [*escroquerie*]. So it's a criminal affair." Thus a simple loan could—with a little digging—easily turn into fraud. A civil matter turned into a criminal case and allowed the gendarmes to become active. There was one problem for the gendarmes though, as Chef Boubacar told me. Complainants always had a clear interest in stressing, overemphasizing, or even inventing fraudulent maneuvers in their stories to transform a civil into a criminal (or at least potentially criminal) affair and have the gendarmes take over the case, and have them work it in their favor. "And this pushes us into ambiguity," Chef Boubacar explained. And ambiguity was not only unacceptable in a gendarme's work, it was also dangerous, he felt. If in the end, it turned out that there was no legal reason whatsoever for the gendarmes' engagement, there could be negative repercussions like countercomplaints, interventions by influential personalities, reprimands from their superiors, or even punishments. "This is why you have to be very careful!" Chef Boubacar told the gendarmes under his watch again and again.

To be on the safe side without pushing back complainants completely, younger gendarmes in particular would send the complainants to the public prosecutor or simply call him and ask for his opinion. And there was no questioning what the prosecutor said. Even if affairs were obviously civil matters, when somebody brought a note written by the prosecutor saying, "See the CB . . . ," gendarmes dealt with it. "Without the piece of paper, it's civil. But with the piece of paper from the prosecutor it's criminal. BOOM! And we have our hands free," as Chef Boubacar put it. The note from the prosecutor not only defined the offence, it also protected the gendarmes from interventions by their superiors and politicians.

All of this notwithstanding, the gendarmes treated many civil affairs anyhow, even though they knew that they had no protection whatsoever from their superiors and the prosecutor.[8] There were several reasons for this. First, the gendarmes had financial interests. Any case, whether criminal or civil was a potential source of additional income, either through unofficial fees (for example for a summons) or through gifts from civilians in response to the gendarmes' having done a good job. These gifts would usually be brought before Adjudant-Chef Souley who would then redistribute parts of them to the gendarmes who had been working on the respective case. Second, and important, the gendarmes (and not only those in Godiya!) sincerely wanted to help people who had been harmed, even if the law, which they often felt was inapt to local contexts, had no sanctions or remedy available for various types of wrongdoing. The real question for the gendarmes was thus not "Is it a case?" but rather "Should we do something about it?"

Hearing (What Kind of a Case Is It? Or: What Should We Do?)

When the gendarmes had decided to "better-do-something-now," they still had to decide about what exactly it was they should do. The big question was whether to send the conflicting parties to trial, or to deal with this case on their own level. The answer depended on what kind of a case they heard in the complaint they were told. This in turn was mainly a formal matter of defining the gravity of the case in correspondence with the legal triad of *crime*, *délit*, and *contravention*.[9] A crime is a serious offence punishable by death or a minimum of ten years imprisonment, a délit a less serious offence punishable by a fine or a prison sentence of less than ten years, and a contravention a minor offence that is punished by a simple fine—a ticket (République du Niger 2003, Art. 1 and 5; Bauer and Pérez 2009, 97–99). The public prosecutor had to be involved in crimes and délits only; the gendarmes handed out tickets for a contravention. These categories reflect the distinction the gendarmes drew between "grandes affaires" on the one hand, and "petites affaires" or "affaires courantes" on the other (see Jeanjean 1991, 84–85). Noncommissioned officers could make decisions regarding contraventions and small "everyday" délits. Big affairs, important délits and crimes, had to be brought to the brigade commander Souley's attention, who would then inform the prosecutor.

Assessing the gravity of the case, the gendarmes paid particular attention to the precise damage caused. In the case of physical harm to the complainant's body or property, this was rather simple for the gendarmes to measure: How large is the field of crops that has been trampled down by a herder's cattle? How much are the stolen goods worth? How much did the treatment of injuries cost? How long is the victim's temporary disability? In the case of immaterial harm, caused for example by slander, the problem of putting a number on the gravity was more complicated. In one case, a woman filed a complaint against another woman who had spread a rumor that the former had HIV/AIDS. For Chef Tahirou, at that time interim brigade commander and quite inexperienced in that position, this was futile and he sent the woman away. Chef Boubacar, however, and all the other gendarmes did not agree with Tahirou, and this led to a heated debate, almost to a brawl between Tahirou and Boubacar. Chef Boubacar explained afterward: "This is a very delicate affair. Everywhere in town, they sullied her name, and if you don't intervene in cases like this, soon there will be chaos! People will start tearing each other to pieces!" Here the relevant category, also put forward by the prosecutor, was "public disorder" (*trouble à l'ordre public*). "Any offence," the prosecutor explained, "is a societal problem. And any societal problem can incite public disorder." So in a sense, the harm caused was always considered beyond the personal damages caused to the complainant and to pose a threat to peaceful coexistence at large. Therefore, gendarmes were extremely cautious when it came to such immaterial, but sometimes-uncountable damage.

Similar to "civil" and "criminal," the categories délit and contravention were not neatly separated and could be transformed into the other. In the case of assault, for example, gendarmes made use of the dividing line between a délit and a contravention, which in their eyes was fixed at ten days of temporary disability for the victim (although the legal article the gendarmes mentioned referred to unintentional harm; see République du Niger 2003, Art. 272); and when consulting with the medical doctor, who was a good friend of Adjudant-Chef Souley, the number of days could be negotiated. The transformation of a délit into a contravention was usually part of the gendarmes' efforts to allow for an "amicable arrangement" because then the prosecutor was not involved and the gendarmes had great leeway in terms of procedure.

Besides the harm caused, the gendarmes paid particular attention to the motive behind the offensive act. Was it committed accidentally, by slight or gross negligence, or by criminal intent? Adjudant-Chef Souley told me in an interview what this "moral dimension" was all about:

> You can commit a serious act in a tolerable situation. And you can commit a less serious act, something simple, but in the spirit of a rogue. Or

you want to mock people, show them that you are better than they are. Or you want to show that you don't respect the law. Or you want to show that you even refuse to admit that the law exists. In this case, even if it's a very small thing, I repress it even more than a serious fault that somebody committed but without malicious intention. This is what I find important. Because there are rogue people, there are people who are incorrigible. At worst they have, or they think they have somebody who can always protect them. Malicious spirits like that I do not tolerate. And whoever the guy is, in these cases I am stone cold. A thief, for example. You see somebody who steals somebody's only ewe. And the guy who stole it, when you go to his place you will see that his father has fifty, perhaps even two hundred cows. And he, this guy, he comes into a village and steals somebody's only ewe? We will impose him a big ticket—to take or to leave and go to prison.

In some way, this is reminiscent of the despotic behavior of colonial commanders, but this is beside the point now. Qualifying the gravity of an offence was not only about what somebody did but also, and more important, why he did it and in which context. When a rich man stole from a poor man, when somebody showed no sign of remorse, or did not show any respect for the law (and those supposed to protect it), the wrong became even *wronger* in Souley's eyes, and thus he was less inclined to find an alternative solution to the dispute. This, again, was regardless of whether the wrongdoer had actually broken the law or not. Thus for the gendarmes it was less important to know what kind of a criminal case it was so that they would know their exact (legal) mandate. It was the other way round: only when they knew what their (moral) mandate was, did they define what kind of a case it was that they just heard.

Law enforcement in Godiya always began with people approaching the gendarmes after something bad had happened to them, with people telling the gendarmes about it and with the gendarmes listening to them and deciding whether they should do something about it and what. It was not like the gendarmes were listening to the omnipresent noise of the social to figure out what sequences or frequencies were illegal. What the gendarmes were able to listen to in the first place had already undergone selection and ordering. The flow of information between civilians and state officials was often severely controlled by local authorities; civilians chose strategically from several available "remedy agents"; they chose how to approach the gendarmes, with whom, and what to tell them. Thus, the stories they brought to the gendarmes' attention had undergone significant prestructuring. Also, when the interaction between civilians and the gendarmes began, there was relatively little bureaucratic form and structure with which the civilians had to conform right from the start. There was no counter, in contrast to other police stations, where they would have to stand in line and where it would have been absolutely clear which officer they had to speak to first; there was no clear separation between inside and outside; the first question the gendarmes asked was always so open and unstructured that everything could be said in response; there were no forms to fill in and no boxes to tick. In short, the complainants were confronted with little external structuring and had plenty of room to shape the interaction themselves.

Now in this relatively open and unstructured interaction, the gendarmes were technically supposed to hear order in what they were told; to make a distinction between civil and criminal matters, between felonies, misdemeanors, and minor offences. Their bureaucratically attuned ear, in other words, was supposed to hear order behind all the noise. Yet this order and the distinction between its separate categories were anything but certain. According to Jean and John Comaroff, this is hardly surprising. Much "traditional" African jurisprudence, they say, "makes no distinction between the criminal and the civil" (2004, 189). Then what happened in Godiya would simply be the continuation of customary legal practice, only this time practiced by uniformed state personnel. Jean and John Comaroff are correct in saying that in civil cases, investigators "are less concerned with forensics than with circumstantial evidence that is socially and culturally sensitive to the context out of which the dispute arose. As a result, questions of abstract reason and legal principle are rendered secondary, and more flexible procedures may be followed" (ibid.). In other words, the gendarmes worked on the basis of a social and cultural rather than legal definition of crime.[10] I think this is only part of the picture. After all, the gendarmes did make distinctions between civil and criminal cases, between felonies, misdemeanors, and minor offences. They did order what they heard according to these categories.

What I think is crucial here brings us back to Egon Bittner. He once said that police officers' vocational ear is "permanently and specifically attuned" to calls of extraordinary emergency (1974, 28). The gendarmes' ear had that sensitivity too, but what counted as an "extraordinary emergency" (and, by extension, as a minor emergency, an everyday affair, a civil dispute, or a mere trifle) was not fixed—and I am tempted to say that this might also be the case for the patrolmen that Bittner was referring to. Perhaps, it was in the process of being fixed, but probably without ever attaining a final state of fixedness. This is the frontier-condition. Both the world and the senses undergo a process of mutual ordering—or attuning. And for the gendarmes, this process unfolded when they were told stories, when they listened to them and tried to figure out what it was that they just heard.

Chapter 5

THE EYE

Surveillance and the Problem of "Seeing Things"

It was one thing for the gendarmes to hear things; it was another to see things. Hearing things—or cases—meant that the gendarmes needed to make sense of the stories people told them, find order behind the noise of the narratives, or put bits and pieces of narrative fragments in order. The gendarmes' ear or, more precisely, their vocational ear, was profoundly shaped by the moral fluidity and factual uncertainty of the frontier-condition. The gendarmes' eye was subject to the same condition, but it not only tried to make sense of what it perceived; it also tried to perceive more. It was constantly trying to reach out into the unknown, and at the end of this reaching out ideally stood the production of knowledge, facts, and truth. The gendarmes' eye, particularly as a device and metaphor for surveillance, is thus at the heart of the frontier as a project of reaching out, pushing forward, and moving beyond.

Surveillance is on the rise in Niger, particularly high-tech surveillance. Since the violent conflicts in neighboring Mali, Libya, and Nigeria, in the early 2010s, US drones and French surveillance aircraft have become visible in the skies over Niger and scan large portions of the Sahel. In close collaboration with their Nigerien counterparts, US and French security agencies intercept telephone calls by alleged members of criminal networks—be it al-Qaeda in the Islamic Maghreb, Boko Haram, or "mundane" smugglers and traffickers; Nigerien officers are receiving more and more US-led training on how to gather, process, and catalogue pieces of intelligence.

Despite all efforts to install and propagate sophisticated methods of surveillance, the street-level work by police and gendarmes, even of those primarily concerned with intelligence work, looks vastly different. Admittedly, both police and gendarmerie have central registers (*fichier central*) as centralized intel-data repositories. They are supposed to store all case files and information about offenders and suspects, their fingerprints, and sometimes even photographs. But they are highly inefficient. During my fieldwork, I found at least three reasons for that: first, only a small percentage of the cases were transformed into written records and then sent for storage and cataloging; second, these documents were hard copies and extremely difficult to comb through for any kind of information matching; and thus third, when a gendarmerie station requested help from a register to identify a given suspect, the central register replied weeks later, if at all. Niger, like most African countries, is a poorly working "registering machine" (Szreter and Breckenridge 2012, 1) and thus not a very efficient "knowledge apparatus" in Foucault's sense (2004, 112). The knowledge of the population, collected in filing cabinets, to govern bureaucratically, identify individuals, and make society legible (see Goody 1986, 116; Scott 1998, 2–3)—the fundamental form of governmental power described by Foucault (2004, 111)—was rather restricted and hardly accessible to the gendarmes. *Herrschaft kraft Wissen*, or domination through knowledge, as Max Weber (1980 [1921], 129) put it, has yet to be achieved.

So while surveillance is visibly on the rise in Niger, institutional knowledge is not. And the gendarmes too had only limited knowledge of the villages and communities in which they worked because they were transferred to a different region or town every three years. Now, what does it mean to exercise state surveillance in a context where both the state and the surveillants seem to know very little about those they want to monitor?

The gendarmes need to maneuver through a landscape that they do not know and without any map. And for this—in order to "see things," as they said—they desperately need help. The gendarmes-as-surveillants maneuvering through an unknown territory is the main focus of this chapter. In this regard, the approach presented here diverges from previous and predominant perspectives on surveillance in two ways: this chapter is neither about the objects and "audiences" of surveillance (see Lyon 2006, 8), nor about the totalizing, subjectifying, and objectifying effects of surveillance as a mode of government and exercising control over (at least specific segments) of the population.[1] States and their surveillance apparatus are often described using the panopticon metaphor made popular by Michel Foucault (1975). It describes a prison structure in which the inmates can be the focus of the surveillant's all-seeing but unseen gaze at any time; as a consequence the inmates become aware of their constant visibility and turn into their own surveillants; power relations permeate and are reproduced in their subjects' bodies (ibid., 202). Yet in a context in which the panopticon seems to have more cracks than walls—more places to hide than to be seen—as in Niger, as in the frontier, such an approach would be misleading. Rather I want to present an account of surveillance that takes the surveillants' perspective as a point of departure: the Nigerien gendarmes' practices and often improvised "ways of operating" in an unknown terrain (see de Certeau 1984, xiv, xix), particularly how they establish and manage relationships with potential informants.

Before entering into the details of these relationships, I put the Nigerien surveillance apparatus in historical perspective, hopefully without being too repetitive. Then, I clarify the role of Nigerien gendarmes' informants in terms of "knowledge brokerage." After that, I present the relationships the gendarmes established with three types of potential informants: "intelligence agents" (*agents de renseignement*), as the gendarmes called them; chiefs and their representatives, the so-called *baruma*; and friends and acquaintances. In conclusion, taking up Michel de Certeau's metaphor (1984, 129), I suggest that where a map of knowledge is missing, even the supposed cartographers' walks turn into improvised and ambivalent moves. The gendarmes rely on guides in an unknown terrain (intelligence agents), on other cartographers who might give them a glance at their own detailed maps (chiefs), and on others' eyes and ears on the ground (friends). Thus the power relations between surveillant and those potentially observed turn out to be much more ambiguous than generally assumed.

Surveillance in Niger in Historical Perspective

Systematic surveillance by state agencies started in Niger during the French colonization, particularly with the arrival of the colonial police in the 1930s. Rather than criminal police work, their main job was to control hygiene, movements, and political opposition to the colonial regime, and all of this mainly in urban centers. After independence, the Police Nationale took over these responsibilities in Niger. Policing outside the urban centers was very different. The gardes de cercle were the main colonial rural police force. Instituted in Niger in 1905, they were recruited from among the Africans in the French colonial army, most of whom were from the French Sudan and the Upper Volta.[2] As a "gendarmerie locale" they served as intermediaries between French colonial administrators and the local population (Tidjani Alou 2001, 101). They were poorly controlled, badly equipped, often lived "off the land," and sometimes radically violated local codes of mutuality, as described by William F. S. Miles (1993, 21–23). However, as they were mostly strangers to the places, people, and languages of the areas of their deployment, they needed the locals to cooperate.

These gardes were auxiliaries of the colonial gendarmerie. In Niger, the first gendarmerie units were created from the late 1940s onward with less than a dozen gendarmes and auxiliaries per unit and roughly thirty French gendarmes plus sixty African auxiliaries in total in the mid-1950s. Niger was "a forgotten, under-administered, under-equipped and under-policed territory" (Cabry 2009, 129, my translation).

Since the French colonial commanders and their African recruits did not speak the local tongue and did not know the areas and the people they were supposed to control, they needed the cooperation of local chiefs, guides, or other intermediaries (Fuglestad 1983, 67). Even after Niger's independence in 1960, the good collaboration between public administrators and chiefs with their knowledge of the local populations and state-backed power to control them was the foundation of effective police work.

The institution of chieftaincy had a hard time under Diori Hamani's one-party rule between 1960 and 1974 in Niger. As Miles notes, Hamani, a typical French-African évolué "looked askance at the chieftaincy as an anachronistic institution, at best old-fashioned and quaint, at worst a potential drawback to modernisation and change" (1987, 251). As a consequence, chiefs were replaced by party committees as intermediaries between the government and the people and excluded from any formal role in the actual governing of the country (ibid., 251–52). The army and gendarmerie were also under pressure. They were increasingly put to work on nonmilitary tasks such as agricultural projects, and Diori turned parts of his party's countrywide youth organization into a party militia that was ultimately supposed to supplant the national army (Higgot and Fuglestad 1975, 394–95; Mignon 1989). Surveillance, particularly of potential civilian, political, or military adversaries, was an essential part of his militia's duties.

This changed after the military coup in 1974. A dramatic increase in state surveillance occurred during the regime of Lieutenant Colonel Seyni Kountché from 1974 to 1987. Kountché established a surveillance regime that was embodied by his powerful secret police, La Coordination (Amuwo 1986, 295–96). Every taxi driver, street vendor, and particularly hawkers roaming public buildings, restaurants, and bars were suspected of snooping on private conversations and reporting to the Coordination (Issa 2008, 142). The result was a dictatorial military and police regime with the total absence of pluralist expression. Hundreds of people were arrested, interrogated, imprisoned, or killed for their political views. This kind of "low-tech surveillance" (Bozzini 2011) may not always have had the intended effects, and its capacity to collect, store, and evaluate intelligence data may be very limited. But Kountché's regime was very efficient in meting out instant and draconian punishments for rumors and hearsay. In other words, it was like many other low-tech surveillance regimes, extremely effective at spreading uncertainty and instilling fear in the civilian population (see ibid., 94, 110). In the late 1980s, things began to change gradually after Kountché's death when the military-controlled, one-party system ended, and was replaced by a period of democratization in the 1990s. Pluralist expression was allowed and the Coordination was suppressed. Both police and gendarmerie were largely discredited and kept a low profile (Lund 2001, 859–60). Systematic surveillance and oppression had come to a halt, the hawker-informants returned to their old trade of hawking.

The next shift took place in the early 2000s and persists until today. After 9/11, Niger, Chad, Mali, and Mauritania were counted among the West African "front-line states" in the global war on terrorism (Davis 2007, 1). Since the abduction of thirty-two Europeans in March 2003 by the Algerian Salafist Group for Preaching and Combat (GSPC), renamed al-Qaeda of the Islamic Maghreb in 2007, the US military presence in the Sahara increased significantly (Ellis 2004, 461; Keenan 2009b, 54).[3] From 2002 onward, Nigerien military and paramilitary forces were targeted by foreign initiatives, participated in joint military operations under US command, and received financial aid and training from US Special Forces (Ellis 2004, 459). At first, this resulted in increased militarization in Niger with a tripling of army and gendarmerie personnel within only ten years (Keenan 2006b, 281; Zangaou 2008, 266). Second, from 2009, France and the United States provided Nigerien security forces with more and more high-technology surveillance assistance and training (Keenan 2008, 19; 2009a, 17).

Since the crisis in Mali triggered by the proclamation of the independent state of Azawad by the National Movement for the Liberation of Azawad (MNLA) in 2012, and particularly since the Islamist group Ansar Dine and the Movement for Oneness and Jihad in West Africa (MUJAO) seized power, things have escalated rapidly. The French led a military intervention in northern Mali and increased their intelligence operations throughout the Sahel; France and the United States have started training and equipping police and paramilitary units to gather and process intelligence more efficiently. They have intensified operational cooperation with local intelligence services and strengthened their own surveillance apparatus in the region; France is operating surveillance aircrafts in the Sahel; the United States is operating unarmed Predator drones from a base outside the capital Niamey. In 2009 and 2010, I talked to diplomats in Niger who expressed fear the Sahel region could turn into a "second Afghanistan." Today, it even has its own name: "Sahelistan" (Laurent 2013).

Niger has also been making considerable investments to strengthen its surveillance capacities. Since 2012, mobile phone users are required to register and provide personal identification details when purchasing or owning a SIM card (as common in most African countries today; Donovan and Martin 2014). This makes it much easier for Nigerien police and intelligence agencies to monitor mobile phone communications—in close collaboration with the United States. In October 2014, Niger's latest investment was a reconnaissance plane, bought to be operated by the country's own intelligence service.

High-tech surveillance is on the rise in Niger; but low-tech surveillance by street-level, generalist police and gendarmes through personal contacts prevails—although barely targeted by international initiatives. First, even pieces of intelligence produced by wiretaps or airborne surveillance need to be verified on the ground. Second, all these high-tech measures are highly selective and punctual in contrast to the vast, predominantly rural country. And thus, third, these high-tech measures are largely useless for most street-level policing agents. The latter need to work with informants, and particularly with ones they can trust.

Informants as Knowledge Brokers

The gendarmes were often strangers in the places where they worked, but communicating with locals was not a big problem. Most of the time, both sides spoke (or at least knew a little) Hausa or Zarma. Only on rare occasions—when the gendarmes were confronted with somebody who only understood a language (i.e., Arabic, Fulfulde, Tamasheq, or Tebu) that none of them understood—would they have to call for an interpreter, mostly a chief or his representative. But even if communicating was quite easy, knowing the identities of the people they talked to and gathering intelligence was far more difficult. Here they needed informants—to locate or identify a person, to understand the context of a particular complaint and the disputants' relationship, to know their families' previous history, and so on. These informants can be thought of as "knowledge brokers"; I borrow the term *broker* from Giorgio Blundo's (2001; 2006) studies of intermediaries in public bureaucracies, although in a slightly modified manner. Whereas Blundo focuses on the role of these intermediaries in the citizens' access to bureaucracies, I focus on the bureaucrats' access to citizens, or more precisely, to knowledge of them.[4] Brokers are those who can draw back the curtain between the local state and its citizens, not only by acting as administrative brokers who provide access to public services (Blundo 2001), but also by acting as knowledge brokers and providing the bureaucrats with information about the citizens they interact with. Administrative brokers help citizens deal with an administration that they don't understand; knowledge brokers allow bureaucrats to deal with a population that they don't understand.

The gendarmes' relationship with their informants was always a balancing act between suspicion and trust. As Sally Engle Merry argues, community intermediaries are "often distrusted, because their ultimate loyalties are ambiguous and they may be double agents. They are powerful in that they have mastered both of the discourses of the interchange, but they are vulnerable to charges of disloyalty or double-dealing" (2006, 40). This resonates well with the three golden rules of intelligence work, which Chef Boubacar, who had learned it from CIA instructors, recited to me:

> Rule number one: Never trust an informant.
> Rule number two: Never trust an informant.
> Rule number three: Never trust an informant.

But, given these rules, what could a gendarme like Boubacar do with a piece of information from somebody he fundamentally distrusted? He could, of course, try to verify this information through independent sources—but in the tight social networks in the rural communities where the gendarmes worked, the existence of independent sources was highly unlikely. In addition, every potential informant had good reason to lie or say nothing at all, since being visibly friendly with the gendarmes, or appearing to be a "double-dealer," could cause stigma and social exclusion and lead to threats and violent attacks on oneself and one's family. This was why potential informants needed to trust Boubacar, Souley, and the others not to make the assistance publicly known and to provide protection in case of trouble. In short, whether the gendarmes were able to bridge the knowledge gap that separated them from the local population depended on their ability to establish networks of trustworthy relationships that involved particular forms of reciprocity (see Beek 2012). In the following sections, I describe the relationships the gendarmes establish with three types of potential informants: "intelligence agents," chiefs, and ordinary acquaintances.

Intelligence Agents

One morning, Adjudant-Chef Souley received a letter from central headquarters in his function as commander of the brigade. It contained a photo, the mobile phone number, and the description of a suspected terrorist's supposed domicile. Souley immediately called one of his agents de renseignement, or intelligence agents, namely Issa.

Souley had about ten intelligence agents dispersed throughout the department, he told me. About half of them were former prison inmates, some of whom Adjudant-Chef Souley had personally jailed and kept in touch with on their release. The others were small-time offenders whom Souley had decided not to send to court after reaching a settlement at the gendarmerie station. Some of these intelligence agents had already supplied him with information, for example about drug trade networks that led to remarkable arrests. Sometimes they were even operationally involved in Souley's work. The former drug dealer, for example, actively helped him smash a group of drug traffickers: Adjudant-Chef Souley stood on the outskirts of town with a handful of gendarmes waiting for his intelligence agent to call him and describe their vehicle as soon as the target group left the bus station. In another case, Adjudant-Chef Souley sent one of his intelligence agents to a town some three hundred kilometers away to gather information about alleged Boko Haram terrorists spilling over from nearby Nigeria.

Men that gendarmes called "les enfants de la gendarmerie," the gendarmerie's children, were a special type of intelligence agents. Issa was one of them. They were unofficial employees who worked at the brigade as cobblers, errand boys, moto-taxi (*kabou-kabou*) drivers, or general handymen. They were often natives of Godiya and thus possessed much deeper knowledge of the place and people than most gendarmes. Issa had been working at the gendarmerie for about twenty years. He began as a "boy" for a former brigade commander, ran errands, did the grocery shopping, cleaned his house, did the laundry, and ironed the uniforms. Bit by bit, he became acquainted with the other gendarmes working at the brigade, and since his former boss was gone, he spent most of his day at the brigade. He told me that his daily job now consisted of sweeping the station's courtyard early in the morning, then washing the gendarmes' cars and motorbikes for tips, and occasionally he would go to town and gather information about people selling drugs or stolen goods. Now Adjudant-Chef Souley gave Issa a specific task. He sent him out to search for the domicile of the alleged terrorist, to casually talk to neighbors and shopkeepers in the same street, and to listen in on conversations in the neighborhood's mosque.

A few days later, when I asked Issa if he liked his job, he said "I like it, and I don't like it." Many people from town think of him as a "secret agent," as a "karen jendarmomi" (the "gendarmes' dog" in Hausa), he said, as somebody who spied on other people's private lives. *Karen jendarmomi* is a pejorative denomination, adapted from the more common "karen dwan," "the custom's dog" for intermediaries between customs officials and their clients who serve as informants for the customs officials and are often involved in the unofficial taxation or nontaxation of transported goods (Bako-Arifari 2001, 49n17; 2006, 188; Olivier de Sardan 2001, 69). Issa did not want to be associated with these kinds of semithugs, as many thought of them.

The distrust with which people looked at him made his life rather complicated and limited his social contacts to his family, close friends, and the gendarmes. When he married his second wife, all the gendarmes donated a little money and visited him in his humble home. This nurtured some people's suspicions. And indeed, time and again, I heard him talk to gendarmes about this neighbor, that merchant, indicating who lived where, traveled where, and was acquainted with whom. Apart from rare intelligence missions, the information Issa provided was of a very general kind, information the gendarmes who were constantly "de passage," as Issa put it, could not have; but these pieces of simple information contributed to the gendarmes' general knowledge of the civilian population they faced.

The relationship between the gendarmes and their intelligence agents was, from the gendarmes' perspective, rather pragmatic. Souley and Boubacar, for example, often gave them mobile phones that they regularly topped up to keep in touch. They also gave them money or clothes (if they were poor), helped them to file a complaint against somebody, and turned a blind eye to dubious activities involving their intelligence agents, in exchange for information. It was a give-and-take relationship, sometimes with explicit and at other times more implicit terms of trade. And yet, trust played an essential role therein because the consequences of such relationships could be terrible. Adjudant-Chef Souley told me about one of his former intelligence agents: a pharmacist who had been arrested for forging documents and almost went to jail. Souley had reached an out-of-court settlement and entered into a privileged relationship with the pharmacist, who was well-informed and whose pharmacy was on the premises of the town's little bus station. And like any bus station, it was a "hotbed of vice," both civilians and gendarmes assured me. Several times the pharmacist had informed Adjudant-Chef Souley about criminal activities at the bus station; and sometimes it led to an arrest. Until one day the pharmacist was found dead in front of his shop, with a bullet in his head. This weighed heavily on Souley's conscience, he told me. According to Souley, in a town as small as Godiya, such crimes do not simply happen. Souley knew that somehow information about the pharmacist being his intelligence agent had gotten into the wrong hands.

Chiefs

Right after Adjudant-Chef Souley had sent Issa to town to search for information about this suspected terrorist, he took out his mobile phone and called Gado—a *baruma*, the representative of a village chief in charge of the neighborhood where the terrorist was supposed to live. Gado was a well-known guest at the gendarmerie brigade. He came there almost every other day. He greeted all the gendarmes with a handshake, knew everybody by name, and sat down on the gendarmes' benches, where no other civilians were allowed to sit.

The hierarchy of chiefs in Niger is parallel to overlapping territorial units of counties (départements), villages/towns, and neighborhoods. The corresponding chiefs were the *chefs de canton, chefs de village*, and *chefs de quartier*. In the case of pastoralist nomads (e.g., Tuareg), the smallest unit of reference was not the village but the group, that is, a cluster of families, and the chief was the chef de groupement (even though the large majority of pastoralist families has become sedentary).

The chiefs and baruma were administrative brokers in that they helped civilians gain access to state institutions, helped them make complaints at the gendarmerie station, or if they were accused of an offence, negotiated in their favor. And they were knowledge brokers in that they knew the people and area under their influence like no one else; their knowledge of people living in their realm of influence proved invaluable to colonial administrators a century ago, and it is still invaluable to gendarmes today. The latter could not rely on or access public registers, and most people in rural areas did not have identity cards. So the gendarmes relied on the chiefs' cooperation when they needed precise information about specific individuals, to identify and locate a suspect, two necessary and crucial steps in any criminal investigation (Brodeur and Ouellet 2005, 48), whether concerning a terrorist or a thief.

Having a chief on their side meant that the gendarmes could gain access to all information required to locate and identify any person under the chief's authority. In criminal investigations, chiefs were like a joker in a game of cards: if you had him in your hand, you would probably win. Chiefs were aware of the importance of their roles, and so were the gendarmes. But not all gendarmes accepted this. One day, during Souley's leave of absence, I accompanied Chef Tahirou, then interim brigade commander, and two gendarmes on a mission to a remote village to arrest a man for financial fraud. It was market day and Chef Tahirou had the driver pull up right on the marketplace. Instantly a knot of agitated people gathered around the vehicle, Chef Tahirou got out and shouted that he was looking for a man named Ali Hassan. At first nobody replied, but then a man came forward and told us that we should come to his house and wait for them to call him. After waiting two hours, Chef Tahirou had enough, decided to leave and forced our host to pay for the gendarmes' "travel expenses" plus gas consumed on the drive to the village. While Tahirou was collecting the money, I talked to the gendarme, Amadou, who was sitting under a thatched roof in the shade, shaking his head in disbelief. "With Souley we never returned home empty-handed," he told me. Chef Hamza later explained to me in an interview:

> There is no authority that can work without the traditional chiefs. For example, we know that this person is somewhere in this area, but we don't know in which camp, or in which section. But we know that he is a Fulani from that area, so we know his baruma. We give him the

summons and he will make some research. On Saturday, he will go to the market and ask around, and then he will tell us his position. So they make our work much easier, much much easier. And even when you are on the ground, looking for somebody, you go and see the traditional chief, he is very efficient, he is very important, he is essential! When you arrive in a village, he will receive you; it is he that will show you everything; if you need somebody, he will say, "We want to see this or that person." Do you, the gendarme know him? Of course you don't. But the chief does know him! And his people will bring him to you or he will give you a guide that will take you to that person.

The chiefs and their knowledge were crucial to the gendarmes' work. But it demanded quite some experience and tact to win over the chiefs, and Chef Tahirou lacked both these qualities. Amadou explained that Chef Tahirou should have, on his arrival in a village and before going anywhere else, gone to the chief's domicile. The chief would have felt respected, important, and proud with the shiny blue gendarmerie truck parked outside his house if the brigade commander had done him the honor of paying a personal visit before doing any other business. After a couple of minutes of casual conversation, Tahirou could have casually asked whether this or that person was around, and before you knew it, the chief would have sent his people to bring this man before the gendarmes. "But bursting in on the market, just like that? Never!" Amadou added. It would not have been the first time that people turned against the gendarmes.

In short, when the gendarmes moved through totally unknown terrain, the chiefs' knowledge was fundamental. And neglecting the importance of the chiefs could prove risky, even dangerous—because it jeopardized the whole investigation, and because the villagers' noncooperation could easily turn into openly hostile opposition. Our arrival on the market place gave us a vivid foretaste of that. In this case, the usually supposed knowledge and power advantage of the surveillants seems distorted, and in other cases, even upside down: some chiefs refused any kind of cooperation with the gendarmes and banned their subjects from talking to state officials altogether—often under the threat of divine punishment. In such, often-remote areas, the gendarmes had no way of finding suspects unless the chief wanted them to find them. They did not even hear of crimes happening there unless the chief wanted them to as well. As a result, in areas where the chief had absolute control over the flow of information toward state officials, the gendarmes were little less than the chief's cavalry: only active when he wanted them to be and then generously recompensed for their services. Adjudant-Chef Souley and his gendarmes were aware of that, but there was nothing they could do about it, Souley said—nothing but try to be on good terms with the chiefs.

Friends and Acquaintances

After having called Gado, the baruma, Adjudant-Chef Souley told me that neither Gado nor his chief had any idea who this man was but that he had already
moved to an unknown location. He had only lived there for a couple of months,
was a nice person who distributed sacks of rice among his neighbors, but he was a
bit strange too, because he did not pray with everybody else in the public mosque
around the corner. That was all they knew. (And this was also the information Issa
later brought back.) This could have been helpful for Souley, if he had learned it
earlier. He told me that he needed to receive information about such occurrences
in real time and from proactive individuals, rather than just on inquiry and after
the suspicious man had moved away. Adjudant-Chef Souley explained this during an interview: "As a gendarme, you need to see things. You need to know what
is happening around you. This is why the contact, the mingling with the population is strongly recommended. You need to know everything. You need to know
everybody. This is how a gendarme can do his work well."

"Mingling" with the civilian population gave the gendarmes what Brodeur
and Ouellet call "connaissance" (2005, 60), a kind of general knowledge about the
people they faced in their everyday work and which was required to contextualize
the fragmentary and inconclusive information received during criminal investigations. But mingling also created friends and acquaintances (see also Bittner
1967, 714), and the latter sometimes informed the gendarmes about particular
events in real time. Adjudant-Chef Souley's way of finding and keeping acquaintances seemed very straightforward. When he tired of sitting at his desk, he would
often take an afternoon drive around Godiya in the brigade's Toyota. Often he
would call me, "Come, let's make a little trip," and we drove around the different
neighborhoods for about an hour, just slightly faster than walking speed; often
he would slow down and greet passers-by or people sitting on the street, sometimes he would turn off the engine and chat with them for a couple of minutes
about their families, their businesses, and casually about news or recent events in
their neighborhood; he would give others a small bill for another round of tea,
then we would continue our trip and our conversation. On one level, strolling
through the village was proactive police work, the prevention of crime by making the presence of police or gendarmerie known, which, according to Bruce
Baker (2007, 340), is very rare in African police forces.[5] But this indeed was, at
least partially, about demonstrating the presence of the gendarmerie's blue Toyota, about managing the gendarmerie's visibility (see Paperman 2003, 398). On
another level, as Souley told me, his tours were just as much about clearing his
head, running a few errands, and, most important, about maintaining friendly
relationships with civilians. One might say that this was part of what in most of

the Anglophone world circulates as "community policing" (Purdeková 2011, 488; Ruteere and Pommerolle 2003).

Adjudant-Chef Souley and all the other gendarmes agreed that having an acquaintance—and thus potential first-class informants—is about being simple, open, and accessible. All you have to do, really, is be a good person. Chef Hamza even went a step further in his effort to find informants:

> I give you an example: In the evening, I leave my uniform at home and take a walk through town. You know these *fada* [a group of men sitting and conversing besides the street], don't you?[6] Anyways, I come to a group and if they are about to prepare tea, I take a couple of francs and pay for it. And if perhaps there's a vendor of grilled meat passing by, I call him, "Hey, bring us meat for a thousand francs." We eat together and chat a bit about everything and nothing, we laugh, and all that. Then we part and tomorrow this very fada will come together again. You come once, twice, three times, and the fourth time you don't come, someone will ask, "Hey, where is this monsieur who has been coming here?" "Ah, this monsieur, you know, he's a gendarme, he's not around, he has probably traveled," voilà, voilà. And when you come back, they will applaud to see you! Yes! Because now you have become familiar to them. Now starting from this, one day one of them might come to you, perhaps because something has happened in his neighborhood, or he has heard something. And that's it: being in a fada is a way to gain mutual trust. You got it? So this very relationship, it is our job to search for it.

And indeed, on several occasions, when I was with Hamza in his *fada* or favorite bar, people told him about this merchant who had just bought ten plots of land with God knows what kind of money, about this soldier who received a big and suspiciously wrapped packet from a bus arriving from Libya, and about that suspicious looking bearded man who had just moved into the neighborhood and did not pray in the little mosque just around the corner. Not in the above-mentioned case, but in many others these tidbits of information effectively led to investigations, sometimes to arrests.

Some gendarmes told me that people would readily and openly talk to gendarmes, if they saw something strange because they lived in a "culture of denunciation" (*culture de dénonciation*). I would not say that this has anything to do with a particular Nigerien "culture" of telling on people. Even though rural Niger is characterized by very strong social control and most actions are public and thus the object of other people's commentary and judgment, many people are highly skeptical of state authorities and would choose not to approach them. But that some people did choose to approach them, I would argue, was the result of the gendarmes' clever way of reaching out, of bonding with them, of opening up to them, of building relationships of trust and reciprocity, not with many, but with enough people to hopefully "see things."

When Adjudant-Chef Souley told me "as a gendarme, you need to see things," he was not talking about visually discerning persons, objects, or practices. Drones and other high-tech surveillance techniques may be able to "see things" in this sense of the word, but they cannot by themselves overcome the problem of knowledge caused by the weakness of Niger's registering machine. Drones may look, but they do not see. They reach out into the unknown, both physically and visually, but they still seem like an echo of the superficial and highly selective demonstrations of state power in colonial times. My aim was to shed some light on what the daily exercise of state surveillance—on the ground, so to speak—can mean in a context where the state seems to know very little about its citizens. In other words: What does it mean for Nigerien gendarmes to "see things"?

State surveillance in Niger has always depended on work with informants. Admittedly, high-tech surveillance is on the rise, the governmental knowledge apparatus is being built up, and the gendarmes' hopes for quicker and better knowledge gathering, processing, and utilization are high. But in a context where this knowledge apparatus still functions badly and where the territory to be controlled is so vast, it is vital for the surveillants to have personal contacts to locate, verify, and contextualize specific pieces of intelligence. The gendarmes in Godiya maneuvered through a landscape that they did not know and without a map, and they did so by reaching out: by establishing and managing a web of relationships with particular knowledge brokers, namely intelligence agents, chiefs, and friends and acquaintances. The gendarmes' relationships with all these had elements of reciprocity; it was always about giving and taking, but neither the gendarmes nor their counterparts always had a clear idea of what they could glean from these relationships; sometimes they did not even expect anything from them.

Informants seemed to fulfill several functions with regards to the gendarmes' knowledge gap. Since the gendarmes often mobilized several informants at the same time, they triangulated specific snippets of information. In other words, their knowledge brokers were like GPS-satellites allowing the gendarmes to locate themselves and others in an unknown terrain. But each of the three kinds of informants had also their specific value. Intelligence agents knew the local terrain and the gendarmes used them as guides, sometimes as one-man expeditions to check on particular events or persons. The chiefs were so valuable to the gendarmes because they had their own detailed maps and a powerful position to maneuver through a terrain that they understood as theirs. If clever enough in their dealing with the chiefs, the gendarmes would get a glance at this map and eventually the chief would push them in the right direction. Friends and acquaintances potentially multiplied the gendarmes' eyes and ears on the ground. All these "knowledge brokers" helped them to "see things."

In this context, and following de Certeau's (1984, 18, 34) line of thought, surveillance in particular and the frontier-project in general does not so much appear like the calculated action conceived of by a powerful state dispositive—a strategy—but rather as a tactical way of operating: the improvised, localized, often spontaneous and makeshift practices of "make do." The strategist conceives the map, controls the map; the tactician has to move through the foreign terrain. And without the map, the supposed strategist, now incapable of "panoptic practice," transforms into a tactician who needs to incessantly capitalize on forces and knowledge that are not his own.

The drones in the skies over Niger may be the symbols of an all-seeing, all-knowing strategist trying to push forward the frontier (which may trigger the highest hopes for some and the worst fears for others); surveillance on the Nigerien ground looks different, and seen in the shadow of the drone may appear amateurish and naïve. However, I am tempted to argue that Niger's relative stability and peace, while surrounded by conflicts and particularly the threat of Boko Haram, can at least in part be attributed to the gendarmes' "seeing things": to the efficiency of their often improvised and makeshift ways of dealing with their problem of knowledge in the frontier.

Chapter 6

THE PEN
Report Writing and Bureaucratic Aesthetics

Writing was part and parcel of the gendarmes' daily work. They were constantly writing daily messages, weekly reports, monthly reports, and particularly investigation reports, so-called procès-verbaux, in which the facts they had established during their investigations were translated into "graphic artifacts" (Hull 2003, 293).

One incident made me realize that I had for months not noticed a remarkable dimension to the gendarmes' writing: Chef Boubacar was one of the first gendarmes with whom I established a friendly relationship that extended beyond the walls of the brigade. About midnight during one of his twenty-four-hour shifts at the brigade, he invited me to have breakfast with him at his house. His shift ended at 7:00 a.m. I arrived at about 8:00 a.m., and we had a nice breakfast. Then he showed me his family photo album with pictures of his wedding, previous posts in the gendarmerie, and of previous girlfriends. As I turned the last page of the album, he handed me a second one. To my surprise, it was not an album of photos but an album of procès-verbaux that he had written during the course of his career as a gendarme. Chef Boubacar had stored them meticulously in transparent sheet protectors, and he presented them just as he had presented the photos: with the same affection, the same tone of voice, the same gestures pointing to this or that particularity. I was surprised, but I did not know quite what to make of his presentation. It took me a few months to become aware of the aesthetic dimension to the procès-verbaux, that is, how the gendarmes tried to manufacture a document that was aesthetically satisfying to them in form, style, and content.

A procès-verbal was a bureaucratic story. In one sense, it was the formalized narrative (or narrative of formulas) that transplanted something that had happened in the practical reality of somebody's lived life into bureaucratic language and rationality. It was the victory of form over life, the closure of the bureaucratic frontier. But in another sense it was still a story that had to be written by someone. At the very least, this someone had to choose words, phrases, and formulas and put them into a sequence with all the authority, responsibility, and profound uncertainty that go with the practice of authorship. Perhaps it is a little far-fetched to call this the victory of life over form; but at least this is life seeping into bureaucracy, constantly undermining the attempted closure of the frontier.

In this chapter, I suggest an approach to bureaucratic work that takes as a point of departure a perspective often adopted by gendarmes themselves when discussing the quality of a procès-verbal: I suggest examining the writing of seemingly purely bureaucratic documents as an essentially aesthetic activity integrated into both organizational and legal rationalities. This endeavor demands some definition of terms. First, I need to be precise about what I mean by "aesthetic activity" and how this concept helps me understand bureaucratic activity. Here I am particularly inspired by Katya Mandoki's (2007) approach to everyday aesthetics. Second, I need to elaborate on what I mean by "writing," and here I adopt a perspective offered by Michel de Certeau (1984). Once I have set out these analytical tools, I turn to the actual writing, correcting, and rewriting of the procès-verbaux, which allows me to ground the gendarmes' aesthetic appreciation of them in their socio-professional environment.

Aesthetics and Bureaucracy

The daily work of bureaucrats is often described as an activity combining official norms, on the one hand, and practical norms (Olivier de Sardan 2008; see also Olivier de Sardan 2004, 149) or routines (Lipsky 1980), on the other. These two aspects reflect the legal and organizational or practical rationalities that guide bureaucrats in their work—and the perceived gap between the two (Hull 2012, 616). What has been largely left out of these descriptions is the aesthetic dimension of bureaucratic work. There are, however, some exceptions. Scholars of organizational studies look for the beauty in organizations (Frederickson 2000) or more generally the "aesthetic categories" (Taylor and Hanson 2005, 1216); they regard organizations as workshops of artistic production (Frederickson 2000, 47–50; Goodsell 1992) or as artistic performances themselves (Strati 1992, 580), and they all seem to engage in a normative effort to promote, value, or reform organizations or administrations in aesthetic terms. Although these scholars look beyond the sphere of pure bureaucratic rationalism, their approaches are somewhat problematic in at least one of the following ways: First, regarding organization as—or comparing it to—art means ascribing a certain value to organizations and what they do and thus is of little analytical value if not grounded in the expressions of the members of the organization (Fratto 1978, 135; Mandoki 2007, 6, 31; Novitz 2001, 159). Second, the beauty, say, of procès-verbaux, cannot be analyzed. "Beauty is not a quality of objects in themselves but an effect of the relation that a subject establishes with a particular object from a particular social context of evaluation and interpretation" (Mandoki 2007, 8). When taking an anthropological approach to aesthetics, the researcher must, thus, "dissolve" any essentialist concept of beauty (Wiseman 2007, 26) and, rather, analyze the context in which an object—here, the procès-verbal—is judged beautiful (or ugly, grotesque, etc.; Gell 1992, 42). Third, analyzing organizations or their output as aesthetic objects masks the fact that such objects come into being only through an aesthetic relation that people establish with them through active ideational, emotional, and sometimes practical engagement (Coote 1992, 247; Firth 1992, 16; Goldman 2001, 188; Mandoki 2007, 12). Unfortunately, these actors—managers, administrators, bureaucrats—the aesthetic relations they establish, and what their everyday aesthetic appetite (Coote 1992, 269; Mandoki 2007, 68) is grounded on have barely begun to be studied.[1] As Pierre Bourdieu (1984) argues, what our appetite strives for is developed on the basis of a specific (social, economic, cultural, etc.) context. Aesthetic appetite is always "embedded" (Ginsburg 1994). Bureaucrats' aesthetic appetite is no exception. And since writing is one of bureaucrats' main activities, it is where their appetite seeks satisfaction.

Anthropologists have also established a link between bureaucratic work and aesthetics. Studies by three scholars are particularly insightful here. Annelise Riles (1998) explores the production, usage, circulation, and aesthetic appreciation of legal documents produced during UN-sponsored conferences. Similarly, R. L. Stirrat (2000) discusses development consultants' work, particularly how the reports they write are judged mainly in aesthetic terms, which he sees as an "exemplification of the values of modernism" (ibid., 42). Oyvind Eggen (2012) focuses on bureaucratic procedures in an agricultural subsidy program in Malawi. He argues that these procedures are carried out according to aesthetic rather than instrumental considerations. In the end, he concludes, the procedures may be inefficient, but they produce the image of a modern state, namely the idea of a legible population and of a professional bureaucracy (ibid., 19). I agree with these authors that a perspective on bureaucratic work needs to take seriously that work's aesthetic dimension, particularly in the case of the everyday production of bureaucratic documents—and not only "when bureaucratic logic and spectacle are joined" (Handelman 1998, xlviii, note 17; see also Goodsell

1997).[2] However, none of them seem to take seriously the perspective of those producing and handling these documents, as, for example, Yael Navaro-Yashin does in her remarkable study of "bureaucracy as an emotive domain" (2006, 282; also 2007). Riles (1998) explores documents as "aesthetic objects" in their own right, without referring to their authors' appreciation of them as such; Stirrat (2000, 41–42) presents aesthetic categories by which consultancy documents are judged but not necessarily by those writing them; and Eggen suggests that "the fact that the aesthetic qualities are not explicitly communicated does not reduce their aesthetic qualities" (2012, 15).

My aim here is not to analyze bureaucratic documents as aesthetic objects or to list features of bureaucratic aesthetics, as, for example, Don Handelman (1998, xlix note 19) does. I am interested in the bureaucrat's direct relationship to the objects of his or her production. I explore how and in which professional context documents are fabricated as aesthetic objects, notably, from the perspective of their authors, and I elaborate on the relationship between aesthetic, pragmatic, and legal reasoning (see Heerey 2003).

Writing

Writing is more than scrawling or typing letters on a sheet of paper or a computer screen. De Certeau insightfully proposes conceiving of writing, *l'écriture*, as "the concrete activity that consists in constructing, on its own, blank space (*un espace propre*)—the page—a text that has power over the exteriority from which it has first been isolated" (1984, 134). Thus, for de Certeau, writing includes three elements. The first one is the blank page, the place of writing, a clean space apart from the messy and fleeting world of speech, which the writer has to manage like an urban planner (ibid.). The second element is the text the writer produces in this virgin space. The author traces words, sentences, eventually a coherent system—the text—and thus fabricates something new, a product distinct from the confused and muddied situation from which it received its ingredients. The third element is the power this product exercises over that same situation. The text organizes, a posteriori, the complexities of everyday life and thus opens up—but also excludes—options for reacting to the ordered mess of lived situations (ibid., 134–35; see also Goodsell 1992, 252; Manning 1986, 299). These three elements can be subsumed under the notions of "form," "style," and "content." The writer-as-urban-planner manages the space of the page, in other words, creates a map, a form that will be filled by the circulation of his or her pen. Its travels may be direct, without detour; they may be hasty, strolling, wandering—they are expressions of style. And what binds the text to the messy world beyond the virgin space of writing, at least in the case of the procès-verbaux I analyze, is its legally exploitable content.

The Procès-Verbal

In the eyes of gendarmes, writing is the most important element distinguishing them from their half-brothers in the police and military: "Gendarmes write!" as most defined the specificity of their work. And indeed, they are constantly writing messages; *comptes-rendus;* weekly, ten-day, and monthly reports; and procès-verbaux.[3] The procès-verbal is distinct from the other genres of texts in its relative openness, which demands the gendarmes' creativity—messages, comptes-rendus, and reports are mostly the result of copying and pasting and filling in the blanks.

Procès-verbaux are characteristic of French legal procedures.[4] They are documents stating a breach of a law and the measures taken in response by gendarmes, so-called *agents de police judiciaire,* a "summary of facts," as Adjudant-Chef Souley put it, that helps the public prosecutor accomplish his or her work.[5] In chapter 4, I noted that not all complaints turn into cases; a similar thing happens during the writing stage: only a small percentage of the cases turn into procès-verbaux. The brigade in Godiya registered 174 cases in one month; only seventeen led to a procès-verbal and were transferred to the prosecutor. The rest were filtered out at the brigade, in most cases through settlements and mostly with the prosecutor's approval (see Oumarou 2011, 201; see chapters 7 and 8).

A procès-verbal functions as a summary. It is an ensemble of information (*simples renseignements)* that is to be transferred to the public prosecutor, who will definitively qualify the offence and launch legal action or close the case (République du Niger 2003, Art. 417; see also Bauer and Pérez 2009, 64); it is the textual entrée into the *fabrique du droit* (law factory; Latour 2002, 85–86). It states every act carried out by the gendarmes: transportation to the scene, observations, measures taken, interrogations, arrests etc. All of these data are collected in one single document, the so-called procès-verbal *unique* (unitary procès-verbal), which is signed by one responsible *officier de police judiciaire.* In France, gendarmes nowadays only write so-called procès-verbaux *séparés* (separate procès-verbaux); they assemble a folder that contains a separate procès-verbal for each act they carry out (one for transportation to the scene, one for the observations, one for each statement, one for each arrest, etc.) and a recapitulatory procès-verbal summarizing the whole case. The advantage of the latter method is that in the event of a legal or procedural error in one of the separate parts, only this part becomes void by law; in a procès-verbal unique, an error renders the whole document legally worthless.

In 2011, a French gendarme was sent to Niger to teach the brigade commanders the newer and more efficient form of procès-verbal séparé. Adjudant-Chef Souley participated in this seminar. He and others said that they were taught this method twenty years ago in their initial coursework and in advanced training courses. But when they returned to their home units as rank-and-file gendarmes, they did not implement it. "Since our bosses didn't know it, we didn't do it," Souley commented. Their "bosses," the ancient brigade commanders, had only been taught to write procès-verbaux in keeping with the old standards. Now Adjudant-Chef Souley put forward more pragmatic reasons for not using the new method: an ensemble of separate procès-verbaux would require much more paper than needed for the unitary form, and, lacking sufficient allocations from their headquarters, at his brigade in Godiya he already had difficulty finding the means to procure the paper they needed for the shorter version.

Writing the Procès-Verbal

There were several steps to writing procès-verbaux. The first one was collecting data such as the names and addresses of victims, witnesses, and suspects, and the gist of what they told the gendarmes in a personal notebook or on a sheet of paper. The second step was a formal interview with them, usually one to four days after the incident. The gendarmes wrote the suspects' statements on loose sheets of paper, sometimes in specific statement notebooks, their *carnets de déclaration*. In the third step, the gendarmes established a first draft of the procès-verbal, usually written in pencil, which, in its form, already corresponded to the final version. This pencil draft was, in the fourth step, proofread by the gendarmes' direct superior, that is, the noncommissioned officer under whose direct authority the investigation was conducted. Corrections and modifications were noted with a pen, expressing superiority over the pencil. The fifth step consisted of rewriting the draft according to the noncommissioned officers' corrections and modifications, now on the computer or the typewriter. A hard copy of this revised draft was then handed to the brigade commander, Adjudant-Chef Souley, who added corrections and modifications with a red pen, the sixth step. In the seventh and last step, the gendarme typed the final version of the procès-verbal, which would then be signed by Souley and sent to various addressees (in the case of a car accident, for example, the public prosecutor, the minister of transport, superior gendarmerie officers, and the archives of the gendarmerie).

Form

"It's the form that counts!" gendarmes often explained when identifying the characteristics of a good procès-verbal.[6] Although there were no official rules defining the correct form, there were strict conventions about what a procès-verbal had to look like, and these conventions were respected, even in the very first pencil draft. For the procès-verbal to be identified and accepted as such, by the author himself as well as by his colleagues and superiors, it had to present several spatial characteristics. Apart from that, there was considerable room for creativity.

Take the front page of a procès-verbal. Conventions dictate that the hierarchical provenance of the procès-verbal appear in the top of the left-hand column,[7] underlined and written in capital letters; beneath it is the running number of the procès-verbal and the date of its establishment; below that is the type of procès-verbal (e.g., *arrestation, renseignements judiciaires*), the addressees, and finally, the brigade commander's signature. In the right column, as the headline "Gendarmerie Nationale—Procès-verbal d'enquête préliminaire" indicates, the details of the specific procès-verbal begin: date; the names of the responsible officier de police judiciaire and the two agents de police judiciaire who worked on the case, all three embraced by a large bracket; their home unit; and mention of the articles of the Code de Procédure Pénale (République du Niger 2007) defining the responsibilities of the officiers and agents de police judiciaire as well as the nature of a preliminary investigation *(enquête préliminaire)*. Finally, the following introductory phrase appears: "Rapportons les opérations suivantes que nous avons effectuées, agissant en uniforme et conformément aux ordres de nos Chefs," a formula already used in nineteenth-century France (Houte 2009, 20).

Since a couple of years before I came to Godiya, most brigades have had access to computers (one per brigade) and printers, replacing mechanical typewriters for the gendarmes' task of writing messages, reports, and procès-verbaux.[8] This profoundly changed the process of writing procès-verbaux. The conventions of form, however, did not change. Whereas on the typewriter, each procès-verbal had to be (or has to be as computers do not work during regular blackouts) written in full length, on the computer never-changing phrases were inserted by copying and pasting—just like Chef Tahirou used an old murder procès-verbal to write a new one—or the proper text of a particular procès-verbal was inserted around fixed space markers (such as never-changing headings and passages) and older text was simply suppressed.

Although some parts or formulations like those at the top of the first page never changed, or were simply copied and pasted or even prewritten, this did not prevent them from being modified according to the gendarmes' personal preferences. He or she changed the font, modified the type size, added or suppressed spaces between letters, arranged the headings, changed the type of underlining, or added space markers.⁹ But if, to be accepted, the procès-verbal only needed to follow the conventions, why manipulate such details? "Because I want it to look nice," Amadou replied, to whom I was about to dictate the preamble of a procès-verbal.¹⁰ "It has to be well-spaced," he clarified.¹¹ When he found that the overall arrangement looked nice, he entered the details. At the beginning of each paragraph, he added "—"; in front of each heading, he added "—:" and after it ":—." In the left-hand column, he separated the addressees of the procès-verbal from the rest of the heading using "//—//—//—//—//";¹² in the right column, he replaced "Vu les articles . . ." with "(((//u les articles." I was quite stunned by this latter kind of coded sign. Later, I found out that replacing letters with other signs has almost become a convention too. Gendarmes from a generation slightly older than Chaibou's, the youngest, had learned to write on typewriters, and thus did not have access to the hundreds of fonts and styles offered nowadays by word processing software. Yet, they had always looked for ways of expressing some creativity in writing procès-verbaux or even simple messages, they said. So, as their superiors apparently had nothing against it, they were creative and wrote "Vu" as "(/u" or "N°" as "/)/°", "/(/°," or, even more eccentrically, as "///)))///°", and the like. Amadou told me such choices were just a matter of personal taste.

What they judged "nice" or "ugly" swung between conventions and their creative modification. Gendarmes learned both conventions and the possibility for creative expression in the brigade. They got a hint of the formal conventions of procès-verbaux during their initial training in the Centre d'Instruction; but they learned the writing of procès-verbaux itself on the job when they were transferred to the brigades and thus were confronted with criminal police work—that is, bureaucratic work—for the first time.¹³ By observing and assisting their superiors, they adapted the conventions their superiors deemed obligatory and nice and began altering them slightly, mostly with the help of formerly unavailable options offered by word processing software.

Chef Hamza told me that early in his career he was regularly praised and rewarded by his superior in front of his colleagues. But he was not rewarded for any heroic work he had accomplished, like catching a long-sought criminal. Rather, his brigade commander very much appreciated his imaginative way of underlining and arranging headings in procès-verbaux. The gendarme Moussa explained during an interview, "You want to make it beautiful, you know. If your boss notices it, he sees the writing, really it's somewhat beautiful! . . . And you will feel proud presenting it to him like that." And brigade commanders were proud too. Adjudant-Chef Souley told me, "If it's beautiful, and he [the gendarme writing the procès-verbal] had the cleverness to do that, I feel proud! And the judge too will find that it's good."

So, there was more to this creativity than the quest for aesthetic satisfaction. Gendarmes, like other street-level bureaucrats, were, in a sense, peer reviewed (see Lipsky 1980, 76). Trying to produce beautiful documents, gendarmes entered into a play between conventions and creativity. If they adopted the inherited conventions and creatively modified them, they might gain respect from their colleagues and, more important, from their superiors, from whom they had inherited the conventions in the first place.[14]

Language Style

Once the blank space of the page has been structured, the writer has a basic map. The next step is the effective production of text, word by word, an activity that is far more demanding than copying and pasting certain objects (such as never-changing text blocks) and that leaves far more room for creativity. The section of the procès-verbal that demands the gendarme's greatest linguistic creativity comprises statements by victims, suspects, or witnesses.

Only in very rare cases did the person interviewed write their own statement. The large majority of the gendarmes' clients were illiterate, and even "intellectuals," as gendarmes called them—these were literates who might be aware of their right to write their own statement—often declined this even though they had been offered the opportunity. Gendarmes told me they often saw "intellectuals" sitting in front of a blank sheet of paper, appearing insecure about what to put into written words and how to do it. They were not familiar with this particular genre of text; they were not familiar with the translation of everyday language into legally exploitable text.

Yacouba told me that there are two styles of writing the statement: some gendarmes try to capture the formulations of the person interviewed word for word, and others start writing only after the person has finished his or her narration. In fact, during my research in the Nigerien gendarmerie, I have never witnessed the first, quasi-shorthand style.[15] This means that when writing statements, gendarmes engaged in a process of double translation: in most cases, they literally translated from a local language into the language of Nigerien bureaucracy, French; but they also translated from oral into written language.[16] Gendarmes often explained that there are two rules regulating this translation activity: put the account in good French (whether or not the person interviewed talks in a local language or in French), and get the gist of it, leave out the detours. "You must not write his whole narration! If you do, it's just waffle. You listen carefully to what he has to say, then you write down what he actually said," as Chef Hamza put it. The interviewee's account is what de Certeau identified as the "fable," "a speech that 'does not know' what it says" (1984, 160), which the gendarme is supposed to translate into legitimate procedural, that is, written, language and give a legal formatting (see Latour 2002, 88; Manning 1986, 298).

But the gendarmes did not accept all written language as legitimate. And the text's legitimacy was a matter of style. Someone writing his or her own statement may use bad French, repeat themselves, insert detours, and express feelings—which gendarmes at times also did: in four cases I witnessed, gendarmes wrote down their own statements in a disciplinary case against them. The translator-gendarme was supposed to filter out grammatical errors, repetitions, detours, and emotions. Yet the statement was written in the first-person perspective, as if the person interviewed had written it and was actually accorded his or her rights to repetitions, detours, and emotions.

As a consequence, most statements appeared very technical in style: short sentences, precise and technical formulations, without emotion. However, even what most gendarmes would refer to as good, crisp, clear style contained disputable elements, namely, military and scientific jargon. One day, I asked Chef Boubacar to explain a sentence I found in a statement by an elderly man who had been beaten by several young men: "These young men descended on me by administering blows with a stick onto me."[17] This description is rather cold and technical. But it contains literary elements that go beyond the demands of short and precise language use. Chef Boubacar said that this hints at the military background of the author of this sentence: "This is our military jargon, it's like it's the gendarme who speaks." He did not hide the fact that the statement was a product of his own writing and did not even want to make the statement appear to be the victim's words, in this case those of a seventy-year-old deaf-mute farmer.

Another phrase on which I stumbled in the observations part of several procès-verbaux was "couché en [lying in or on] décubitus dorsal," referring to a dead body. The instructor from the French gendarmerie became aware of this formulation as well. He had never seen it written in a procès-verbal in France and looked it up in a dictionary. "This is ridiculous!" he shouted at his audience of forty brigade commanders. He told them forcefully, "Keep it simple! He was lying on his back. Full stop!" The brigade commanders, however, seemed to like it. Sitting in the audience, I heard one of them murmur, "Mais c'est joli ... [But it's nice ...]." Then the French gendarme continued reading the procès-verbal and came on: "The lifeless corpse bathed in a sea of blood ..." and he shook his head in despair.[18] Most gendarmes were constantly concerned with finding the right, the best term or phrase. Thus they spend a considerable amount of time browsing through French dictionaries; like Chef Tahirou looking for a phrase to appropriately describe how the murderer had killed the two girls—"scalped" or "chopped."

Repetitions, detours, and emotional expressions were generally banned. Yet some gendarmes, mostly young ones like Moussa, included them in statements they wrote and met with harsh criticism from their superiors. The latter felt that they had not yet completed their on-the-job training in writing "good" procès-verbaux (although even Adjudant-Chef Souley now and then added a "Dieu merci" to a witness's statement). More ambiguous was the use of metaphors, part of what some gendarmes pejoratively called "literature." I followed several discussions about the term *volatiliser,* "to vanish into thin air." A phrase I often read in statements was "le voleur s'est volatilisé." Chef Boubacar, for example, noted that a thief is neither a leaf nor a bird and, thus, cannot vanish into thin air. Yet others observed that if one can administer blows of a stick onto someone's head, a thief can also vanish into thin air. In both cases, the issue was not about authentically reproducing the narrative, but about aesthetically appropriating it. This appropriation became apparent in minimal modifications, for example, from "I lost my permit" to "I mislaid my permit" or from "during the census" to "in the course of the census."[19] These and similar modifications—"administered blows" and "voleurs volatilisés"—all unveil the authors' deep involvement in the text, in a sense, the aesthetic relation they established with the story they were about to write down. Whether through jargon or through "literature," the author appropriated the oral statement through the translation he or she carried out, transforming the text into a personal creation and making it one that writer and reader consider nice.

Gendarmes wanted to prove to themselves, their colleagues, and their superiors that they justly carry the reputation and the self-image of writing intellectuals. (It is thus not surprising that in one remote and isolated brigade, gendarmes spent every day, from dawn till dusk, for months and months, sitting in front of their office playing Scrabble.) The demonstration of language skills was a question of *gendarmique* self-esteem. If they wrote in a style that was not appreciated by their superiors, they would be reprimanded in front of all of their colleagues, and being reprimanded for a lack of language skills was very upsetting for gendarmes, whose professional self-esteem is essentially based on writing skills. Also, a procès-verbal that is commonly regarded as beautifully written will be appreciated even at the hierarchical level above the brigade. This is why, although they did not comment on the form of the document, brigade commanders like Adjudant-Chef Souley also engaged in discussions of language style. Seldom did Souley pass on a procès-verbal without having effected at least some minor modifications—even if he only added a "Dieu merci" to a witness statement or turned a "lost" into "mislaid." In the end, it was his procès-verbal; he was the one who submitted it to the superior echelon (except when he was on temporary leave and Chef Tahirou was the interim brigade commander). And if a procès-verbal was written in bad French or was too "literary," the chief secretary of the regional commander would call the brigade commander to convey his superior's disapproval.

Content

From a legal point of view, one might argue that content is the most important aspect of procès-verbaux. Yet gendarmes manipulated content in multiple ways. First, they invented small facts, such as the time of an interrogation or the year and place of a witness's birth, if these data have not been gathered in the course of the investigation. With regard to the time of interrogations, for example, gendarmes were extremely meticulous. Chef Tahirou noted for the beginning of the murderer's interrogation as "10 heures et 02 minutes," the ending as "10 heures et 28 minutes," although he had not even taken his statement properly. When the writing of the procès-verbal took place sometime after the investigation, gendarmes also used such precise time specifications although they usually remembered the time of day only vaguely.

Second, gendarmes adjusted facts to keep their actions within legal boundaries. For example, they routinely noted that they had informed the person in custody about the right to consult a lawyer and that the obligatory medical examination of the suspect will be delivered after receipt, which I have never yet witnessed. Furthermore, they practically invented the hours of a person's entry into and exit from custody and thus pretended never to exceed the forty-eight-hour legal maximum that they can detain a person, which in fact happened regularly.[20] In other words, the story of the procès-verbal represented not only the facts that the gendarmes had established in their investigation, but also a faultless fiction of their work. This appears to be a universal phenomenon in police work and has been demonstrated for French gendarmes (Mouhanna 2001, 42), Taiwanese police (Martin 2007, 684), and British police: "Reports are assembled in ways that portray the actions taken by the police as standing in a 'correct' or sanctionable relation with court-honoured standards of law-enforcement" (Meehan 1986, 75; see also Innes 2002, 79; Nelken 2009, 266, 272).

Third, and somehow encompassing the first two points, the facts that the gendarmes had established, and thus the true story recorded in the procès-verbal, were less ambiguous than the stories they collected during their investigation. As a result, the offence became more serious. Two cases illustrate this practice. In the first case, two pastoralists were accused of beating up a farmer. Adjudant-Chef Souley changed the witness's statement from "I have not seen that he was beaten" into "I don't know the actual perpetrators because they were many."[21] The original version was obviously conceived of as a sign of ambiguity in the dramaturgy of the procès-verbal. In the original statement, the witness admits to not having seen the beating; the modified statement conceals the fact by referring to a large group of people who may have beaten the man. Thus, the lack of proof in the original statement was hidden; the facts the gendarmes had established were truer than that. The procès-verbal and the story told in it became less ambiguous.

In the second case, a young man was accused of raping a girl who died as a consequence of an infection she acquired through this act. The deceased girl's parents, however, made clear that the sexual intercourse was consensual. The gendarmes were the only ones qualifying the young people's intercourse as rape. The young man's date of birth was noted as "around 1990"; the girl's age was noted as "about 12." Neither the parents of the young man nor the girl could give their children's exact ages, yet the gendarmes chose nineteen for the boy and twelve for the girl and thus produced a most unfavorable constellation of circumstances for the young man. Slightly older than eighteen, he would receive the full punishment prescribed by the Code Pénal (République du Niger 2003, Art. 45–47), made all the more severe because the girl he is said to have violated was younger than thirteen years (ibid., Art. 284). Adjudant-Chef Souley also slightly modified the young man's statement. The girl, whom the young man claimed he did not know ("I only know her by sight"), had become a well-known neighbor ("I have already known her because she was our neighbor.").[22] From a number of discussions I had with gendarmes about similar cases, I learned that they deemed the rape of a well-known neighborhood girl even more perfidious than the rape of a stranger. The crime became more serious. I do not suggest that the gendarmes merely tried to incriminate the young man in this case or the men who supposedly beat up the farmer—even though gendarmes repeatedly stated that "if we write, it is because we want to lock them up, not let them go," contrary to what the police would do. But, beyond that, the more serious the crime and the more unambiguous its description, the more aesthetically satisfying they found the story put forward in the procès-verbal.

This wish for coherence is also a reason why gendarmes, particularly senior gendarmes like Yacouba, Chef Hamza, and Adjudant-Chef Souley, were somewhat reluctant to accept the separate procès-verbaux. They told me that it was much easier to produce a coherent story within a unitary procès-verbal. And coherence is what counts, they said; even the public prosecutor would prefer unitary procès-verbaux because of their coherence, which makes cases appear rather simple.

The public prosecutor, principal addressee of the procès-verbal, was aware of most of the rewriting. Thus, he told me in an interview, he was extremely cautious about the legal exploitability of procès-verbaux. He asserted that statements were often distorted, and the gendarmes' preliminary definition of most crimes and offences was not very well founded; rather, the pieces of information laid out in the document often seemed to perfectly back up the definition the gendarmes chose to apply. The gendarme Amadou put it bluntly: the truth value of procès-verbaux was comparable to an adventure comic strip. This is an exaggeration, but it reflects the dissatisfaction some gendarmes felt about the gap between, on the one hand, their self-representation as true public servants (see Lentz 2010) and, on the other hand, their realization that they are dishonest (see also Hills 2013, 83; Meehan 1986, 78) and constantly overstep the rights of civilians by taking advantage of their illiteracy.[23] Amadou's colleagues, however, were not so critical. They knew that they would, as Innes put it, "'smooth reality' in order to construct a narrative" (2002, 78); but this was not equal to a distortion of the truth—and they knew what the truth was because they had already established the facts.[24]

On a different note, although gendarmes took their role as auxiliaries of the public prosecutor very seriously, they were aware of the purely informative character of the procès-verbal. They knew that they are not the ones who convict a person; they knew that they did not control the outcome of their work (see Lipsky 1980, 78). Here the other addressees of the procès-verbal became important, or as Meehan (1986, 75) put it, the "internal career" of the document gained significance (see also Hull 2008, 505). Besides the public prosecutor, at least one superior in the hierarchy, in most cases, the commandant de groupement, was a direct addressee of the procès-verbaux. Superior officers in distant, air-conditioned offices, most of whom had never worked in a brigade and thus knew hardly anything about the daily work of writing procès-verbaux, would find on reading unambiguous procès-verbaux that the gendarmes in the brigade had done good investigative work, and the more serious the crimes managed in the brigades, the more impressed (or proud) are the superiors (see Mouhanna 2001, 42). In addition, monthly statistics demonstrating the management of crimes underline the quality, institutional legitimacy, and social value of the work done in the brigade (see López 2007). It is thus little wonder that the gendarmerie's clearance rate, which is based on official reports such as procès-verbaux, was an impressive 99.56 percent in 2009.[25]

Written language is never a neutral means of expression, not in scientific publications, not in bureaucratic documents such as procès-verbaux; its authors always engage in some kind of literary reasoning (Knorr Cetina 2002, 176). Martin Innes is thus absolutely right in arguing that the "arrangement of the case material into a narrative form by the police needs to be understood as an artful construction" (2002, 78). In this chapter, I have suggested that to better understand bureaucratic activity, we have to admit that beyond its formalistic rationality and beyond institutional, material, and social constraints (or incentives), there is an aesthetic dimension to it.[26] The gendarmes are not exceptional: from discussions with friends and colleagues in Niger who work in and on hospitals and development projects (particularly Dr. Moha Mahaman), I learned that medical personnel who write reports and fill out patient files also strive for aesthetic satisfaction; scholarly literature suggests that the same could be said about bureaucrats elsewhere in and beyond Africa (Hull 2012; McKay 2012; Navaro-Yashin 2006, 2007; Stirrat 2000). And from brief fieldwork in a German police station, I learned that, there too, some types of formatting, language style, and content are appreciated more than others. Weber (1980 [1921], 664) argues that bureaucrats necessarily engage in creative activity and demonstrate a good deal of devotion to it. I tried to take this creativity seriously and explored it, since the gendarmes themselves expressed it when they were writing and discussing the stories they put together in the procès-verbaux.

What I have endeavored to make clear is the parallel and mostly complementary existence of aesthetic, pragmatic, and legal reasoning; they are all part of creative bureaucratic activity, and are often difficult to separate. Chef Boubacar's album of procès-verbaux in transparent sheet protectors reflects multiple things at the same time: legal outcomes, pragmatic concerns, and aesthetic appreciation. Going through the album, Boubacar explained how and for what offence somebody was or was not convicted; he underlined the legal function and value of these documents. He also explained that he pragmatically collected them as a professional archive because his organization did not provide him with written guidelines for writing different kinds of procès-verbaux (preliminary investigation, in flagrante delicto, legal information, military information, administrative information, different criminal offences); his album served as guide where his organization did not—it was, in Agnès Badou's terms, a result of the "domiciliation de la bibliothèque du service" (2013, 33). And the album and Boubacar's way of presenting it to me reflected his aesthetic appreciation of procès-verbaux as well as his self-esteem as a gendarme.

Focusing on the aesthetics at play in bureaucrats' daily work, particularly in writing bureaucratic stories, may be one way to fill (or rather move beyond) the gap that scholars of bureaucracy often perceive between official norms and informal practices, between legal and pragmatic reasoning. Aesthetics of form, style, and content are not mere decor overlaid on the legal or pragmatic function of documents; bureaucratic aesthetics embrace all at the same time, and only in this combination do procès-verbaux and other documents gain aesthetic value in the eyes of their authors and readers.

It is thus no contradiction that bureaucratic aesthetics are at once personal and impersonal, predictable and unpredictable, legal documentation and poetry; they connect people, domains, and worlds through translation while making their separation blatantly obvious. It is the aesthetic of the frontier.

Part III

POLICING LIFE, OR BUREAUCRATIC DRAMA

Chapter 7

DRAMA WORK

Law enforcement was just part of the gendarmes' daily activities. In fact, it was a minor one. Yes, Souley, Boubacar, Amadou, and the others did want to prove to themselves, their colleagues, and superiors and to the civilian population that they were professionals, intellectuals, and incorruptible bureaucrats. But they also wanted to help people live in peace. They were not so naïve as to hope for total and everlasting harmony, but they did their best to help people resolve disputes that might otherwise easily escalate and cause far greater damage to the local community as a whole. The gendarmes' aim was to repair social relationships before they broke entirely apart. And they did this even in purely civil affairs, although they were legally bound from intervening in such cases.

Scholars of policing often argue that the moment somebody thinks about going to the police to file a complaint, or when that person threatens to do so, indicates an irreparable rupture in the social relationship between the disputants. This idea is built on the widely held assumption that civilians worldwide go to the police only when all other available means of resolving (or ignoring) a dispute have failed.[1] And yet, irretrievably ending a social relationship is rather one of many modes of handling disputes than the precondition for going to the police or court (see Nader and Todd 1978, 9). When civilians came up the hill to the gendarmes in Godiya, this was not necessarily their last option, neither was the social relationship between them terminated. It put pressure on their relationship, of course; but at the same time they entered into a rather special, somewhat intimate kind of relationship because they were forced to confront each other, enter into face-to-face interaction, and precisely this often prevented the relationship from breaking apart.

"You see," Chef Hamza explained, "these people are condemned to live together. So if you separate them, this is not good. You must try and reunite them." He told me about a particular case from a few years earlier that he remembered quite vividly.

> One day, two families came here over some small thing, and they had for more than six months never even greeted one another. And they live in the same neighborhood! All the time the women attacked one another, the children attacked one another. And they were direct neighbors! This is not a life! I told them that your closest relative is always your neighbor. If you get sick or something happens at your house, it's your neighbor who will know it first, even before your relatives! I told them that and we were talking until 9 in the evening! Eventually they understood one another. And then? Voilà, two weeks later they came back and said, "Really, now we are doing really fine!" Wallahi! They even gave me ten thousand francs.

Adjudant-Chef Souley put it in a nutshell: "You should never leave black spots in the community." Except when confronted with severe crimes, the gendarmes saw their function as resolving conflicts and thus restoring social order in the disputants' community. Not only is this reminiscent of many precolonial styles of court procedure and judicial process (see Gluckman 1973 [1955]; Nader 1969), in a sense, it is also the raw matter on which Victor Turner's metaphor of the social drama is built (Turner 1979, 83; 1980). When taking a close look at how the disputing parties and the gendarmes maneuvered through the different steps of this "secular ritual" (Moore and Myerhoff 1977, 4), it seems like the search for redress and reintegration means first and foremost that all parties needed to establish a consensus about how they would interact with one another—which roles they were to adopt. Here the dramaturgical skills of the gendarmes were key. Establishing a consensus meant distributing mutually compatible roles among the parties in such a way that everybody could save face and meaningful interaction was possible. Only within the frame of such "orderly interaction" (see Goffman 1983; Rawls 1987) is it possible to find an amicable solution to the social drama.

From this perspective, arranging a dispute means, first of all, establishing consensus in the interaction order. Yet, the power to define the roles of the participants in the interaction was unevenly distributed because the stage on which this drama was performed was a legal one, with the permanent possibility of legal prosecution—which meant a threat to both parties. In principle, civil disputes belonged to the realm of le social, as Chef Boubacar often explained; but les textes and *la loi* were still there, ready to be put to use. In this kind of "social drama on the stage of law," if you wish, the gendarmes hardly worked or presented themselves as law enforcers but as mediators. They used the ambivalence and possibilities of the frontier-condition not so much to invoke the state of exception (although at times they did threaten to do so during the early stages of so-called arrangement)—quite the contrary. The gendarmes did reach out, in a sense, not to extend the grasp of the state but to keep things separate that would otherwise become very dangerous. While their bureaucratic work is based on the translation from le social into les textes, from life to form, in these arrangements, the gendarmes allow for a clear separation of the two. Thereby they allow for a connection that goes far beyond the production of mutually compatible forms and formats (i.e., pressing life into a bureaucratically exploitable form), namely toward the creation of mutually compatible forms of sociality (i.e., between the persons embodying and those facing the state) and morality (i.e., when legal morality and local morality stand in sharp contrast with each other).

Prelude: Breach, Crisis, Search for Redress

Michelle, a good friend of mine, told me about a problem she had with the previous tenant of the house she was living in. He had not paid his last electricity bill; therefore the electricity company had threatened to cut the electricity to her house several times, so that she was compelled to pay the outstanding bill plus arrears fees, in total sixty-five thousand francs CFA. She and her boyfriend Chris, with whom she shared the house, had repeatedly tried to contact the previous tenant, Pierre; but he had been putting them off for months. They also had contacted the landlord to talk to Pierre and find a solution, but in vain. And because Michelle and Chris felt they had not been taken seriously and had been messed about with, they were considering filing a complaint at the gendarmerie. But they were afraid of Pierre. They told me that he was an ex-soldier, a big guy with a quick temper. He had a family and all; a nice wife and three children and they did not want to punish them by filing a complaint and dragging him to the gendarmerie. When Michelle asked me for my opinion, I told her that I would mention the issue to the gendarmes and find out what they suggested. The next day I talked to Adjudant-Chef Souley about their problems and qualms. Souley said that they should not worry. I should bring them here and he would give them a proper summons for Pierre—"en bonne et due forme."

Michelle and Chris experienced a breach, entered the crisis stage, and sought redress (see Turner 1980, 150–51). They had at first, in the "conflict stage" (Nader and Todd 1978, 15), tried to resolve the issue directly with Pierre, then consulted the landlord thereby expanding the dispute to a third party, but this did not work either. When they were considering a complaint at the gendarmerie, it was not so much about the money. Of course, they wanted their money back, but they also wanted to teach Pierre a lesson, use the gendarmes as a threat and symbolic punishment to make him take them seriously, perhaps even apologize (see Merry 1979, 919; Nader and Todd 1978, 22). They wanted redress in terms of their personal standing—gain the respect they felt they deserved. This episode was truly about a breach of a norm, and the missing money was just a symptom. They were also aware of the threat of further escalation, which could, in their view, result in violence by Pierre; and they knew that the gendarmerie could simply work by the book, establish a report, and send them to court. This is rarely the preferred outcome (see Merry 1979, 902). This is why intermediaries play an important role at this stage of the disputing process. In most cases, the dispute had already been brought before a chief, an influential neighbor or any other third party, with the aim of finding redress and compensation. If these did not succeed, they would often serve as intermediaries. They gave counsel as to which options of redress were available, which should be avoided and how to go about choosing one. I as an intermediary helped Michelle and Chris find an option; I helped them prepare the terrain for their complaint; I reduced their uncertainty in the face of the gendarmerie and the "legal funnel" (see Bierschenk 2008); and by presenting the issue to the gendarmes I preset the roles of the complainants and suspects.

Day 1: Preparing the Stage of Law— Complaint and Summons

Three days later, Michelle and Chris came to the brigade. They called me on my mobile phone when they were close so that I could meet them in the parking lot. They were visibly anxious. I accompanied them across the courtyard to the brigade building and when we climbed the two stairs to enter, the gendarme Chaibou addressed us and greeted the pair of them. I told him that they wanted to file a complaint. Chef Tahirou was just passing by, heard this and led us straight into one of the chef's offices. He sat down behind the desk and invited us to take our seats. I took the chair beside the desk, Michelle and Chris the chairs in front of the desk. I explained to Chef Tahirou what this affair was about and he got up and took us straight to the brigade commander Adjudant-Chef Souley, whose office was next door. Souley was alone so we entered right away. Chef Tahirou invited us to take a seat. I sat a little to the right of Souley's desk so as not to block his view of Michelle and Chris who were sitting just behind me. Chef Tahirou was standing beside the desk, between Souley and us. He explained to Adjudant-Chef Souley, nodding towards me: "He brought us an affair." I told him that it was the affair I had mentioned a few days earlier. He remembered and asked Michelle and Chris whether the landlord was unable to sort this out, whether they had tried speaking with Pierre, and how long this problem had been going on. Chris explained the details of the case in a calm but agitated way. "We just want our money back, that's all." Souley decided to hand them a summons for Pierre. "Soldier or ancient soldier, he is not above the law." Chris then expressed his fear of Pierre's reaction when handing him the summons. Michelle seemed intimidated as well and was frowning and had an anxious look in her eyes. But Adjudant-Chef Souley reassured them that there was no need to worry. "When he sees that it's the gendarmerie, he knows what it is." He suggested summoning him for the next day at 10:30 a.m. Michelle and Chris agreed and everybody shook hands and said goodbye. I left the office with them and told the gendarme, Chaibou, that the brigade commander said to issue a summons for them. Chaibou opened the complaints register and wrote down the details that he requested of Chris. They included names and phone numbers of the complainants and the name and phone number of the summoned. Then he wrote the summons, stamped it, and handed it to Chris. "So we will all come together tomorrow. And Mirco will listen to you and decide on the affair!" I laughed loudly, Michelle and Chris only reservedly. They thanked the gendarme and said goodbye. I went with them to the parking lot to see them off, and I tried to calm them down. I told them to call me as soon as they had handed over the summons to Pierre.

The spatial arrangement of these interactions can be described in terms of different communicative qualities. The parking lot was the space for personal talk and for hopes and fears. This was also where the gendarmes spoke in private with relatives, friends, and acquaintances that came by either to just visit them or as a party to an ongoing dispute. On the doorstep to the brigade building we entered another space, one in which interaction with the gendarmes began. We were directly addressed by the gendarme Chaibou, who immediately tried to identify the visitors' roles—were they just my friends and visitors, were they suspects, witnesses, or complainants? We were then formally received in the chef's office, but the complainants did not talk and were not addressed. Chef Tahirou dominated the interaction through his questions to me, the intermediary, and his aim now was to qualify the kind of complaint they brought to the gendarmes. Chef Tahirou then decided to bring the case directly to the brigade commander, the office in the center of the brigade. With each step, the gendarmes tried to get a more nuanced grasp of Michelle and Chris's roles.

At this stage, the moment of the first contact with the gendarmes, I as an intermediary played a central role for both the complainants and the gendarmes. Michelle and Chris did not know where to go, whom to talk to, and how to present their case. They were extremely nervous about presenting themselves, which role the gendarmes would play, and how to confidently maneuver through this specific type of interaction so alien to them. I met them at the parking lot, greeted them, and tried to make them feel comfortable—to reduce the threat inherent to the legal setting. This seems to be a rather typical function of intermediaries in public bureaucracies in Africa (Blundo 2006; Tidjani Alou 2006, 167). Then I guided them through the courtyard, presented their issue to the first gendarme who approached us, then explained the problem to Chef Tahirou in more detail, then to the brigade commander. It was no coincidence that I was placed—and placed myself—right in front of the brigade commander's desk, as his principal interlocutor. The brigade commander addressed Chris and Michelle only for further details about the dispute, whether they had already confronted Pierre or had tried other remedy agents. By placing myself between the complainants and the gendarmes, I protected Michelle and Chris's presentation of self in this environment so unfamiliar to them. But I also assisted the gendarmes: not only did I guide the complainants, I also presented the matter in the appropriate format, namely a complaint; through this, I helped the gendarmes qualify Michelle and Chris's roles. I also transmitted the brigade commander's order of issuing a summons to his subordinate. I was in part complainant, in part gendarme—part of both worlds at the same time. This is exactly what happened with most of the intermediaries, be they chiefs, their representatives, local politicians, or gendarmes as friends of the complainants.

At this stage, nobody had explicitly decided whether the issue at hand would be treated as a social drama or a legal procedure—it was a bureaucratically ambivalent situation. This is what made the situation difficult to grasp from the complainants' perspective. They came to the brigade stating through me that they wanted to file a complaint, which is the formal opening of a criminal case. This was the only way to gain the gendarmes' ear. In the conversation with the brigade commander, however, they said that they only wanted their money back, and that Pierre had treated them disrespectfully. After hearing a complaint,

Adjudant-Chef Souley usually asked: "Me kake so?" ("What do you want?"). (If the complainants had not mentioned this of their own accord.) Here it became clear that the case had not been fully appropriated by the gendarmes but that they heard the complainants' wish. I have never heard a complainant say that he wanted his opponent to be legally prosecuted or put into prison (see also Spittler 1980, 158). They merely wanted material compensation or moral redress. Even though invoking the law as the factor legitimizing their action ("he is not above the law"), the gendarmes said between the lines that they were ready to manage this problem as a social drama and not start a legal procedure. A case was formally opened (a complaint was issued, an entry was made in the brigade's complaints register), but the gendarmes insinuated that it did not have to be formally treated nor fully appropriated by the gendarmerie. This was particularly clear when complainants had to hand over the summons personally.

> In the evening, Michelle called me. They had just gotten home from Pierre's and, Michelle said, it did not go very well. Pierre's wife had let them in, the two children were playing in the living room, and Michelle and Chris waited for Pierre to come home from work. When he entered the living room, he immediately asked them "What do you want?" and Michelle and Chris asked him to talk with them in the courtyard. They didn't want to hand him the summons in front of his wife and children. The three of them stepped out and when Michelle and Chris gave him the summons, he looked at it, turned around without a word, got into his car and drove off. Michelle was scared. When they got home, she saw that the door handle to their house was broken off. True, it had been cracked for some time, but Pierre could also have smashed it. Had he entered the house? It turned out he had not, but Michelle's fear remained.

When Michelle and Chris handed over the summons, they were extremely careful as to how they did it. They made sure to protect Pierre's face vis-à-vis his family. This is not exceptional behavior. Those who hand over summonses were often careful as to how to perform the handing over. Either they put the summons in an envelope so that only the recipient could see it; or they handed it to the recipients' *chef de quartier*, who would then make sure that the recipient received it discretely and support him in the disputing process. Again, a sign that the social relation has not been dissolved but merely irritated. Otherwise, care for the opponent's reputation would be of no concern. However, the moment of handing over the summons, or rather the moment the recipient realizes that he is being handed a summons from the gendarmerie, represents another major irritation of the social relationship between the two parties. From Pierre's perspective, this breach set the crisis in motion. And when Pierre turned away silently, he gave them a taste of what schism might feel like. In terms of the interaction order, this irritation stemmed mainly from somebody's realization that he or she had been ascribed a role—that of a suspect summoned by the gendarmerie, that of a wrongdoer, etc.—without having had the opportunity to have a say in it. On some level, through the complaint and the summons, the crisis between Michelle/Chris and Pierre was amplified. But it was also, on another level, taken out of their hands. The gendarmes had given them an appointment; the summons was issued, an entry made in the complaints register—there was no turning back.

Day 2: Hearing and Confrontation

Michelle and Chris arrived at the brigade a couple of minutes before 10:30 a.m. I was already there. We stood in front of the building waiting for Pierre. Chef Tahirou saw us standing there, greeted us amicably and invited us to take a seat in the front office. While we were waiting, I talked and joked to the gendarmes Nouhou and Omar who were going about their daily business: writing reports, taking witness statements, receiving complaints. At about 11:15 a.m. Adjudant-Chef Souley came out of his office, saw that Pierre had not arrived yet and asked Michelle for his phone number. He jotted it down on a post-it note and went back into his office. A few minutes later, he came out saying "I called him. He's coming." He arrived at twelve o'clock and greeted everybody briefly. I got up and shook hands with him, and he went straight into the brigade commander's office. Souley was with somebody and told Pierre to wait outside. He went out into the courtyard again.

When the people left Adjudant-Chef Souley's office, they left the door open and we entered. Pierre, Michelle and Chris sat in front of the desk; I stood by the closed door, where Chef Tahirou had been standing the day before. After a brief silence, Adjudant-Chef Souley pointed at Chris, still without saying a word. Chris then retold the story in crisp, clear French while Pierre played silently with his mobile phone. After a few questions of detail by Adjudant-Chef Souley, he pointed to Pierre who then told his version of the same story. He talked agitatedly and loudly, verbally invading the room. He kept glancing at Adjudant-Chef Souley and me with wide-open eyes and gesticulating wildly. When our eyes met, I nodded attentively and understandingly. The longer his narration, the more complicated everything seemed. At some point, he said that the landlord still owed him half a month's rent. He had apparently paid for a full month although he had left the house earlier in the month. "C'est très simple!" Adjudant-Chef Souley replied and asked for the landlord's phone number. "This is the *commandant de brigade* of the gendarmerie..." He presented the issue at hand to him briefly and told him that the problem could not be resolved without him and asked him to come to the brigade the next day at 10:00 a.m. The landlord agreed and Adjudant-Chef Souley told everybody to meet again the next morning. He ended the meeting with "that's it. See you tomorrow."

After having waited an hour for Pierre to arrive, Michelle and Chris were not sure whether they were still in a good position. They felt that the gendarmes had not been as strict with Pierre as they had hoped. Pierre had arrived late, needed to be reminded by the brigade commander not to miss the meeting, and had not even been reprimanded. Pierre was granted considerable time autonomy, and thus a say in when interaction was possible. Control over time is regarded as one of the main features of police and other bureaucrats when dealing with civilians (Lipsky 1980, 61–65), and here the gendarmes ceded it partially to Pierre. This showed Michelle and Chris that the gendarmes were not simply "their" gendarmes (see Hornberger 2004); and this showed Pierre that he was not in such a bad position after all. When he showed up, he greeted everybody briefly and went straight to the brigade commander. He demonstrated spatial autonomy—opened a door Michelle and Chris had not and would not dare open without being invited to do so. Having been told to wait outside, he stepped into the courtyard; he did not wait in the same room as Michelle and Chris, giving them another foretaste of schism. In a sense, the gendarmes voluntarily gave up a small portion of their temporal and territorial advantages that were at the base of their control of the interaction order (see Katovich and Reese 1993, 402).

In the brigade commander's office, the dramaturgical consensus finding started off with the disputants trying to adapt the roles they wanted to adapt or refusing the unwanted ones. Chris, given the first word, spoke calmly and in remarkably clear and elaborate French, thus demonstrating his confidence and that his status, being a young migrant student from a neighboring country and perhaps twenty years younger than Pierre, was nonetheless considerably high. He strengthened his role as a serious and respectable complainant. Pierre, by contrast, was not so comfortable with the role he had been ascribed from the outset. He was agitated, talked loudly, was searching for eye contact with the brigade commander and myself. As he had no intermediary with him, he tried to find allies to stop him being cast in the role of the bad guy. That the landlord still owed him some money (although this had little to do with the unpaid electricity bill) gave the brigade commander the opportunity to expand the conflict and seemingly transfer some of Pierre's guilt to a third party who was absent from this interaction situation. He granted Pierre some of the claims with regards to the definition of his role: he too was a victim of injustice.

At this stage, no mention of the law was made whatsoever, and no bureaucratic procedures were applied. The landlord was invited to join them the next day, no summons was issued, no declarations were taken, and nothing was noted down in case registers. Although it was clear to everybody that they found themselves on the stage of law, with the threat of the uniform and the law being omnipresent, gendarmes made no explicit reference to this threat. They often even calmed everybody down, telling them to not be afraid. Chef Hamza used to tell intimidated disputants: "There is no difference between us and you! We will talk, we will arrange, and that's it!"[2] He thus verbally minimized the powerful role of the gendarmes as those who could easily define a person's role, and those who could—due to the porosity of the civil/criminal divide—at any moment turn the social drama into a legal procedure.

At this level, a consensus, both on the dispute and the drama level, has not been reached yet. At some point it even seemed out of reach:

> After Adjudant-Chef Souley had concluded the hearing, Pierre was the first to get up and out; he left without a word. Michelle and Chris had also gotten up, but Chris addressed Adjudant-Chef Souley again. Pierre heard this and came back quickly. "What you are about to tell are lies!" he shouted at Chris. A dispute broke out between them, Souley was still sitting behind his desk quietly looking at both, and suddenly the dispute stopped and everybody went out, Pierre a bit faster than the rest. I followed him quickly in order to calm him down; but he shouted me down. Chris caught up with us, barged in and shouted at Pierre. Pierre then shouted back that Chris had threatened him the last time they had talked over the phone, that he would not respect him, and Chris shouted back even louder, insults flew back and forth, and I stepped in between the two trying to deescalate the situation. "I'm ready for anything!" Chris shouted and Pierre replied, "Even here and now!" I pushed Chris back and I told Michelle to hold him back. I then took Pierre by the arm to take him aside and show him my sympathy, but they both shouted me down. I was wondering what the gendarmes might think of my behavior. I pulled Pierre by the arm and pushed Chris further back, and I accompanied Pierre out onto the parking lot and to his car. I tried to talk to him calmly but I had a hard time getting a word in edgeways. I told him that we were here "to get on well with each other," that it was

the landlord's fault having pocketed two months' rent, that "tomorrow we will find a solution," that there was "no problem," and I realized that I was talking just like a gendarme. He merely wanted to be treated with respect, he told me, and not the way Chris, "this boy," had been treating him. He got into his car; we shook hands twice through the open window. "We'll keep in touch," he said as he drove off.

As Pierre felt Chris would denigrate him further in front of Adjudant-Chef Souley even when he was not present, the conflict escalated. The escalation was already hinted at when Pierre came back into the brigade commander's office but was quickly transferred into the courtyard. And it was not about the money, it was about the role Pierre refused to accept: a villain who does not deserve the respect one shows to respectable persons. He presented himself as a respectable man, a good business-man, and twenty years older than Chris. My own role shifted slightly from supporter of Michelle and Chris to Pierre's ally. Even I felt that Chris had not accorded him the minimum of respect. But Chris, I felt, was also disrespectful to the gendarmes and me by making a scene in front of the brigade. He did not accept the interaction order at the brigade: it was not a space for fighting. Gendarmes often intervened when disputants started to fight or yelled at each other in the courtyard.[3] Time and again they made it clear that the case had been taken over by the gendarmes, that they would do their work, and that it was also a question of good manners not to behave in such a crude way in front of gendarmes. "This is not a bus station!" gen-darmes often told them in reference to the noisy, bustling, and seemingly chaotic atmosphere there. These were some of the few moments in which gendarmes truly imposed the authority they could exert over the interaction order.

Whereas the intermediary was almost absent during the hearing and the con-frontation, in situations where the crisis seemed to escalate, as between Chris and Pierre in the courtyard, he was essential. He was more than the complain-ants' or suspects' biased supporter; he was also responsible for his clients' correct conduct in a space to which he had introduced them; he was standing in for the gendarmes' roles, for respect for the interaction order defined by the gendarmes.

Day 3: Trial and Judgment

The next day, Michelle and Chris arrived almost punctually, just a few minutes after 10:00 a.m. Fifteen minutes later, the landlord arrived and we greeted him with a handshake. Pierre arrived another fifteen min-utes later. He greeted everybody with a handshake, was calm and smil-ing friendly. We all chatted as we waited in the front office.

When another pair of disputants had left Adjudant-Chef Souley's office, we entered. The landlord was offered a chair in front of Souley's desk, behind him sat, from right to left Chris, Michelle and Pierre; I was again standing in front of the closed door. Adjudant-Chef Souley said nothing and nobody else was sure whose turn it was to talk first, including me. After a brief silence the landlord started talking, took a document out of his briefcase and handed it to Adjudant-Chef Souley, then he took it back again, asked Souley for a pen, read through a couple of paragraphs and marked them with a cross. Adjudant-Chef Souley interrupted the landlord and began explaining what the two parties had brought before him: the dates of Pierre's move-out and of Michelle's and Chris's move-in.

With the landlord present, Adjudant-Chef Souley reduced the pressure on Pierre who was very responsive to that; after all, now the landlord was the bad guy and Pierre a victim as well. When Pierre talked, he mentioned Chris as an ally against the landlord who had tricked them both. Chris, in contrast, presented himself as the landlord's ally and tried to move the focus from the rent pocketed by the landlord to the electricity bill that Pierre had not paid. Adjudant-Chef Souley interrupted the discussion. "It's very simple. It's very, very simple," he said. He recapitulated the move-in and move-out dates, the dates up to which and from which date on rent was paid, and drew a diagram to explain this to Chris, who was still focusing only on the electricity bill and how the landlord pocketed the double rent for a half month. Chris still did not seem to understand. "Give me 25,000," Souley said to him. He took the notes (representing half a month's rent) and demonstrated the flow of money from Pierre to the landlord and from Chris to the landlord. "Do you understand?" he asked Chris several times until he finally nodded.

Adjudant-Chef Souley recapitulated again: Pierre had been paying rent until September 20; Michelle and Chris started paying rent on September 5; the landlord received the double rent for fifteen days, or half a month, thus 25,000 francs CFA. The landlord must now add fifteen days to Michelle and Chris's right to the house (put differently, when they stop paying rent, they can stay for another fifteen days). Finally Souley turned to the unpaid electricity bill plus arrears fees of 65,000 francs CFA. As Pierre had paid 15 days of Michelle and Chris's rent, this left him with outstanding 40,000 francs CFA to be given to Chris. Everybody in the room nodded. Adjudant-Chef Souley told Pierre to pay on Monday morning at the brigade. Pierre replied that he could give it to them later this afternoon or tomorrow, but Souley interrupted him harshly: "No, no, you bring that here, we are the witnesses!" and he pointed to his wide-open eyes. Then Adjudant-Chef Souley turned to Michelle and Chris and said, "He will bring the money Monday morning. I will give it to Mirco, since we are together." Michelle and Chris did not understand and asked whether they would come here and get the money. "No, no," Adjudant-Chef Souley replied, "This is between us," and he pointed his finger at me.

"Ok, it's settled!" Adjudant-Chef Souley concluded. The others got up, thanked and shook hands with Souley. I held the door open and left the office last. Michelle and Chris were waiting for me in the courtyard; Pierre and the landlord had already gone to the parking lot, without shaking hands with Michelle and Chris. I told Michelle and Chris to catch up with them, "You need to shake hands in the end!" The atmosphere was calmer in the parking lot and the handshakes were amicable. I went on to chat a bit with Pierre. "Are you a gendarme?" he asked me. "Almost, " I replied jokingly. "There is no 'almost'!" he said as he got into his car. When Pierre and the landlord left, I talked to Michelle and Chris and asked them whether they were satisfied." Well . . . I'm waiting . . ." Chris said. "I'll be satisfied when I hold the money in my hands."

All in all, Adjudant-Chef Souley was a very competent arranger. First, he remembered all the sums and dates Pierre, Chris, and the landlord had been juggling around with. After appreciating all the pieces of evidence he "told them the truth," which here meant telling all the participants what their "true" roles were. And he made sure that everybody in the room understood what the truth was—particularly Chris, the complainant. The initial problem, so the conclusion, was an accumulation of unfortunate circumstances. Adjudant-Chef Souley presented the facts in such a convincing way that the final option of resolution appeared almost self-evident. Nobody who had listened to his explanations could be against it. And second, with the expansion of the conflict to the landlord, Adjudant-Chef Souley gave everybody the opportunity to save face—and ultimately to agree to the consensus established in the interaction order. And yet, in the end Pierre had to pay the money Michelle and Chris had asked for in the first place.

In cases in which the gendarmes seemed more disinterested they handed the responsibility of finding a consensus over to the disputants and their intermediaries. After the hearing and the confrontation and after telling them the truth, gendarmes invited the disputants to find a consensus between them. "Go and find an agreement!" Chef Boubacar used to say to them. The disputants then met in the parking lot or behind the brigade building and talked, often for hours. When they had found a consensus, one of them, usually the intermediary, would come back to the brigade commander or another noncommissioned officer, who had heard and judged their case, and present the result of the negotiations. If the gendarmes thought that the agreed on compensation payment was fair and just, the case was settled. If it was not, the gendarmes would send them away, rebuking them for wasting their time, or they would threaten them with legal prosecution, thus to turn this civil affair into a legal case (see chapter 4).

The final resolution to the conflict was always a verbal one. In the case presented here, Adjudant-Chef Souley declared: "Ok, it's settled," and that was the end of it. Sometimes he was more explicit when mentioning the resolution to the conflict, the rehabilitation of order. Then he would give the disputants extensive moral lessons about what they had done wrong, how they should live peacefully together, and he ended his speech, after a brief pause of silence, with the phrase: "To, yanzu ba kome tsakaninku!" ("Now there stands nothing in between you!").[4]

Epilogue: Compensation and Redress

The transaction was completed two days later, on Monday afternoon. Pierre was supposed to bring the money in the morning, but by 1:00 p.m., Adjudant-Chef Souley had to call and remind him, so that he finally arrived around 6:00 p.m. When Pierre came, he seemed cheerful and relaxed, saluted me in military style with a big smile on his face; then we shook hands amicably and chatted and joked like old friends. He told me that he himself wanted to file a complaint against somebody who owed him some 800,000 francs CFA, but not today. He was in a very good mood while he was in Adjudant-Chef Souley's office. Here again, he saluted in a funny-military way, Adjudant-Chef Souley smiled and did the same funny gesture. Pierre sat directly in front of the desk; I sat to his left, just a bit further away. Pierre immediately handed Souley five 10,000-franc CFA notes. Adjudant-Chef Souley counted them twice. He said that there were 50,000, but he only needed to pay 40,000. Souley handed me the 40,000 and put one 10,000 note on the desk. "What is that?" he asked. "Normally this is for you," Pierre replied. Adjudant-Chef Souley pushed the note in Pierre's direction and he took it instantly. Then Pierre pulled an impressively thick wad of notes out of his front pocket. "Ah, he has a lot of money!" Adjudant-Chef Souley said in my direction. Pierre handed him a 5,000 note and Souley thanked him and immediately asked "and him?" pointing at me. Without hesitation Pierre handed me also a 5,000 note. "But no . . ." I shyly replied but took the money anyway. "Okay, we're settled up!" Souley immediately concluded. Pierre and I got up and out of the office. I told him that I would be here if he came back for his own troubles the next day.[5]

This transaction was rather unbureaucratic. No documents were signed, no complaints withdrawn, no receipt handed out. Adjudant-Chef Souley's conclusion, "We're settled up," is much more remindful of smoothing out minor disputes among equals than of closing a police case. This also suggests that the problem now solved was not one between Pierre and the complainants, but one between him and Adjudant-Chef Souley.

In other cases, particularly when a lot of money was involved, the redress and compensation became very formal. Then both disputing parties signed a contract with the gendarmes as witnesses, custodians, and enforcers of the contract. Gendarmes did not perceive this as illegal or extralegal. They conceived it as "transactions" prescribed by the code of criminal procedure (République du Niger 2007, Art. 6), which cancel "l'action publique," the legal prosecution. A lot of cases ended with such an "engagement," a written contract that specified which sum of money was to be paid until when, in how many installments, and the dates of payments. The gendarmes would ensure that the installments were brought on time and they kept the money until the agreed on sum had been paid in full. Then they would call the recipient to come and collect it. If the debtor did not bring the money to the gendarmes, they had a legal case against him because he had not fulfilled his contract with the gendarmerie. An engagement—written or unwritten as in Pierre's case—was "a consensus before the law," as the gendarmes called it, and they thought of themselves as the guarantors of this consensus. This was possible because, in their eyes, it was an engagement vis-à-vis the gendarmerie, not primarily vis-à-vis the complainant. "Now this is an affair between you and the gendarmerie," they often told the debtors. Part of the engagement the debtor would sign was the phrase "in case of noncommitment, I will be subjected to the rigor of the law."[6] They cited article 184 of the Code Pénal that defined the refusal to respond to a summons. "This also covers the engagements. So if he doesn't honor his engagement . . . article 184!"

Pierre gave Souley the 40,000 francs plus 5,000 francs for each of us. What for? Perhaps for not turning the social drama into a legal procedure or perhaps for allowing him to save face. In other words, perhaps it was for Adjudant-Chef Souley's being a good arranger. Not only did he arrange, in the sense of repair, or "gyara"—a key Hausa term often used by the disputants themselves—the breach that had brought them to the gendarmes in the first place, he also made an arrangement, in the sense that he managed to creatively arrange the roles distributed and taken over in the drama setting so that the participants felt largely at ease, eventually, and the collectively produced outcome was a satisfying one for all participants.

Settling a dispute does not mean to "negotiate nothing," as Kemp et al. (1992) suggest. It means, first of all, establishing consensus. All participants in the dispute described—gendarmes, disputants, and intermediaries—needed to find an agreement in terms of the roles they adopt and imposed on others to make interaction orderly and thus meaningful. Only then was an "amicable arrangement" possible, as well as reintegration. Eventually, in the case of a successful arrangement, the gendarmes will have ideally restored peace on two levels: one, between the disputants themselves—when Chris and Michelle ran into Pierre at a filling station weeks later, he even invited them to have dinner at his house; and two, within the larger community.

From beginning to end, arrangements were bureaucratically ambivalent situations. They had a bureaucratic opening through the filing of a complaint, the issuing of a summons, and the entry in the complaints registry. They were also accompanied by bureaucratic elements specific to the office environment in which they took place. And a lot of these arrangements also had a bureaucratic closing, namely a signed contract of commitment. On the one hand, such bureaucratic traces or graphic artifacts (Hull 2003) rendered the transformation of social dramas into legal procedures not only (theoretically) possible for the gendarmes, but also painfully tangible for the complainants and suspects. On the other hand, the fact that the gendarmes by far exceeded their legal mandate by dealing with purely civil cases made them highly vulnerable to interventions or disciplinary complaints by well-connected or legally trained *parents-amis-connaissances* that the disputing parties might mobilize. Bearing this tension—the vague and yet permanent threat of legal prosecution, while being the least favorite outcome for all parties involved—is the toll demanded by the frontier. It is also testament to the realm of possibilities that the frontier offers, including the possibility of sheer and unbureaucratic human drama.

Chapter 8

REPAIR WORK

It has become a common observation by scholars of policing, that, as Waddington (1999, 5, emphasis in original) put it, "the characteristic feature of policing is *under enforcement of the law*—not its enforcement." Under-enforcement is mostly understood as the occasional (or frequent) *non*enforcement of the law, depending on the police officer's discretionary decision to turn a blind eye to particular situations. The gendarmes in Godiya also often chose not to enforce the law. Just as often, however, they chose to truly *under*-enforce it—that is, enforce it, but not fully. In most cases, this meant turning a délit into a simple contravention (a criminal into a noncriminal offence), or a contravention into a mere warning. This happened mainly in the course of what they called "amicable arrangements"—the out-of-court settlement of cases.

The Hausa term for such arrangements is *gyara*. Literally it means "to repair." "Don Allah, a gyara," "I beg you to repair," was probably the single, most common phrase spoken during my ethnographic research in the Nigerien gendarmerie. With this phrase, civilians begged the gendarmes not to send them to court and possibly into prison but rather to allow them to make amends instead. The victims knew that going to court meant that they had to spend months (and a lot of money) traveling back and forth between their homes and the courthouse, which was often dozens if not hundreds of kilometers away. In Niger, as in other West African countries, courts work often painstakingly slowly and cases are routinely adjourned (for Niger, see Oumarou 2011, 240–48; Tidjani Alou 2006; for Benin, see Bierschenk 2008, 117). The victims did not know when and if they would eventually be compensated. For them it was a terribly insecure investment. So usually both parties wanted the gendarmes to allow for an extralegal settlement of the cases. And indeed, most cases were eventually settled by the gendarmes and outside the courts, even when a criminal law had been broken.

The Nigerien gendarmes usually tried not to stick too closely to the book, producing bureaucratic cases, files, and sending everything to court. One of their primary aims was gyara, to restore peace, whether they were confronted with purely civil affairs (for which they had no legal mandate to resolve) or criminal cases. As Chef Hamza explained this to me, "Making noise" is not good. "You must try and reunite them." Adjudant-Chef Souley said that "you should never leave black spots in the community." Thus, instead of applying the law indifferently, the gendarmes rather tried to find alternative solutions to disputes and conflicts. When no law had been broken, the aim was to forge a consensus between the parties. The gendarmes would merely serve as guarantors of this agreement, which generally took the form of financial compensation. When a criminal law had been broken or rather when the gendarmes came to that conclusion, they as the "soldiers of the law," as they called themselves, also felt offended. A law has been broken, and what is broken needs to be restored.

To achieve what the gendarmes understood as justice, that is, to repair the harm and restore the law, all parties had to lower their expectations, including the law. The Nigerien penal code (Code Pénal) and code of criminal procedure (Code de Procédure Pénale) both originate and still contain elements dating back to the colonial era. Penal codes in Niger and other French-speaking African countries have rarely been modernized, so the gap between legal proscriptions and social notions of justice is particularly wide (Bierschenk 2008, 114; Oumarou 2011, 13, 185). According to the gendarmes, these outdated and "foreign" laws were largely inappropriate for policing the life worlds of the people they confronted. This process could be seen as a prime example of discretion-led under-enforcement—a process which, as many scholars have shown, is a necessary principle of police work everywhere.[4] In this article, however, taking the gendarmes' perspective and the notion of gyara seriously, I suggest that what appears as the under-enforcement or restraint of the law from one perspective may from another appear as the correction, or "repair," of the law. What the gendarmes thus repaired, I argue, was not only the relationships between conflicting parties, but the law itself. True, this is a particular kind of repair. The gendarmes often only produced makeshift solutions for more serious problems, just like the *mai gyaran moto* or *mota*, the mechanics for motorbikes or cars that I have met in Niger. The repair was hardly ever permanent, nor removed the cause of the damage, nor improved the substance of your car; but it allowed you to continue on the road—at least for some time. With this, I try to do what anthropologists may do best (e.g., Bierschenk et al. 2016): propose a change in perspective. In that sense, it is not the application of the law that is deficient, as metaphorically expressed in "under-enforcement," but the law itself. As I will show, from that perspective the gendarmes not only have the power to declare the "state of exception" and reduce people to "bare life"; they can reduce the law to "bare text"—in an "exception to the state," if you wish.

I will develop my empirical argument by examining one particular case of assault and battery and only afterward conclude with a discussion of its theoretical implications, drawing mostly on Aristotle's concept of *epieikeia* as the "rectification" of the law and Max Gluckman's (1973 [1955]) description of the "norm of the reasonable man" as necessary for bridging the gap between "law in general" and "law in action." Cases like the one I present here were part of the bread-and-butter business of the gendarmes in Godiya.

Harm and Offence

One morning a sixteen-year-old boy came to the brigade; he had cuts and bruises and his face was swollen. When he came closer, Chef Hamza recognized him as a peddler who sold coffee, tea, and bread at the local bus station. Without waiting for the greetings and out of concern for the boy, he asked him what had happened. A mechanic who also worked at the bus station had beaten him up, he said in such a timid voice that Chef Hamza and I barely heard him. The mechanic had ordered and drunk a coffee and eaten a piece of bread and refused to pay afterward. The ensuing argument quickly turned into a fistfight and the mechanic, perhaps in his mid-twenties, was much stronger and beat up the boy badly. Chef Hamza asked which mechanic it was. The boy did not know his name but described the workshop where the bully worked and Chef Hamza's hunch turned out to be right. He got visibly angry: "How often have we had him here, this thug? His relatives come, we hit them with a fine of 12,000, 8,000, 12,000 and every time they pay for him!" He told the gendarme, Moussa, to give the young man a summons for the mechanic.

Not only had the mechanic breached his commercial contract with the boy when he ordered and consumed coffee and bread without paying, but he also beat him up afterward. In legal terms, it was the délit assault and battery (*coups et blessures volontaires*). The Nigerien penal code states that "every person who has willfully injured or struck, or committed any other violence or assault, shall be punished with imprisonment of three months to two years and a fine of 10,000 to 100,000 francs or one of these penalties only" (République du Niger 2003, Art. 222, my translation). The mechanic had clearly broken criminal law; according to the gendarmes there was no doubt about that. But Chef Hamza was also offended. He knew the mechanic who had already been summoned to the brigade several times. He was well aware that the mechanic had been released just as often with a fine, which his relatives paid.

In similar cases, gendarmes often sent away the complainant, dismissing the incident as mere brawls among young adults, nothing unusual, and that, "it was not worth" putting their time and energy into this kind of "futilities." The gendarme Amadou explained that this was the difference between a good and a bad gendarme: "You should never say, 'It isn't worth it.' Even if the damage caused is small, you should never say, 'It's a futility.' Otherwise the poor would never recover their rights." Some gendarmes were more inclined to take over cases in which a lot of money was at stake. That meant that the gendarmes had a prospect of additional income after a successful arrangement. But a good gendarme should not limit his motivations to possible income; he should himself also feel offended both in his role as the defender of justice and through his empathy with the victim. Since most gendarmes came from similarly poor and rural areas, they were particularly sensitive to their "rural brothers and sisters" difficulties, needs, and expectations, they said. Justice, however, was a rather diffuse thing. And it should perhaps, as Laura Nader (1990) reminds us with regards to "harmony," be understood as an ideology with political implications. As I have shown elsewhere, in this context justice is like security first and foremost about the protection, care, and definition of the community (Göpfert 2012, 66). So even when the gendarmes were not very empathetic with the victim, they were at least sensitive to whether somebody willfully disrespected communal peace and thus the gendarmes' ambition to maintain it—that is, the core of their professional identity (Beek and Göpfert 2013b, 113–15). Chef Hamza's anger was not so much caused by the fact that the mechanic had beaten up a younger boy, but rather by his constant disrespect for the gendarmes and the law and the fact that he could count on his relatives' support. In this light, the mechanic had done three things: he had caused harm to the boy, broken the law, and offended the gendarmes.

Hearing and Judgment

The injured boy came back to the brigade about one hour later, followed at a short distance by the mechanic. Chef Hamza called them to come near and they squatted down in front of him. He asked the boy to repeat what had happened. He was very shy, and was barely audible, stuttered and kept touching the cuts on his lips. "Ya isa, [That's enough]," Chef Hamza interrupted him harshly and pointed to the mechanic. "This talk is not true," the latter started. He had not even finished his first sentence when Chef Hamza interrupted him harshly. "Baka miji ba ne!" [You are not a man!]" Only here you have courage because you know that your relatives will pay for you. But down there, beating up this child?" Chef Hamza got up from the bench and said, "Man, that's a thug, lock him up." Moussa got up and took the mechanic into the building, wrote down his name, profession, date, and place of birth, names of his mother and father and locked him into the cell.

When the two parties were assembled at the brigade, the collective hearing started. As usual, the complainant spoke first, then the suspect. After that, the gendarmes delivered a judgment, a clear definition of roles. The boy was the victim; the mechanic was not even treated as a suspect but as guilty, a bully and a thug—not only vis-à-vis the boy, but also in relation to the gendarmes. The judgment was first verbalized, and then materialized when Chef Hamza had Moussa detain the mechanic. Moussa noted the mechanic's particulars in the arrest registry, forced him to take off his shirt and shoes, and locked him into the cell. In most cases, after they had uncovered the truth and defined the role of the offender, the gendarmes routinely incarcerated the offender. This had several effects. First of all, the mechanic or any other person who was put into the cell was forced to take on the role ascribed to him. He was no longer in a position to negotiate with the gendarmes or at least have his version of the story heard. And the complainant was reassured by the gendarmes' judgment in his favor.

But it was unclear whether the mechanic was now being held by the strong grip of the law or just by the gendarmes. To put it in Jan Beek's (2011, 201) terms: had the gendarmes' already drawn the register of formal law enforcement or was this some sort of instant punishment as part of the register of sociality? It could be either or both: the initiation of a legal procedure or the gendarmes' violently punishing him in response to what they perceived as a threat to their status (see Alpert and Dunham 2004, 172–76; Conti 2009, 411–13). Or was it just a humiliating exercise in social discipline (see Choongh 1998, 227)?

At this point, both parties could not know how the gendarmes would proceed: write a report or find an arrangement, in other words, enforce the law or not. To the boy and the mechanic it was not clear which role the gendarmes had adopted. If the gendarmes were themselves unsure which role to take on, they would call the prosecutor (depending on their personal relationship with him)—the formal head and supervisor of any criminal investigation. The latter would then tell them to find an arrangement, to merely fine the offender or make the procedure, depending on the national or regional *politique pénale*, a "policy relating to particular offences" (Hodgson 2002, 236n39), but also on his own workload and his trust in the gendarmes' abilities as arrangers (because he would not want to take the blame for possible backlashes). In short, during the hearing, the gendarmes made a full assessment of what has been broken and might need repair, but also whether it could be fixed at all.

"What Do You Want?"

Shortly after the mechanic had been locked into the cell, Adjudant-Chef Souley came back from some errands. Chef Hamza directly approached him and told him about this affair. Souley sat down on a bench beside the boy and asked him what had happened. The boy, still squatting on the ground, talked so shyly that Souley urged him to speak up several times. Then he asked Chef Hamza whether the mechanic had already confessed. Hamza and the other gendarmes present said that whether he had confessed or not . . . "We know this thug" Souley then asked the boy "To, me kake so? [What do you want?]," but the boy could hardly talk. Seemingly intimidated by Souley's impressive bodily presence and aura of authority, he was staring at the ground and nervously touching the wounds on his face and did not say a word. Adjudant-Chef Souley told him to go to the hospital, have his wounds taken care of and come back with the receipts for the treatment. When the boy left, Adjudant-Chef Souley explained that this is what the mechanic always did: pick a fight with younger and weaker boys, preferably those like this one, who were strangers in the town and had no relatives here, who worked hard just to earn their daily bread.

The mechanic was in the cell; this looked like enforcement. Then Adjudant-Chef Souley uttered the central question: "Me kake so?"—"What do you want?" The gendarmes asked this question in all cases except for cases of severe crimes, such as murder or kidnapping. In the latter case, the gendarmes made clear that their activity had nothing to do with the complainant's request but with their legal or superior moral mandate. When they asked, "What do you want?" the gendarmes insinuated that all their ensuing activities depended on the complainant's choice. Sometimes a second one followed the question: "Kana so an kai shi prison?"—"Do you want us to put him in prison?" Or they said: "In kuna so an kara . . . bashi koma gida!"—"If you want that we proceed, he will not return home." This implied that the gendarmes' strict law enforcement depended on whether this was the complainant's will. I have never witnessed somebody replying, "Yes, they should put him in prison." Putting somebody in prison would in most cases mean social disaster. It would mean stigmatizing somebody as an intrinsically dangerous person and of absolutely no social value. Furthermore, it would put enormous pressure on the prisoner's family; an imprisoned man could no longer look after his family, instead they now had to look after him. And since in the rural communities where the gendarmes worked, there was almost always some kind of relationship between the families of the victim and the offender, even if only an ethnically based joking relationship (see Tamari 2006; Verne 2004), the prison option had to be absolutely avoided in order to prevent social rupture. Again: "Never leave black spots in the community!" Civilians thought quite similarly, and this is why they too always opted for arrangements. Only when everybody agreed that the offender was, in fact, of no social value and of intrinsic danger to the whole community did civilians urge the gendarmes to take that person away—and thus draw the boundary of the community.

The gendarmes seemed to leave it to the complainants' discretion which exact role they would adopt: that of the law enforcer, punisher, mediator, and so on. With this, I suggest, they tried to grasp popular ideas about the gravity of a given offence. In other words, they tried to understand popular conceptions of right and wrong and of who was and was not perceived as being part of this local community. A superior officer once told me that the gendarmes, in their interface position between the law and the people, and in order to do a good job, had to "find an understanding with the population. They have to study: What is their vision of security and justice? And by doing that, they adopt, even without being aware of it, a client-centered perspective." The gendarmes knew very well that civilians could easily interpret the indifferent application of the law against fundamental local convictions as misuse of power, and they would call a march on the gendarmerie station. Although I have never witnessed but only heard stories about a protest march, I was struck by how seriously the gendarmes appeared to be concerned with them.

Preparing the Repairs

A couple of minutes after the boy had left to seek treatment at the hospital, Adjudant-Chef Souley asked Chef Hamza exactly which mechanic they had locked up. Hamza described the location of the workshop he was employed in, what last affair had brought him here and who his father was. It turned out that Souley also knew both the mechanic and his father; he had his phone number and was about to call the father when Chef Hamza said: "Ga shi, [There he is]," pointing at an elderly man walking toward the brigade. Souley put his mobile phone in his pocket and waited for the man to come closer. He came, respectfully greeted the gendarmes and said that he had learnt that his son was here. "Don Allah a gyara," he said in Hausa, "I beg you to repair." Adjudant-Chef Souley replied harshly: "Tsoho, irin wannan fitina bamu yi gyara! [Old man, we don't arrange this kind of disobedience!]"[1] The father then squatted down and began complaining about his disobedient and useless son, about how he was sick of him getting into trouble and that he should instead marry, have children and live a decent life. Chef Hamza got up from the bench, walked toward the building and called the man, "Ka zo!" to follow him. He opened the cell door and said that they could talk for a bit in the courtyard.

When Adjudant-Chef Souley dialed the number of the mechanic's father, even though he hung up when he saw the man coming toward the brigade, he wanted to have the suspect's ally come to the brigade. In most cases, however, Adjudant-Chef Souley or other brigade commanders did not have the phone numbers for suspects' relatives. Then the gendarmes slowed things down by not writing the case file quickly, extending the limbo in which complainant and suspect found themselves. Usually this meant that the gendarmes kept the suspect in custody for forty-eight hours, the legal maximum; sometimes longer. During these two or more days, one or more of the suspect's relatives or his or her neighborhood chief, would come to the brigade to talk to the gendarmes and beg for an arrangement: "Don Allah a gyara!" They would also talk to the complainant and their family and beg them to withdraw their complaint. They knew that they had to negotiate with both the complainant and the gendarmes. However, the gendarmes would always say that in this particular case, an arrangement was impossible. And then they would wait.

If nobody came to support the suspect, the gendarmes allowed him or her to contact supporters themselves. Although they were in custody, most of the time they were not confined in the cells but rather allowed to sit in the courtyard. They could not leave the brigade (although about once a month somebody did run off) but they received visitors, talked to the complainant, and could even use their mobile phones. Sometimes the gendarmes would even top up the suspect's phone and allow him or her to charge its battery in the brigade's office. Some had installed their chargers, as if they were living in the brigade: the charger was constantly in the multiple socket outlet and the cord coiled around the leg of the office table, plugging and unplugging their phones every few hours. When a gendarme working in the office heard it ringing, he would even get up from the computer and hurry to bring it to the suspect sitting in the courtyard.

Most of the suspects' telephone conversations were about money. The suspects tried to find friends and relatives who would help them pay compensation to the complainant. "If you have some money, bring it here!" I heard some of the detainees say on the phone. Others were more offensive; they tried to mobilize contacts that would help them refute the allegations made by the complainant. "I'll counterattack," a suspect once said to himself while he was searching through the directory on his phone. A counterattack could also mean that the suspects tried to mobilize people that would use their influence and intervene to make the gendarmes work in their favor (see Beek 2012, 559–60). The gendarmes did not like such interventions; but enabling them was a way for them to identify influential friends a detainee might have. Sometimes the interventions were so intense that, as Christian Lund (1998, 208) describes with regards to land disputes in eastern Niger, it was "not the power of the litigants that was confronted, but the powers that they were able to mobilize." Interventions by these "powers" would cause the gendarmes trouble if they occurred after the arrangement had been reached. When it occurred during the consensus finding, the gendarmes could still adjust the strictness and clemency of their judgment so that they would not offend the influential relatives of the parties, but do them a favor and without appearing as puppets of the powerful. When the intervention occurred after reaching the arrangement and closing the case, they had to justify why they had not worked by the book, and they had to defend the judgment they had made during the arrangement. In some cases they even had to reopen and revise the case; and in order not to burn their fingers again, they would quickly write a report and forward the case to the prosecutor for him to deal with the interventions.

Allowing the suspects to use their phones and simply slowing things down was a way for the gendarmes to suggest that an alternative, extralegal solution, a repair, to the conflict might be possible. But it was also a way for the gendarmes to make sure that when restraining the law, they would not hurt themselves. To paraphrase a policeman Jeffrey Martin (2007, 687) cites: the arrangement, just like the law, is like a knife. And each gendarme had to be a "skillful surgeon if he himself is not to lose control of the blade."

Repairing the Harm

The boy came back in the afternoon with a couple of plasters on his face and a plastic bag with some medication. He did not talk to any of the gendarmes; he just sat down on a mat in the shade and waited. When Adjudant-Chef Souley came back from a break, he asked the boy for the receipt for his treatment, glanced at it and handed it back to him, and told Amadou to take the boy's statement. Amadou got his *cahier de declarations* from the office, sat down on a bench and asked the boy to sit beside him. When he had finished, he handed the notebook to Adjudant-Chef Souley, together with the receipt for over 2,500 francs CFA for the medication the boy had bought. Souley read through the declaration and stopped at the last paragraph, which he read aloud: "I press charges and I demand the sum of 50,000 francs as compensation." "You want 50,000 francs?" Souley asked him angrily. All the gendarmes started laughing. "You know exactly that he doesn't have this kind of money! Do you want to create him still more problems?" He asked Amadou to bring the mechanic. When he came out of the cell, rubbing his eyes in the bright sunlight, Souley told him to give the boy 5,000 and to bring it to the brigade tomorrow morning. "Why did you beat up this child? Isn't he your little brother?" And if he ever caused any trouble again in Godiya, Souley would make sure that he would be taken to prison. "We have your name! If tomorrow somebody files a complaint against you, by God, you will not go home!" Then he sent him away with his father. The complainant was still sitting there unsure what to do. After a while, Adjudant-Chef Souley walked toward him and gave him a 5,000 franc note. "Now there stands nothing between you! Do you understand? It's over!" The boy thanked him and the other gendarmes and went away.

Souley imposed an arrangement that in his eyes was just and satisfying for all participants. The boy received compensation of five thousand francs for his medical expenses and his pain and suffering. In most cases, however, the arrangement was negotiated between complainant and suspect via intermediaries, families, or chiefs. But they were never allowed to negotiate right at the brigade.[2] "You will talk some place else," Adjudant-Chef Souley used to say to them, "somewhere under a tree, somewhere in town, some place where nobody can hear you, and I don't even want to see you. I don't give a damn about it!" Had the two parties reached a consensus, they or the chief negotiator, in most cases a representative of a chief, came back to the brigade to present the result to the gendarmes. The consensus contained the amount of compensation the perpetrator would pay to the victim. This usually covered the victim's medical expenses, the estimated price of the stolen or damaged goods and the victim's expenses while searching for the suspect or coming to the brigade. If the brigade commander felt that one of the parties had somehow been pressured into accepting the consensus, which meant that the brigade commander deemed the amount of compensation too high or too low, he again threatened to write a report and forward the case to court. This is also what he did when the parties had not reached an agreement.

In such cases, Adjudant-Chef Souley said, "I use a bit of pressure. I talk to them with red eyes and unsettle them, that I will write the report, and then you will see that they start to think."

In the case of the boy whom the mechanic had beaten up, the two parties did not negotiate. The boy was much too young to negotiate with the mechanic's father and he had no relatives in town who would support him and negotiate in his stead. The gendarmes asked him how much he wanted in compensation; and Adjudant-Chef Souley then rebuked him for demanding far too much. In view of the boy's medical expenses of 2,500 francs and the fact that his injuries were not serious and that the mechanic was almost as poor, Souley felt that compensation to the amount of 50,000 francs was grossly unfair (and unrealistic); 5,000 francs was the right sum to repair the harm caused. As the boy had no other option, he simply had to agree; the mechanic and his father had no choice but to agree because anything was better than being sent to court and possibly to prison.

The resolution was always the same: a moral lesson and the gendarmes' stressing that the problem was solved once and for all, that all ill will had been removed. Sometimes the moral lesson Adjudant-Chef Souley gave in the court-yard of the brigade took some fifteen minutes and was for every other civilian and every gendarme to hear. Everybody would stop talking and listen. In a defamation case, he talked about how to behave toward your neighbor, live peacefully together, that your closest relative is your neighbor; in the case of alleged adultery he talked about the difficulties of being married but that family was, after all, the highest good you could have; in the case presented above, he told the mechanic to be peaceful and have sympathy with his "little brother" who struggled just like him to earn enough to have something to eat in the evening; and in almost every case he ended by saying that now nothing stood between the two parties. The gendarmes had repaired the harm, and they had at least tried to repair the relationship between the victim and the offender, and thus peace was maintained within the community.

Closing the Case

When the two opposing parties had reached an agreement, perhaps the harm was repaired, and maybe the relationship between the two as well. But the law had still been broken. An agreement between the conflicting parties was only the precondition for a full arrangement. Once, I asked Chef Hamza whether the withdrawal of a complaint was sufficient for an arrangement and he replied harshly, "Whether there is a complaint or not, we don't give a damn! If he has offended the law, the state has to regain his rights, too!"

For the gendarmes, this meant that the offender had to be punished in some way. In cases of severe crimes this was simple: the offender had to be brought before the court and sent to prison. In cases they tried to arrange, the gendarmes themselves punished the offender. They put the offender into the cell at the brigade, like they did with the mechanic. The gendarmes often explained this as a means of correction, "to intimidate them so that tomorrow they will not do the same thing again," as Chef Hamza put it. This corrective intention notwithstanding, incarceration also had a purely punitive dimension (see Beek and Göpfert 2013a, 488–89). In addition to that, the gendarmes would have most offenders pay a fine—a monetary "reparation." The amount of the fine was at the discretion of the gendarmes and could also be negotiated. Often the offender, his family, or his chief would plead to reduce the fine; and the gendarmes themselves were careful not to impose too high a sum because they did not want these civilians to feel as if their treatment was grossly unjust. Then they would complain, often with the help of influential friends or relatives, about the gendarmes' misconduct, which could land the gendarmes in enormous trouble. Whether the offenders received a "reçu"—a "receipt," as the gendarmes called the tickets they handed out—and thus whether the money went into their own or the state's pocket was another question and depended on whether the gendarmes felt there was a high risk of complaints later.[3]

Imposing a fine at the brigade meant in most cases that a délit was downgraded to a contravention, the category for the least severe offences punishable by mere fines. The mechanic though, who had beaten up the boy and thus clearly committed the délit of assault and battery, did not have to pay any fine. In other words, the délit did not turn into a contravention but it simply dissolved. This was an instance of extreme under-enforcement; or an example of how the gendarmes repaired the law, not because it has been broken, but because they felt it was inherently deficient.

Repairing the Law

There is always a gap between law and action. The law because it is general and has a totalizing claim, is always and necessarily in tension with concrete, practical reality. Aristotle in the Nicomachean Ethics (Aristotle 1925) thus introduced the notion of epieikeia, which is translated as "equity," "correction," or "rectification" of the law (Shiner 1994, 1247, 1252) or "Berichtigung des Gesetzes" in German (Gadamer 1999 [1960], 323). In this sense, applying the law demands that a good judge with the virtue of equity not apply it à la lettre. "In restraining the law, he is not diminishing it but, on the contrary, finding the better law" (Gadamer 1975,

316), or even finding "justice which lies beyond the written law," as Roger Shiner (1994, 1247) cites Aristotle. "Written law inevitably falls short of the standard of applicability that it wears on its linguistic face. Written law speaks universally and absolutely, but it has no right to do so. Equity corrects that deficiency" (ibid., 1255).[4] Max Gluckman in his seminal analysis of the judicial process among the Barotse calls this the "norm of the reasonable man." According to this norm, "the judges may develop and even alter the law" (Gluckman 1973 [1955], 160) in order to bridge the rift between "law in general" and "law in action" (ibid., 291; see also Aubert 1969, 288).[5]

The gendarmes in Niger, however, went beyond what for Aristotle was epie-ikeia and for Gluckman was the norm of the reasonable man. They not only had to bridge the gap between law and action; they also had to apply a law that they deemed inappropriate for policing the life worlds of the people they confronted. So what they did was gyara: repair work. Anyone who ever had their car or motorbike repaired at a small garage in a West African rural town or village knows what repair work there means. Most of the time, the mai gyaran moto, or mota, the mechanics for motorbikes or cars that I have met during my stay in Niger, produced only makeshift solutions for more serious problems: a hole in a car tire that they sew up by hand, a V-belt that they replaced with a homemade cloth-belt and so on. The repair was hardly ever permanent, nor removed the cause of the damage, nor improved the substance of your car; but it allowed you to continue on the road—although you never knew for how long. It could be, depending on the kind of repair, for a few hours (then you would be angry), a couple of weeks (that was good!) or even months (that was great!). Sometimes the local makeshift V-belt was better adapted to the harsh climate in the Sahel and worked for even longer than the imported original.

The gendarmes' repairing the law was similar. It was neither permanent nor had any consequences for the written and codified law of the penal code. There was no such thing as a feedback loop through which the gendarmes' repairs would alter the "concrete law" (Benda-Beckmann and Benda-Beckmann 2006, 13), for example, the law against assault and battery.[6] Rather, what they repaired was the law as a totality, as described by Bruno Latour (2010, 254). According to Latour (ibid., 255), "It is as if there were no degrees in law: either one is fully into it, or one is not in it at all and begins to talk about something else." The gendarmes would perhaps try to prove Latour wrong. They talked about the law and many other things at the same time, things they subsumed under the label "the social." The gendarmes never drew the register of formal law enforcement alone; they asked the complainants what they wanted them to do; and they always took nonlegal aspects into consideration making it hard for civilians to predict how the gendarmes would proceed.

The gendarmes are in a sense the gatekeepers of the legal machinery.[7] They were the ones who decided what would enter (or be excluded from) the chain of legal-bureaucratic translations, inscriptions, and purification (see Latour 2010, 253). By doing so, the gendarmes prevented the legal machinery from getting clogged up with too many cases, as prosecutors assured me time and again—in a kind of preventive repair against system breakdown and, at the same time, for the creation of the organization's external boundaries (Bierschenk 2008, 118–19; Luhmann 2013 [1983], 41). Not through purification but the "contamination" of the law with what they called "the social," the gendarmes repaired the law as a totality, and in their eyes, decidedly so for the better.

In this chapter, I have demonstrated how the gendarmes arrived at settlements when criminal law was offended, how they repaired the relationship between the disputants, that between the designated offender and the law, and thus how they repaired the law itself. When I asked the gendarmes about these arrangements, they referred to different moral and pragmatic considerations. First, keeping a case at brigade level and finding an arrangement opened up the possibility of substantial additional income for them. Second, even the prosecutors preferred arrangements to strict prosecution. "Arrange this at your level," he told them over the phone, or "impose a fine on them" although the case was ostensibly more severe than a simple contravention. One prosecutor told me that "a reconciliation is better than a good ruling" because a ruling would clearly define who was right and who was wrong; and this would eventually lead to the rupture of the relationship between the two parties—something that had to be avoided at all costs. Third, the gendarmes said that they respected the wishes of the civilians who brought their problems to them. "The people who come to us to file a complaint, they themselves ask for an arrangement," Chef Hamza explained. As they knew that going to court would do nothing but delay their compensation, if they are compensated at all. Fourth, and perhaps most important, the gendarmes often felt that strict law enforcement was unjust. But contrary to the often-stated claim that the sense of justice among police officers and gendarmes translates into them making decisions that serve the privileged and exclude the marginalized (see, for example, Corsianos 2001, 114), the gendarmes were much more equitable and sensitive to the rural communities' needs and expectations—not least because most gendarmes had similar backgrounds. In Adjudant-Chef Souley's words:

> Applying the rigour of the law, for the poor this is . . . this means creating situations that are yet more disastrous than the act the guy has committed. You have to understand some things, follow certain norms.

Especially when you're a man of the law. Because it can happen to everyone. Today we are in a world that is . . . ignorant. People all the time, all the time, even while they're eating they will commit an offence! [he laughs] And how do you . . . ? You cannot be rigorous. I don't want the victim to be left alone, but I also do not want that the offender is overly penalized. Really, people have always opted for peace. And that's what makes us try and find arrangements.

From a state law-centered perspective, what the gendarmes did during these arrangements appears as the under-enforcement of the law. They used their discretion not to do what the law dictated. The application of the law was deficient. From a different perspective, they did what they felt morally obliged to do. They repaired a law that they deemed unjust. Not its application, but the law itself is deficient. If Marilyn Strathern (1996, 522) argues that "law" cuts into a limitless expanse of "justice," then the gendarmes would argue that they, in search of justice, cut into a limitless expanse of law.

In short, what I suggest is a change of perspective. To leave aside the paradigmatic law-centered perspective for a moment and adapt one that is more sensitive to those actors' views and practices that have to apply the law on a daily basis. This, in itself, is not revolutionary, particularly with the ethnographic studies of policing à la Bittner (1967; 1974) and Skolnick (1966) in mind. Yet the little twist I propose means to also take seriously local concepts of law enforcement, dispute settlement, and the search for justice, in this case: gyara, repair work. This is neither to shift responsibility (or deficiency) from one side to the other, nor to absolve police officers or gendarmes from occasional arbitrariness and abuse of power, nor to hide the fact that the gendarmes' repair work was, pure and simple, illegal (which in some cases caused them not only profound yet vague inner troubles but also concrete and painful disciplinary procedures). This is merely to give an example of what an "anthropological criminology" may have to offer to broader criminological debates about crime, punishment, and the application of the law.

What is at stake, here in the frontier, is the nature of the law and the state itself. True, the frontier allows for intermingling and flows. Yet in the logic of bureaucratic government, such flow means contamination and simply must not happen—for the sake of the law. In the logic of the frontier, also the grip of the law needs to be controlled—for the sake of justice. True, the gendarmes have the power to declare the state of exception and act outside the law in defense of law; but they also have the power to declare an "exception to the state." The gendarmes can decide when to reduce people to bare life, and they can decide when to reduce the law to "bare text." The state of exception is supposed to defend the law, the exception to the state to defend *from* the law. And the result of their actions is not a mere aberration of the central model, an incomplete implementation; it is right here at the frontier, where what is considered the law and the state is made and remade over and over again. It is right here where the prevailing moral standards become palpable. Thus, it is here at the frontier that the value of the modern state, of bureaucracy, and of the gendarme Amadou's work must be judged. Due to this condition, the gendarmes themselves were tragic figures in a space of ambiguity and uncertainty. How they dealt with this is subject of the following chapter.

Chapter 9

TRAGIC WORK

Members of any bureaucratic organization who are in contact with people are caught between abstract norms that guide and sanction their actions and the concreteness of practical reality. This is an irresolvable tension. Bearing it is what it means to work in the frontier. It is the "if-then" idiom of general precept versus the "as-therefore" one of the concrete case (Geertz 1983, 174); the "law in general" versus "law in action" (Gluckman 1973 [1955], 325; see also Moore 2000 [1978]); the "government of laws" versus "the government of men" (Sykes 1969, 336); perhaps ultimately the "image" versus the "practices of the state" (Migdal and Schlichte 2005, 11, 35), or simply the "ideal type" versus "human action" (Weber 1980 [1921], 2–4).

This tension is reflected in the gendarmes' talk about their daily work. They often moaned that they are stuck between legality and illegality, theory and practice, the rules and routines, les textes and le social. I agree with Richard Rottenburg (1995, 20) in that the metadistinction of formal versus informal (or rational versus socioculturally embedded) is, from the bureaucrats' point of view, irrelevant. Each side is just as rational and socioculturally embedded as the other. But how do the gendarmes maneuver in between the two?[1]

The bureaucrats' maneuvering in the frontier-space is often described as a matter of discretion or corruption, two terms particularly prominent in research on police work. According to Michael Lipsky, the discretion of street-level bureaucrats is necessary because they "work in situations too complicated to reduce to programmatic formats" and thus need leeway between "compassion and flexibility on the one hand, and impartiality and rigid rule-application on the other hand" (1980, 15–16). Thus understood, discretion is a necessary effect of what Jonathan Wender describes as the "bureaucratic paradox," particularly accentuated in what police officers and gendarmes do: "Though it is their official role as bureaucratic agents that first brings them into the presence of their fellow human beings, that role is precisely what often must be transcended in order to truly ameliorate the given predicaments at hand" (2008, 4). As a result, and particularly in arrangements, the gendarmes constantly break the bureaucratic norms that are supposed to structure their daily work. According to Hamani Oumarou (2011, 252), working on the Nigerien judicial service, this is precisely what keeps the judicial machine running. However, both the civilian population and scholars of bureaucracy can easily perceive this as corruption, he adds.[2] I agree with Colin Leys (1965) in that the term *corruption* is of little value as an analytical concept. Used as such, it is part of a moralistic discourse that takes the binary divisions of legal/illegal and public/private for granted and as a necessary cornerstone of a duly and justly functioning state. It either reproduces Max Weber's ideal type or compares African states with preindustrial Europe, where this ideal type has not been completely achieved yet (see Scott 1969, 315–16). Corruption should interest scholars of bureaucracy and policing rather as a discourse in which popular knowledge and expectations of the state become tangible.[3] I want to take seriously the perspectives of the gendarmes and civilians, the tension between "cooperation" and "corruption" (Martin 2007, 690; Mouhanna 2001, 39), and thus the profound tension at the core of the state as "both disinterested and corrupt, just and coercive, participatory and removed" (Poole 2004, 61).

In this chapter, I attempt to go beyond these dialectic binaries and focus on the space in between—the space in which the gendarmes find themselves, particularly when they orchestrate arrangements. The first step to doing so is to acknowledge a second dimension to the bureaucratic paradox, one that is due to the particularities of the police profession, namely, their different audiences; the second step is to make sense of this tension in terms of a space of profound uncertainty in the "bureaucratic drama"; the third step is to understand the gendarmes' maneuvering through it—how they present themselves and try to arrange themselves with their different audiences, and as a consequence perceive themselves as tragic creatures in the bureaucratic drama.

The Gendarmes in the Bureaucratic Limbo

According to Dominique Monjardet (1996, 9), an influential French police sociologist, a particular feature of police organizations is their threefold character: they are an instrument of state power and as such receive orders from public authorities; then they are a public service and can be called on by anybody; and they are a profession that develops its very own interests.

> Triple determination that has no reason to melt into perfect harmony. To the contrary, these three dimensions can clash as separate, competing logics of action. The everyday functioning of the police is the result of perpetual tensions (conflicts, compromise) between these three logics, and any "theory" of the police (and there are some of them) that acknowledges only one of these as the function or reason of the police is handicapped for it is unable to account for all the observed practices. (1996, 9; my translation)

For the gendarmes in Niger, this triple determination means that they are, first, accountable to the two public authorities that sanction their daily work, namely the Minister of Defense—ultimately represented by their superior officers—and the Minister of Justice—represented by the public prosecutor in whose jurisdiction they work. Second, they are accountable to the civilians who contact them for their services. Third, due to the difficult working conditions and limited career options, they have their own professional interests. And one of their most prominent interests, the one they mentioned time and again, was "to please them all." "We struggle to please the justice system, the population, and our bosses," as Adjudant-Chef Souley put it in an interview.

The gendarmes were thus not only caught in the tension between ideal and practice; they were also caught between different and often conflicting expectations from the public, the prosecutors, and their superiors. Positioning themselves clearly on either side, including the technical bureaucratic one, would create enormous problems for them. In that sense, during arrangements, the disputing parties not only found themselves in a condition of liminality, but the gendarmes too were liminal creatures. In contrast to "classical" Turnerian social dramas with liminal spaces, the gendarmes' liminality was not pushing toward status transformation, and the drama did not dissolve and turn into redress or schism; the space of ambiguity in which the gendarmes found themselves—that is, the frontier—was a permanent one and the gendarmes could only struggle to alleviate the tensions and uncertainties that went with it.[4]

One of the consequences of the gendarmes being caught in this space of merging and blurring distinctions was their frustration as professionals who wanted to do good. A lot of gendarmes told me that their work was not about justice anymore; "justice is dead," Amadou once said in a moment of deep disappointment after another case was dismissed due to a call from headquarters. It was not even about applying the texts, the one feature they always put forward to distinguish themselves from the police, the military, and the National Guard. "If you always want to apply the texts in your work, you will have great difficulties. You cannot work with the rigor of the texts," Amadou said. "If you do it anyway, immediately there will be a phone call from Niamey and you will be transferred right away. Or you will at least be asked, 'What have you done?' There are people who only apply the texts, but no one will give them the stripes." "Stripes" was Amadou's reference to the shoulder badges gendarmes receive when they advance up through the corps' hierarchy. When their superiors were dissatisfied with a gendarme's performance, they could easily prevent him or her from advancing; all the gendarmes' greatest fear was to be blocked. And applying the texts was, according to Amadou, not a way to please the superiors.

All bureaucrats are confronted with the basic bureaucratic paradox (see Wender 2008), and most bureaucrats are confronted with different and conflicting expectations. But unlike police officers in Germany, for example, the gendarmes in Niger could not find refuge in their organization and protection in bureaucratic procedures. Quite the contrary, they felt abandoned. Only few superiors above the level of adjudant-chef would step up and protect a gendarme who had made a wrong decision when arranging a dispute and had to expect repercussions. So they indeed had to please them all, and they did so by carefully choosing different ways of presenting themselves vis-à-vis the population, the prosecutors, and their superior officers; one element of this presentation was the distribution of money.

Being caught in this limbo and trying to please everybody, the gendarmes "need to know how to walk on eggshells," a superior officer explained. In the following, I try to look at this "walk on eggshells" through dramaturgical lenses similar to Peter Manning's (1982) and Simon Holdaway's (1980). Building on Erving Goffman, Manning explores how police officers "selectively present aspects of themselves" and of their behaviors, combined with specific "symbolizations referring to those behaviors . . . which are likely to produce certain effects in others" (1982 [1967], 235); Holdaway calls this a "dramaturgical analysis of how police maintain an occupational imagery" (1980, 88). Only here it will be a multidimensional imagery, since "the others" are the gendarmes' different audiences: the civilian population, the prosecutor, and their superior officers. This is the "bureaucratic drama" times two: the gendarmes' selective presentation of self toward their different audiences, and their selective reference to bureaucratic procedures in their attempt to alleviate the tensions and minimize the uncertainties of the liminal space in which they work.

Force Humane / Force Inhumane

The gendarmes wanted to please the civilians for two main pragmatic reasons. When the complainants and suspects were both satisfied with the gendarmes' work, they were more likely to give them a gift afterward. And when they were not satisfied with the arrangement the gendarmes orchestrated, they were more likely to appeal to an influential friend or relative to complain about the gendarmes on a higher hierarchical level within the gendarmerie or at the prosecutor's office. Influential friends or relatives were part of the so-called "PAC," the *parents-amis-connaissances*—relatives-friends-acquaintances—a popular dictum in Niger to refer to personal relationships that one mobilizes to gain personal advantages. Gendarmes mobilized them to be transferred to "juicy" or "relaxing" gendarmerie posts (see Badou 2013, 219) or to gain information about the announcement of career opportunities such as competitive exams for advancement, about job offerings related to UN missions abroad, about special training opportunities, and the like. Civilians mobilized them to intervene in their favor. The result were *rebondissements*, as the gendarmes called them, backlashes; the most common backlash was a telephone call the brigade commander received from either a superior officer or the prosecutor. They would simply ask, "What has happened?" And since the gendarmes had not followed the official procedure, they could have difficulties explaining and justifying their actions.

The gendarmes presented themselves toward the civilian population selectively as sympathetic persons providing a service and as strict and indifferent bureaucrats. An important aspect of their image as service providers was what they called the "charte d'accueil" or "welcome charter." The gendarme Moussa explained this in an interview:

> You see, the gendarmerie has its way of doing things. It is not clear that you will get what you want. But we will not send you away. You yourself can see it, concerning your stay with us: Did you get what you wanted to get? Perhaps you didn't get it, but you were welcome. But we didn't frustrate you. So this is what we call "welcome charter." We made you feel welcome. That's it. This is why I said that when a guy comes we make him feel welcome. Don't you see what we do? We offer them a seat. We ask them what they have come for. We sit on the desk and leave the chair to the guy. So that he's comfortable and expresses himself. We don't beat people. We don't insult them. We don't threaten them. We will ask him what he wants, and perhaps we can help him, perhaps we can't. But this guy will be very glad! Because we respected him. And tomorrow he will feel comfortable coming back again.

Moussa exaggerated a little. The gendarmes did not receive all civilians with the same sense of hospitality. But most of them did indeed adopt a respectful and polite attitude vis-à-vis civilians. Almost every day, I saw them arrange chairs, benches, and mats under the shade in front of the brigade, for civilians to sit on. They shared tea with some civilians, even detainees; they shared their food with them, even if only the leftovers; sometimes they even gave them money. Once, an elderly complainant had spent over two hours waiting at the brigade for the suspect to show up. When he got up to leave, the gendarme Omar gave him four hundred francs to pay for a taxi. "This is an old man the age of your parents. You can't make him walk all the way home."[5] Another day, there was a young man accused of theft at the market; but the victim did not turn up, so the gendarmes sent him home after a couple of hours; Yacouba gave him 350 francs and then said to me: "This is a poor guy. He only wants something to eat." The gendarmes' behavior at times resonated extremely well with their slogan of being a *force humaine*, a human force. Being welcoming, respectful, and polite, the gendarmes knew that this way there would be fewer complaints and more gifts.

The gendarmes depended on these gifts. They received virtually no endowments from their organization, neither paper, printers, fuel, boots, or uniforms. They had to procure it on their own—with the money they received as gifts or by taxing technically free services. Some of the gifts were quite impressive: in Godiya, a local retailer donated a computer to the brigade while a local mason built the little mosque in front of the building. Oumarou calls this state of being for the Nigerien judiciary the "débrouillardise" (2011, 205), a state of permanent make-do and resourcefulness. But the gendarmes never asked for gifts of money (contrary to Nigerien police officers, as taxi and bus drivers told me in interviews). The gendarmes' behavior was in this respect remindful of how Verne (2004, 179) describes the "scrounging" (*Schnorren*) of persons of superior status from those of lower status in a rural Hausa community in Niger. The big one (*babba*) would never explicitly ask for a gift from the small one (*karami*). Even the handing over could be problematic: if there was a baruma as intermediary whom the gendarmes were acquainted with, he would, after the successful arrangement, bring the money to the brigade commander, hand it over in his office, invisible to everybody else; then "receipts" were not necessary. If the concerned party had to pay directly, tickets were obligatory and the gendarmes would only levy a tax of 10 percent of the sum in question—this 10 percent went without a receipt. It is fundamentally contradictory, Verne (2004, 179) continues, to explicitly demand respect and money at the same time—except in the context of service delivery. And the respect from the civilian population was something the gendarmes would not want to jeopardize. I asked Amadou in an interview whether he was proud of being a gendarme and he replied:

> I am very glad to be a gendarme. I am proud to be a gendarme. Vis-à-vis the society, vis-à-vis the respect that I embody. But on the other hand, how can we be proud to be gendarmes if we know that our bosses are toothless tigers or even crooks? Yes, we are proud, but not thanks to them. It's because of the population. Every time they have a problem

they will come to the gendarmerie because they trust us. This is why we are proud. And we must do everything to keep that image. If it were for the gendarmerie, we would not even get up in the morning.

What the gendarmes interpreted as civilians' signs of respect could also be fear of the powerful and opaque legal funnel as described by Bierschenk (2008, 119), and the expectation of uncertainty in the face of possibly disinterested and coercive bureaucrats—as representatives of a fundamentally ambivalent state (see Poole 2004). Gendarmes could, indeed, also be less welcoming. Then they took on the role of the distant, indifferent bureaucrat. As Michael Herzfeld put it, "Indifference is the rejection of common humanity. It is the denial of identity, of selfhood" (1992, 1). It is, in a sense, the inversion of the force humaine. When people arrived at the brigade, some of them were sent away immediately. The gendarmes would explain that they were by law not authorized to accept civil complaints. They would send these complainants either to their neighborhood chief or to the civil judge at the local court. Only when the prosecutor sent them back to the brigade with a signed and stamped note, a minimalistic *commission rogatoire*—meaning when he officially tasked them with the investigation of this case (Bauer and Pérez 2009, 67–68)—would they take on the case.

When they took over a case right after the complaint, the gendarmes always undertook some kind of bureaucratic procedure, and in most cases they also commented on it in front of the civilians: "The legal procedure is like a bullet. Once it takes off, there is no turning back." When they handed out a summons, they made an entry in the complaints registry; when they put somebody into the cell, they made an entry in the arrest registry; when they took somebody's statement or testimony, they wrote it down in the statement notebook (*cahier de déclarations*). Sometimes they even wrote the whole procès-verbal, only to keep it in their drawer after they had achieved an arrangement between the parties; they merely added a sentence stating that the complainant had withdrawn his complaint, including the complainant's signature. The reason they did so, although they knew that most cases ended in an arrangement, was to protect themselves "in case it explodes afterward," but also to show the civilians that a diversion from the legal procedure was possible only thanks to the gendarmes.

With or Despite the Prosecutor

The gendarmes' positioning toward the prosecutor was equally ambivalent. They wanted to have a good relationship with him because as their direct superior in judicial matters he had considerable control over their work. Every arrangement produced at the brigade meant one less case for the prosecutors. Quite similar to the gendarmes, the prosecutors also complained about the ever-rising demands on them and the insufficient resources to manage them (Oumarou 2011, 213). "If the gendarmes manage to get a withdrawal of a complaint, they have helped the judge," a prosecutor told me.[6] "Arrangements keep the judicial machine running," as Hamani Oumarou (2011, 252; my translation) puts it, but can easily be perceived as the result of illicit negotiations and money transactions with one of the parties. Therefore, arrangements and also those the prosecutors produced in the form of a *non-lieu*, a dismissed case, could cause trouble. Arrangements produced by the gendarmes, who had no legal mandate to dismiss cases, meant that the prosecutor did not have his auxiliaries under control, or that he was their accomplice. And when the prosecutor received a call from his superior in Niamey and was asked "What happened?" he also might struggle to explain, especially when he was not even aware of a particular case. He would then in turn call the brigade commander to ask the same question. The gendarmes wanted their judicial superior to protect them from critical backlashes, and therefore they had to please him.

Sometimes the gendarmes called the prosecutor right after receiving a complaint, sometimes only when the procès-verbal was established. In other words, sometimes they were his swift and diligent auxiliaries, even in matters that did not fall under their competency, such as arrangements; sometimes they were merely his reticent prefabricators of legal cases. When I was in Godiya, I witnessed the transfer of the old and the arrival of the new prosecutor. As a result, the practices of informing the court changed drastically. It all depended on a good collaboration between the brigade commander and the prosecutor, the gendarmes assured me time and again. Adjudant-Chef Souley elaborated on this in an interview:

> You need good collaboration. You need to be straightforward with each other. If it is an affair that you want to arrange, you don't need to inform him all the time. Otherwise he himself will think you are incompetent. The one [prosecutor] who left, all the time he says, "You have tickets, just use them! Everything you can arrange, you can arrange." Or just "detain him at the brigade." And when there really was a backlash, he would protect us. We worked together very well, we even became friends. We used to spend our evenings together with our families. Just today we talked over the phone. He thanked me for the two cases of Guinness I sent him. But the new one [prosecutor], well . . . When he came, I studied him. Everything he wants is procedure. Every time. When you inform him, he will say no, no, no. He will tell you to write the *PV*. Where will this end? He is going to piss us off? *PV* for anything? Instead

of tickets? You rush to make a *PV* although there is a solution that the people themselves suggested? Since I've noticed that this is it, okay, I take all my time. If in the end it doesn't work out, all right, I make a *PV*, I transfer them [to court], and that's it.

According to Adjudant-Chef Souley, it all boils down to the level of trust between gendarmes and the prosecutor. When they collaborated well, the work became much easier for both. The prosecutor could rely on the gendarmes to help him limit his workload, and he could also rely on getting a portion of the money the gendarmes received after successful arrangements. Certainly, Adjudant-Chef Souley gave him more than a couple of cases of Guinness, the other gendarmes assured me. The gendarmes could rely on the prosecutors' support when they tried to find an arrangement and thus tended to overstep their legal preroga-tives; and they could even rely on his protection in case there was some form of backlash. When the relationship between the two was characterized by distrust, as with the new prosecutor, he would not allow for arrangements. The result was, however, not that the gendarmes did not arrange cases anymore; they only did it without informing the prosecutor; and now they had to be even more care-ful in their arrangements, to take all their time, to make sure that neither of the disputing parties would cause a backlash afterward. In short, they needed a good relationship with the prosecutor in order to work calmly. If this was not possible, they minimized the contact to him.

Resourceful Subordinates with an Air of Efficiency

Gendarmes had very limited contact with their superior officers. They were in distant, air-conditioned offices in the regional or national headquarters, and came to the brigade once a year for the annual inspection. The gendarmes only contacted them through radio messages informing them about arrests and fin-ished procès-verbaux and through monthly reports summarizing a month's investigations and the number of tickets handed out.

Although their professional contact was limited, the gendarmes made consid-erable effort to please their superiors, simply because they depended on them in almost every matter to do with their professional life, from the allocation of funds and working material to postings and advancements. For the gendarmes, pleasing their superiors meant causing them as little trouble as possible. And trouble meant for an officer being asked to intervene in the daily running of a brigade. Every time I was at the regional or national headquarters visiting superior officers, there were lines of parents-amis-connaissances outside their offices waiting to have their problems dealt with. Any discontented party of a former arrangement, or an influential relative of this party, was another potential candidate in the line. The general attitude toward arrangements on any superior level seemed to be: "Arrangements, in any case, this is not official. We are not aware of this. But as long as there is no backlash, we don't care," as a superior officer put it. Interestingly, Adjudant-Chef Souley adopted the same position toward arrangements orchestrated by his own gendarmes; for him this was a sign of trust in his gendarmes, similar to the trust a prosecutor should, according to Souley, have in the brigade commander.[7]

Others queuing outside the officers' doors were not dissatisfied with the gendarmes' work, but they wanted their officer-relative to intervene in their favor in an ongoing investigation. Adjudant-Chef Souley received frequent calls from a superior officer in the regional capital or from Niamey requesting him to "help" his relative who was about to file a complaint or who had just been summoned as a suspect. Then the gendarmes could take over the role of their superior's friend and thus "help" him. As a result, the outcome of some arrangements was not equitably achieved but imposed in accordance with the particularistic interests of one of Souley's superiors. However, the gendarmes could also present themselves as the prosecutor's diligent auxiliaries—another reason why a good relationship with him was essential. Adjudant-Chef Souley explained:

> Sometimes, even if it's merely a cousin of one of the bosses, he will try to intervene to help his relative, even if he has offended the law. But when there is the piece of paper from the prosecutor, or I have informed him, voilà, I'm following the prosecutor's orders! Now they are forced to pull out and let us do our job. Whatever the strength of the person, his power, he will say, "Well, okay. Since it's at the court, I stop." Then we are free and we will not have our hands tied.

As soon as they informed the prosecutor, the decision to dismiss or push forward a case in favor of a superior's relative, thus the decision to break bureaucratic norms, was no longer up to the gendarmes. This was particularly important for the gendarmes when a superior officer intervened in favor of the offender. "Never say 'no' to a superior," was the rule of thumb; "but if it's awkward, you can find another way," the rule continued.[8] Here the "other way" was the bureaucratic norm of informing the prosecutor. With his help the gendarmes did not have to refuse a favor to their superior, neither did they break the law.

A different way to please the superiors was by presenting themselves as "cash cows." This could, again, be in the form of a friend or an efficient working unit. To work efficiently meant first and foremost to mete out sufficient tickets and thus earn sufficient money for the public accounts. If this were not the case, administrative authorities like the governor of a region or the prefect of a department would ask the regional commander why a particular brigade paid so little money into the public account last month. This meant that either the gendarmes at this brigade had a particularly lazy month, or that they had imposed fines without handing out the "receipts," that is, tickets. And only those fines with a receipt were paid into the public account at the end of the month. This happened when Adjudant-Chef Souley was on a two-week leave of absence and Chef Tahirou, second in command and thus interim brigade commander, pocketed most of the money; which caused Souley serious trouble and thus Tahirou himself. Adjudant-Chef Souley was furious, "When I came back, there was not a single franc to pay into the public account. This means that he has not given any tickets. People cannot understand this, the command cannot understand this, and they rebuked me for that!" The gendarmes were under pressure to pay a relatively stable sum into the public account of the department they were working in at the end of each month. This money, together with the money collected by customs and tax officers, was used to pay the public employees in the department: hospital employees, teachers, etc.; and when the account was not balanced, the prefect would telephone the regional commander, and the regional commander would telephone the brigade commander.

Presenting themselves as efficient, however, was not an easy thing for the gendarmes who were blatantly underequipped. According to Chef Boubacar, the reason for this was not that the gendarmerie lacked money:

> There is no work equipment. Look at our office: the computer, someone donated it. This is what we work with. We are the ones to pay for the paper. Not to mention the uniforms, the rangers [boots]. You [as a gendarme] have to pay your fuel to move. When you go on a mission, you pay for your food. For all this there is a budget that comes every month but never reaches the personnel. And our bosses, they are over there and they stuff themselves. So we have to cope and be resourceful. And if we don't, they will say that you're not willing to work, that you have no professional conscience. And on top of that, they will get angry and transfer you someplace. So we do have to cope and be resourceful. But if the thing blows up, they will say that they are not aware. They will say that they have never told you to do that. They protect themselves.

The gendarme Amadou put it in a nutshell: "Il faut faire semblant" ("You need to pretend"). To phrase it differently, in this drama and vis-à-vis their superiors, the gendarmes deliberately played the role of the proud, motivated, and undemanding subordinate, although on the "backstage" they were utterly frustrated. And their frustration grew even stronger with every private call they received from their superiors. Except for a few calls that a superior made to give a gendarme, who was his friend, relative, or classmate, insider information about upcoming announcements for advancement *concours* or for participation in a UN peace mission, most of these private calls were about favors requested by a superior.[9] These favors could be about ordering a "commission de brousse," some goods that were much cheaper in rural areas (e.g., firewood, bootlegged fuel, bush meat, animals), or about contributing money to a superior officer's marriage, to the marriage of his daughter, to his grandson's baptism, among other things. Sometimes they did not even call the brigade, but expected a more or less fixed sum at the end of each month. It was all about "gestures," Adjudant-Chef Souley told me:

> If you see a CB who is really appreciated [by the superiors], if they say "Oh, this one is good," it's not because of his work, eh! It is because of his gestures. Mirco, I don't hide anything from you. This is one of my problems with the officers. Okay, from time to time when I want to, in order to please you. That's it . . . it is a matter of formality. But I don't make it a principle. You will not tell me that this is mandatory. No, no, no. That's not even part of the job, it is informal. And there are officers who make it an issue! The commander he even made a [disciplinary] report. In reality, it is because of that but he sought another pretext. He said I did not report to him on time. . . . This has nothing to do with the work. It's as if they say, "Go and extort money from these people, I will extort money from you as well."

These were favors the superiors explicitly or implicitly requested of the gendarmes in the brigades. The gendarmes could, if they were ready to deal with the possible consequences, refrain from doing such favors. The consequences could be a disciplinary report for professional misconduct, as in Adjudant-Chef Souley's case. And because the gendarmes constantly overstepped bureaucratic norms, there were an infinite number of possible pretexts for a disciplinary report. Other negative consequences could be an exclusion from information relevant for advancements, advanced training offers, and the like. This was the one thing all gendarmes wanted to avoid. They could only take their chances and disappoint a superior when they were certain that other officers or friends in the officers' front offices would keep them in the loop.

Superiors could request money from the gendarmes in the brigade slightly differently and via "bons," a kind of credit. The superiors knew that there was a lot of cash at the brigade, by the end of the month up to 500,000 francs in a regular brigade territoriale as in Godiya, some 3 million francs in units where the gendarmes were also on traffic duty. Thus time and again superiors called and said "bring a ton of cement to my relative . . . Make a *bon*," Souley explained. "Or 'bring this sum to this parent.' They know that it's not my own money that pays for the cement. So we write it in the form of a credit. But they will never pay it back." Since the gendarmes collected this money through fines—with receipts—they were obliged to pay them into the public account by the end of the month. And it was their responsibility to cover the hole such credits left in the brigade's cash box. "You must never leave a hole!" they always said. This proved disastrous for one brigade commander that I spent some time with. His superiors had taken so many bons from him that he was barely able to fill the holes with the money he received as gifts. As a result, when he retired most of his personal savings were gone, although his last posting was at one of the most affluent and "juiciest" brigades. He then spent weeks driving around the country, calling on his former superiors to repay some of their credits, but alas in vain.

During the first week of my fieldwork in the Nigerien gendarmerie, I asked an officer what he thought was the distinctive feature of the gendarme. "It's our house culture. Do you know what the culture of our organization is? You need to juggle. We do nothing but juggle. And you will see this in the construction of the individual." I did not understand what he was talking about until months later, when I saw that the gendarmes were caught between the rules and routine, public and private, les textes and le social, juggling the expectations of civilians, prosecutors, and their superiors—and how they struggled to come to terms with these.

The gendarmes had pragmatic reasons to please them all, but it was difficult to please everyone at the same time. The gendarmes presented themselves as uncomplicated, swift, and diligent auxiliaries or as reticent prefabricators of legal cases toward the prosecutor. They presented themselves as dutiful auxiliaries of the prosecutor, as cash cows or friends toward their superiors and as sympathetic or indifferent toward civilians. They were both a force humaine and a force inhumaine. This is not only a sign of the "bureaucratic paradox" Jonathan Wender (2008, 4, 190) had in mind; it is also a manifestation of the frontier. To make sense of the gendarmes maneuvering through it, I suggested the term *bureaucratic drama*: the gendarmes' or the bureaucrats' selective presentation of self toward their different audiences. But there is another term related to "drama" that resonates even more with the gendarmes' feeling of frustration: the tragedy. "How could it come to this even though nobody wanted it?" was how Julia Eckert phrased the key question of the tragedy.[10] Some gendarmes said it was because of the bosses, as outlined above; some argue it is socioculturally embedded (Olivier de Sardan 1999, 36); others, like the gendarme Amadou, are simply disillusioned:

> You know, Mirco, sometimes you are drawn this way, you are drawn that way. . . . You know, if you find yourself in such a situation . . . really . . . it's discouraging. . . . Mirco . . . I've been searching, I've been searching

> . . . but I haven't found the reason for these problems. But you do see the result, don't you? Everyone thinks of himself before taking care of the institution.

This resembles what Blundo and Olivier de Sardan (2006a, 95–96) describe as the absence of control and the established administrative practice of "every-man-for-himself-ism." I do not think, however, that the gendarme is in a "bubble, which he sometimes shares with one or two others and in which he organizes his activities in a way that appears most convenient to him"—with impunity (ibid., 95). Quite the contrary, the gendarmes were confronted with so many expectations and control mechanisms, even though they were not the official channels but "informal accountabilities" (Owen 2013, 59), that they were extremely cautious about doing what appeared most convenient to their audiences—precisely because they did not enjoy impunity.

The bureaucratic drama thus created both *communitas* and isolation at the same time. It created communitas among the gendarmes through their shared sense of frustration (see Turner 1989 [1969], 96–97; 1985, 124). But it also caused a sense of isolation as tragic creatures, with neither catastrophe nor catharsis in sight. The gendarme as a bureaucratic Sisyphus: a frontier figure tasked with the impossible project of closing the frontier.

POSTSCRIPT
On the Significance of the Frontier

Sometimes the gendarmes formatted stories about peoples' lives to fit the needs of the bureaucratic form; sometimes they kept these forms and lives apart, thereby allowing for mutually compatible kinds of sociality and morality. The one produced, one might say, separation through connection, the other connection through separation. And between these conflicting bureaucratic and humanistic projects stood the tragic figure of the gendarme—the protagonist of the frontier.

The frontier-space is not only the borderland between life governed by public institutions and life outside of the state's grasp; it is also the site where bureaucracy and the world it is charged with managing meet and the tension between the two becomes tangible. It is the space between bureaucratic form and lived life. This tension then gives birth to a particular condition of doing and being. As a borderland full of frictions and fluctuations, the frontier provides constant threats and guarantees, constraints and possibilities, can be both brutally destructive and profoundly empowering. If anything, it keeps its inhabitants constantly on their toes. In contrast to borders and borderlands or peripheries and margins, the frontier has a direction and a force—a vector, so to say. It represents the constant attempt to push forward. In other words, the frontier is a project that aims to extend its reach beyond its confines. The stakes attached to this project are considerably high, here, where intermingling and flows can be both brutal and empowering, where the law needs to be both defended and controlled, where people can be reduced to bare life the law to bare text, where the "state of exception" can be played off against the "exception to the state." Again, it is right here where the prevailing moral standards become palpable, and it is right here at the frontier that the value of the modern state, of bureaucracy, and of the gendarme Amadou's work must be judged.

Since its use by Frederick Jackson Turner in the early twentieth century, the notion of the frontier has been largely discredited, and rightly so. Turner's frontier is an overly simplistic and ethnocentric concept that wholeheartedly disregards the fate and perspective of those who were subject to the frontiersmen and women pushing forward. It is a historical-analytical manifestation of racism and imperialism. And yet, the notion of the frontier offers something that related notions such as border, boundary, periphery, and margin don't. Understood (as I have tried to sketch throughout this book) as a *space*, a *condition* and a *project* with particular *stakes*, the idea of the frontier can be of heuristic significance for our understanding of bureaucracy, the postcolonial condition, and for the project of anthropology and social theory.

The Bureaucratic Frontier

There was a profound tension at work in the gendarmes' daily lives as bureaucrats. "Mu da ku duka daia ne," they would at times tell anxious civilians to calm them down: "We and you are one and the same." The gendarmes had this strong sense of belonging, of oneness with the people around them; and yet, split into first and second person—"we" and "you"—there was a clear distinction between them. They were the same, and yet they were not.

The nature of this dividing line is something that many ethnographies of public bureaucracies have been struggling with. To most, the solution was to argue that the state is embedded in wider social structures and possesses blurred, obfuscated, or shifting boundaries, centers, and margins.[1] All these metaphors imply a more or less clear division of state and society. However, I would like to follow Timothy Mitchell and argue that what appears as this fundamental divide should be understood first of all as the "effect of detailed processes of spatial organization, temporal arrangement, functional specification, and supervision and surveillance" (1991b, 95)—in short: an effect of concrete governing practices. Second, as I have tried to show, this divide is not only the effect of governing practices such as police work; it's at the heart of it. There is no outside to this divide. Of course, there are moments when one side seems stronger than the other, when les textes are more visible than le social (and vice versa), but there is never one without the other. The state does not merely *have* boundaries, margins, or frontiers; the state *is* the frontier—a space where two worlds collide and merge at the same time: two worlds that appear to be in constant and irresolvable tension with one another. Only in brief and elusive moments, as in the phrase "We and you are one and the same," do we get to see both sides at once, do we hear the frontier speak, and do we get a clear glimpse of the gendarmes' and all other bureaucrats' daily ontological conundrum. It is a frontier-space that cannot be closed; rather it is the horizon that moves with them.

All bureaucrats work in that frontier-space and have to deal with abstract norms that guide and sanction their actions on the one hand, and the concreteness of practical reality on the other. In the case of street-level bureaucrats, this is rather obvious as they work on the outer fringes of their organizations and in direct contact with the "other side." But also those in back offices, without contact to their civilian counterparts, find themselves in a similar place, even if only in their own daily role-switching from private person to public servant and the conflicting normative orders or systems of meaning. The space of bureaucracy is the frontier between form and life. And because there is no solution to this tension, there is a profoundly tragic potential to it. This tragedy becomes even more tangible in the postcolonial condition.

Global Frontiers

Borderlands, spaces of flux and in-betweens have always existed, but they have probably never had a reputation as bad as today. Bridges went out of fashion; walls are now setting the trend. There is, of course, Donald Trump and his ludicrous plan to build a giant wall on the US-Mexican border. But there is also the massive resurgence of border controls, if not throughout Europe, then at least at its eastern and southern fringes, with tangible effects even in Niger. The European Union's border regime, embodied for example by FRONTEX (the European Border and Coast Guard Agency), but also by "development aid" and "technical assistance" regarding the equipment and training of border police has been continuously pushing forward, from the northern banks of the Mediterranean to its southern banks, to the Sahara, and now to the southern border of Sahel countries like Niger. And perhaps even worse, there is a massive surge in radical, right wing, antimigration movements such as the German "Patriotic Europeans Against the Islamization of the Occident" (Pegida) and the white nationalist "identitarian movement" throughout Europe, with their racist and neofascist ideology of "ethnopluralism" and the threat of the "great exchange."

In all of these instances, the perceived threat is one of the "Other" pushing backward. The "Other" doesn't respect the fact that "our" imagined frontiers have been closed. From the perspective of the protagonists of these movements, this is also a kind of repair work, of course. They want to keep domains, people, and histories separate to not get them dangerously entangled. But in doing so they are far more naïve than the gendarmes ever were. Amadou, Adjudant-Chef Souley, and even Chef Tahirou never thought that their repair work was anything more than instantaneous bricolage—a makeshift solution to a given problem. They never said they would or could produce a permanent separation of these worlds (les textes versus le social). Neither were they so naïve as to think that they were the only protagonists in that play. Nor did they think that the choice was merely between separation and connection. They knew perfectly that what was intended as a connection on one level may turn out to be a separation on another, and vice versa.

There is quite some humility in that understanding. Perhaps it was the very condition of their work environment in Niger, a "frontier country" in the old sense of the word that caused the gendarmes' sense of meek realism. Working in and on the edge of the desert, where a vast and uncontrollable openness spreads out people, things, and stories, not even the proudest and cockiest of all gendarmes would ever think that this frontier is one that can be closed.

Before the end of colonialism (and perhaps again before the end of the Cold War), the nature of global connections seemed rather straightforward, all frontiers appeared closed. Hierarchies were clear; levels of agency were clear; affiliations and allegiances were clear; the directions, kinds, and rates of exchange were clear. Everything appeared unambiguously in control. And suddenly it was not. Let me be clear: the control and certainty that colonialism and capitalism promised to the metropoles were to a large extent illusory, as many simple descriptions of the world are; yet bit by bit, this illusion waned and both hopes and fears took over. And they still remain. The certainty of the map with borders gave way to the openness, flows, and frictions of borderlands. Through the acceleration and intensification of communication technology, global mobility, and neoliberal capitalism, these borderlands were no longer more or less stable spaces of uncertainty and potential. They turned into frontiers to be closed, defended, or pushed forward.

It may be an open question (and perhaps depends on one's perspective) whether these postcolonial or neoliberal frontiers are regarded as being pushed forward or backward or whether they have been widening and spreading out ever since. What is certain is that any attempt to achieve clear-cut connection or separation appears illusory at best and fatally destructive at worst. Anthropology, science of the "contact zone" (Hastrup 1997), is not immune to this condition.

Disconnections in the Contact Zone

Kirsten Hastrup once described anthropology as the theoretical practice in and of the "contact zone, that is the zone where cultures meet, and horizons fuse" (1997, 352). I quite like her take on this, first, for it recognizes anthropology as both theory and practice; and second, because it takes the shared experience of humans in the contact zone—the shared experience of relativity—as the starting point that not only leads to conceptual relativity (instead of ontological incommensurability). Ultimately, it gives rise to "a language of perspicuous contrast, which is neither theirs nor ours, but a separate language in which we can formulate both their and our lifestyles as alternative possibilities" (Hastrup 1997, 366). In other words, anthropological theorizing takes place in a third space, though not one of total hybridity, but of confident eccentricity.

What if we thought of the contact zone not as a zone where horizons fuse, but where one horizon might be pushed against the other? Or where horizons might be kept separate? Traditionally, anthropology has been pushing forward its horizon toward foreign and exotic places (and unfortunately some still hold this as the hallmark of anthropology) and the fusion of horizons often was more of a rhetorical device than actual stance. Even without such exoticizing ambition, isn't the aim of all social theory, as Charles Taylor (1985, 92–94) put it, to make sense of "what is really going on"? To push *our* understanding beyond the surface of (both our and their) common-sense descriptions to get at the implicit and defining understandings that underpin *their* practices—whoever "they" are?

Anthropology's contact zone, at least how I experienced it with the gendarmes in Niger, is not only one where both sides at times push and pull at each other's horizons, it is also a zone where separations are made, where repair work is done. And in many respects, the repair work I did was not so different from that done by the gendarmes. The choice of stories I looked for, listened to, and wrote down and also the connections I drew and disconnections I kept between them, was influenced by my "vocational ear" and "sense of justice" just like the gendarmes'. This is probably why I did not write more about some gendarmes' abuse of power and avarice. I did meet gendarmes who were abusive and violent, and those whose vocational ear was exclusively attuned to the sound of money. They were few in number, and I did not have friendly relationships with them, but they existed. Nevertheless, I suggest that the study of idealists like Adjudant-Chef Souley, Chef Boubacar, Amadou, and the other gendarmes in Godiya can help us make sense of the profound tension the gendarmes struggled with: that they broke the law to be just (see also Kirsch 2010, 155).

My sense of justice was probably also the reason why I did not draw much clearer connections between the gendarmes' contemporary practices and the exploitative routines and despotic attitudes of their colonial predecessors. I could have mentioned that in many instances Souley's behavior as brigade commander heavily reminded me of accounts I had read about the arbitrary rule of some French colonial officers. Yet it felt like highlighting such parallels and implying historical continuities would not do justice, first, to the agency, subjectivity, and morality of Souley, Amadou, and the others; and second, it would smother the surplus historicity of each moment I observed, "the potential, the not yet, or not ever, manifest: the possible" (Hastrup 1997, 362). Like the gendarmes, I knowingly disconnected domains, people, and histories that might otherwise get dangerously entangled—so that we can get on with the work of "repair," of making it better and more just. I somehow took theorizing about the gendarmes' world seriously as a practice that could potentially change it—in whatever minuscule way.

It is almost too banal to say that the line between theory and practice is a bit fuzzy. According to Charles Taylor (1985, 106), we live in an "inescapably theoretical civilization": we are all convinced that there is more to social interaction (and practices in general) than can meet the eye, something that needs to be laid bare in theory. Practices seem to push us to uncover their theoretical foundations. People reach for theories to make sense of a practical world that is in large parts opaque to them. What is more, theorizing is a practice, too! So, in a sense, theory pushes into practices and practices into theory. Few other disciplines seem to take this tension as seriously as anthropology.

All in all, then, the place of anthropology is a rather peculiar one. It is a contact zone of horizons and a meeting point of theory and practice. Yet I think this experience of copresence does not lead to either fusion or contrast, connection or disconnection, but to both at the same time. This tension is what dominated the gendarmes' daily lives; and it is what dominates the theoretical practice of anthropology in the frontier.

Notes

1. A HANDFUL OF GENDARMES, TWO WORLDS, AND THE FRONTIER BETWEEN

1. All quotations from the gendarmes are drawn from interviews or field notes. They were recorded in French or Hausa; these are my translations. All names are pseudonyms.

2. These practices included, of course, the leeway and discretion bureaucrats have due to their position within the organization, social status, resources, and so forth, as already shown by Lipsky in his study on American street-level bureaucrats (1980).

3. Many scholars of policing worldwide have pointed out that accessing and participant field research in police organizations is always—to put it mildly—complicated (see particularly Behr 2003; Dieu 2008, 49; Ericson 1989; Marenin 1982, 385; Monjardet 2005; Punch 1989; Van Maanen 1981).

4. Laboratoire d'Etudes et de Recherches sur les Dynamiques Sociales et le Développement Local.

5. Within the National Gendarmerie there is a functional division between the Gendarmerie Mobile and the Gendarmerie Territoriale. A superior officer directly accountable to the high commander (*haut commandant*) heads each section. The primary function of the Mobile Gendarmerie is antiriot and public order policing, and the gendarmes live in the barracks at the eight regional headquarters. Administratively, the gendarmerie is divided into three *légions* (Niamey, Agadez, Zinder), eight *groupements*, which correspond to the country's eight administrative regions (Agadez, Diffa, Dosso, Maradi, Niamey, Tahoua, Tillabéri, and Zinder), and seventeen dependent *compagnies* in charge of all fifty-nine *brigades territoriales*. In addition to these brigade territoriales, one brigade specializes in criminal investigations in each legion, the so-called *brigade de recherches*, and three to four so-called *brigades mixtes*, former *brigades routières*, work as traffic control units, now also in charge of judicial and administrative police work.

6. In 2008, the percentage of women in the Nigerien gendarmerie was at about 4 percent (Zangaou 2008, 266); recruitment numbers from 2012 reflect this trend (2012: 17 women out of 425 recruits).

7. The correct form of address for both *maréchal des logis* and *maréchal des logis-chef* is *chef*.

8. In 2013, the whole Gendarmerie Nationale had personnel of about six thousand gendarmes, all ranks considered. These are distributed across three *corps* (ranked highest to lowest): officers (*officiers*), noncommissioned officers (*sous-officiers*), and gendarmes. According to legal stipulations, 5 percent should be officers, 25 percent noncommissioned officers, and 70 percent gendarmes (Ordonnance N° 99– 62 du 20 décembre 1999), but it was impossible for me to verify these numbers. Officers are recruited through a competitive exam open to university graduates as "direct entries" or among noncommissioned officers with a baccalaureate. They are the commanders of a *compagnie, groupement, and légion* or at the national headquarters. Except for extraordinary nominations such as Chef Hamza, noncommissioned officers, such as Souley, Boubacar, and Tahirou, are recruited among those rank-and-file gendarmes who have obtained two professional diplomas (Certificats d'Aptitude Professionnelle: CAP-1 and CAP-2) and a varying number of years of experience (this varies between two and four years, depending on a ministerial decree) also via a competitive exam. They then do six months of advanced training in the gendarmerie's Centre d'Instruction in Niamey. Rank-and-file gendarmes are recruited through exams

among men and women with a junior secondary school diploma (Brevet d'études du premier cycle: BEPC) and not older than twenty-five (for men) or twenty-three (women) years. When they are accepted, they receive six months of military training together with army soldiers (Formation militaire commune de base); then they have six months of professional gendarmerie training in their duties as *police administrative, militaire,* and particularly *judiciaire.* Afterward, they are sent into a brigade as *élèves-gendarmes* for six months on-the-job training. The gendarme Chaibou had just been promoted from élève to a full gendarme. Only gendarmes and noncommissioned officers work in the brigades. In her dissertation, Agnès Badou (2013) gives a vivid, multifaceted description and analysis of the recruitment and advancement processes for the gendarmerie and police in Benin, as well as the gendarmes' and police officers' strategies for dealing with radical uncertainties linked to their advancement. The strategies of the gendarmes in Niger are basically the same.

9. It is a fiction in the sense that it is something made; see Clifford 1986, 6; Geertz 1973, 15; Latour and Woolgar 1986, 41, 257.

2. A HISTORY OF THE GENDARMERIE IN NIGER

1. A remarkable exception is Raison-Jourde and Roy 2010.

2. Notable examples include the edited volume by Bat and Courtin (2012a) and Joël Glasman's monograph (2014).

3. Some argue that this is true of the French gendarmerie (Dieu 2008, 31–39; Luc 2005, 20–23).

4. According to Fuglestad (1983, 110), for the French, Niger was like a penitentiary colony to which officials were exiled.

5. However, some *méhariste* units were twice this size (Dramé 2007, 156).

6. For more details, see the descriptions of méhariste activities by Bouchez (1910) and Duboc (1946) from the colonial period.

7. See Décret N° 61–63/MI/NFO, JO Niger N° 49, 09.12.1961.

8. See Loi N° 60–46 du 01.08.1960, JO Niger N° 12, 01.09.1960. According to Baulin (1986, 52), at that time, the Nigerien army consisted of six officers, 48 noncommissioned officers and 164 rank-and-file soldiers.

9. The first seven cercles were Niamey, Madaoua, Zinder, Gouré, N'Guigmi, Agadez, and Bilma (Fuglestad 1983, 80).

10. For vivid descriptions of these requisitions, see Olivier de Sardan 1984, 135–43, 163–71; and Spittler 1978, 52, 60.

11. See Charlick 1991, 36; Fuglestad 1983, 81; Mann 2009, 333; Roberts 2005, 60–62; Spittler 1982, 66.

12. See Arrêté général relatif aux pensions de retraite et gratifications de réforme des *gardes de cercle,* 28.08.1920, JO AOF N° 822; Arrêté 6366, 23.11.1950, JO AOF N° 2508.

13. See Arrêté 5219, 19.08.1952, JO AOF N° 2786.

14. For detailed accounts of the gendarmerie's French history, see Dieu 2002 and 2008; Emsley 1999; Farcy 2001; Gleizal 1993; Houte 2008; Lignereux 2008; Lizurey 2006; Luc 2005.

15. If not mentioned otherwise, the facts and figures on the colonial gendarmerie in the following paragraphs are drawn from the detailed account by the historiographer of the French colonial gendarmerie, Gérard Cabry (2009).

16. In its final state, French West Africa comprised Côte d'Ivoire, Dahomey (later Benin), French Sudan (later Mali), French Upper Volta (later Burkina Faso), Guinea, Mauritania, Niger, and Senegal.

17. Décret N° 46–1900, JO Togo, 01.10.1947.

18. Décret N° 45–1343, JO Togo.

19. In 1948, the Gendarmerie des Colonies was transformed into the Gendarmerie Outre-Mer.

20. Décret N° 53–347, JO Togo, 16.03.1953.

21. Décret N° 53–274, JO Togo, 01.05.1953.

22. Most litigation was still treated by chiefs and their own policelike force, the *dogari*, often on horses, uniformed, and armed with small leather whips, *chicottes* (Spittler 1978, 146). They earned an additional income by settling disputes. Canton chiefs earned around a thousand francs as judges, lower-ranking chiefs who functioned as advocates for their subjects or as intermediaries earned around five hundred francs (ibid., 47).

23. See Décret N° 45–1343, JO Togo, 16.09.1945.

24. Temps du Niger N° 368, 14.08.1961.

25. The number of French gendarmes gradually decreased; they had often been officially congratulated, decorated for their services to the Nigerien armed forces, and then seen off, as on one occasion reported by the journal *Temps du Niger* (08.08.1966): "Après avoir remis à chacun sa décoration [officiers de l'ordre national; chevaliers de l'ordre national; chevalier de l'ordre du mérite], le ministre [de la défense nationale] Noma Kaka a vivement remercié les officiers pour la bonne volonté et la compétence qu'ils ont déployées malgré les conditions de vie et de travail dans la reconstitution de l'armée nigérienne. 'La reconnaissance est une vertu chez les Nigériens, aussi soyez persuadés que vous ne serez pas oubliés quand vous regagnerez votre patrie,' a dit en conclusion M. Noma Kaka en s'adressant à ceux d'entre eux qui quittent définitivement le Niger."

26. See Décret N° 77–30 PCMS/MDN, JO Niger 01.03.1977.

27. Arrêté N° 30 PRN.DN.DG, JO Niger 01.07.1962; *Temps du Niger*, 19.06.1962, N° 634.

28. *Temps du Niger* 23.08.1962, N° 684.

29. Décret N° 62–178 DN, JO Niger 15.09.1962.

30. See, for example, JO 1958 N°1; JO 1961 N°20; JO 1966 N°17.

31. Décret N° 63–129/ORB, JO Niger 15.08.1963.

32. Décret N° 79–28 PCMS/MDN, JO Niger N°7 01.04.1979.

33. Décret N° 82–156/PCMS/MDN/MI, JO Niger N° 21, 01.11.1982.

34. French: "L'armée a été discréditée au cours de la conférence, humilié, de façon que quand tu portes la tenue, on dirait qu'on peut nous cracher dessus" (Interview).

35. See Arrêté n° 14/MDN/DGJM, JO Niger N° 7, 01.04.1997.

36. Loi N° 97–42, JO Niger N° 24, 15.12.1998; Ordonnance N° 96–005, JO Niger N° 24, 15.12.1998; Abdourhamane 1999, 89–90; Deycard 2007, 132–34.

37. In March 2003, the Algerian Salafist Group for Preaching and Combat GSPC, renamed al-Qaeda of the Islamic Maghreb in 2007 (Keenan 2009a, 14), abducted thirty-two Europeans (see Keenan 2009b, 54–56). Since then, the US military presence in the Sahara augmented significantly (Ellis 2004, 461), and some observers suggested "that US policy towards the Sahara may have had the perverse effect of stimulating militant activity" (Ellis 2007, 22). The anthropologist, Jeremy Keenan, gave intriguing insight into this self-fulfilling prophecy (2004, 694; 2006a, 9; 2007; 2009a; 2009b). From 2008 onward, the frequency of kidnappings in Niger increased rapidly: in December 2008 (two Canadian diplomats kidnapped near Niamey were released); January 2009 (three of four European tourists kidnapped near the Mali-Niger border were released and one was executed); September 2010 (seven foreigners kidnapped in Arlit, in Niger's uranium mining zone; three released, four French people were released after three years in 2013); January 2011 (two French people kidnapped in Niamey were killed during an attempt to rescue the hostages).

38. The members of the PSI were Chad, Mali, Mauritania, Niger, Nigeria, and Senegal; TSCTP added Algeria, Morocco, and Tunisia.

39. Since 2013, probably since the French military engagement against militant groups in northern Mali, there is even a proper term for this region cutting across several countries: "Sahelistan" (Heisbourg 2013, 10–11; Laurent 2013).

40. Arrêté N° 90/MDN/DAAF, JO Niger N° 17, 01.09.2005.

41. A similar tendency can be seen in the other corps, with annual recruitments of army soldiers, national guards (until 2010: Forces Nationales d'Intervention et de Sécurité FNIS), and police of also about one thousand elements each.

3. A STORY OF A MURDER, NO TRACES, AND NOTHING TO REPORT

1. French: R-A-S, "rien à signaler."
2. French: SIR, "sur interrogation réponse."
3. French: "Il a scalpé le cou de la fille" (field notes).
4. French: "haché avec une hache" (field notes).

4. THE EAR

1. This point has been underlined, for example, by Feest and Blankenburg 1972, 19; Goldstein 1960; Ignatieff 1979, 445; Monjardet 1996, 38; Reiner 2000, 19; Waddington 1999, 38.

2. Rijk van Dijk (2001, 565–66) describes a similar practice called a "voodoo oath" that Nigerian prostitutes in the Netherlands had taken.

3. On the popular semiology of money transactions, particularly in terms of manducation, see Blundo and Olivier de Sardan 2006b, 121–22.

4. This has been underlined by scores of policing scholars, e.g., Baker 2005; Benda-Beckmann and Benda-Beckmann 2006; Benda-Beckmann et al. 2009, 4; Hills 2009, 19; 2013; Jensen 2007, 49; Loader 2000; Pratten 2008, 4; Reiner 2000, 4–6.

5. Richard Roberts also made this point in his historical study of disputes and colonial courts in the French Sudan (2005, 16–17, 232).

6. "Voir M. le CB de Godiya pour dresser procédure de . . . ," d'arrestation, for example.

7. Beek (2012, 556) describes a similar routine in the Ghanaian police as a discretionary strategy to not produce cases.

8. A key incident often referred to by gendarmes occurred in the early 2000s, when a handcuffed detainee lost his hand after a wound on his wrist had become infected. He was detained illegally but legitimately, according to all gendarmes who told me this story. But it was not a criminal case. Human rights' associations then filed a complaint at the public prosecutor's, and the gendarme on duty was severely punished and put on trial. Superior officers of the gendarmerie then explicitly forbade engagement in civil matters.

9. Since these categories can only inappropriately be translated into felony, misdemeanor, and minor offences, I will stick to the French terminology.

10. A similar point has been made by Buur 2006, 754; Jensen 2007, 49; and Nader 2003, 65.

5. THE EYE

1. In the last couple of years, a number of researchers, often inspired by Foucault's (1975) reflections on surveillance, have presented highly insightful accounts about the effects of surveillance as a mode of governing in Africa. See Bozzini 2011; Donovan and Martin 2014; McGregor 2013; Purdeková 2011. To my knowledge, there is no ethnographic account of the practices of surveillance as perceived by those who use them.

2. Dramé 2007, 52; Arrêté général relatif aux pensions de retraite et gratifications de réforme des gardes de cercle, August 28, 1920, JO AOF N° 822; Arrêté 6366, November 23, 1950, JO AOF N° 2508.

3. Between 2008 and 2011 the frequency of kidnappings in Niger increased rapidly: December 2008 (two Canadian diplomats kidnapped near Niamey; released); January 2009 (four European tourists kidnapped near the Mali-Niger border; three released, one executed); September 2010 (seven foreigners kidnapped in Arlit, in Niger's uranium

mining zone; three released, four French still kept hostage); January 2011 (two French kidnapped in Niamey; killed during hostage rescue attempt).

4. Ericson also uses the term *knowledge broker* in a different way: for the police officer who "produces and distributes knowledge for the risk management activities of security operatives in other institutions" (1994, 151). My understanding of knowledge brokers is closer to and includes what Jan Beek describes as "friends of the police" (2012, 561–62).

5. According to Manning (2001, 88), also police organizations of the global north are more concerned with the here and now than with the prevention of criminal acts. This is, to some extent, also true of the Nigerien gendarmerie. In the brigades where I was, gendarmes did not systematically patrol their areas for which they were responsible. Gendarmes went on extended patrols in remote areas only a couple of times a year, in collaboration with the National Guard, the military, forestry, or customs officers. Other than that, patrols only took place on the brigade commander's initiative.

6. *Fada* is a Hausa word originally designating "a chief's council chamber." Today, the term is applied to any gathering of young men on the street, which is usually preparing tea, or sometimes rice with beans, listening to music and chatting until late at night. For their role in urban security see Göpfert 2012.

6. THE PEN

1. For a remarkable exception, see Gagliardi 2003.

2. This brings to mind Achille Mbembe's reflections on the "aesthetics of power," first expressed in his 1992 article "Provisional Notes on the Postcolony." However, I am not interested here in a broad aesthetics of power but in only one of its configurations in a specific socio-professional setting and from a specific perspective. For a critical and intriguing discussion of Mbembe's thoughts, see Karlström 2003.

3. French: "Le gendarme, ça écrit!" (field notes).

4. In France, procès-verbaux were introduced in the gendarmerie during the late eighteenth century and then universally implemented in the early nineteenth century (Houte 2009, 5). Since then, it has been mandatory for every gendarmerie candidate to be able to read and write. Gendarmes were supposed to write down everything they did and record every piece of information they gathered, and over time they became better trained in writing (ibid., 5–10). Their literacy was an important marker of their distinction from the police, who, if they wrote at all, only scratched notes on bits of paper in bad handwriting and with whom gendarmes did not—and in Niger still do not—want to be confused (ibid., 11, 19).

5. French: "Résumé des faits."

6. French: "C'est la forme qui prime!" (field notes).

7. République du Niger; Ministère de la Défense Nationale; Haut Commandant de la Gendarmerie Nationale; Gendarmerie Territoriale; Légion X; Groupement de Y; Brigade Z.

8. Computers were not allocated to brigades by headquarters, so brigade commanders had to pay for hardware, software, and maintenance out of the brigade's limited budget.

9. Variations on one heading include PREAMBULE, P R E A M B U L E, *P R E A M B U L E*, **PREAMBULE** and—: P R E A M B U L E :—.

10. French: "Parce que je veux que ça soit joli" (field notes).

11. French: "Il [le procès-verbal] doit être aéré" (field notes).

12. Other basic examples of space markers are /=/=/=/=/=/, ~~~~~~~, and a line of dots or hyphens.

13. After their initial instruction, most gendarmes are transferred to units with military and public order functions, namely, the *escadrons,* where they follow on-the-job training.

14. Jan Beek discusses the absence of clear official guidelines, which allows for creativity in daily police work, even beyond writing (2011, 202–5).

15. The same seems to be the case in the Nigerien National Police (Oumarou 2011, 196).

16. Pascal Singy and Fabrice Rouiller (2001, 652) indicate that only roughly 25 percent of Nigeriens understand French; see Singy and Rouiller 2001, 655–56, on the French language in the Nigerien legal system. Since the gendarmes' responsibilities lie mainly in rural areas, the percentage of francophone people who enter into contact with them might be still lower.

17. French: "Ces jeunes gens ont fait irruption sur moi en m'administrant des coups de bâton."

18. French: "Le corps sans vie baignait dans une mare de sang."

19. From "J'ai perdu mon permis" to "J'ai égaré mon permis" and from "lors du recensement" to "dans le cadre du recensement."

20. This happened not because of mere disrespect for the rights of people in custody but also because of the constraints of the gendarmes' everyday work. According to the Code de Procédure Pénale (République du Niger 2007, Art. 71), the forty-eight-hour period of detainment in police custody begins in the moment of apprehension. Yet, if a person was arrested in a small rural outpost that did not have a vehicle and had to be transferred to the nearest brigade which sometimes meant traveling more than a hundred kilometers of bush path, the legal procedure could often be launched only one or two days after the initial arrest.

21. This change was to an SIR (*sur interrogation réponse*), that is, an answer given to a question asked by the gendarme to elucidate certain aspects perhaps not mentioned in the statement but, nevertheless, important for the investigation. In French, the change was from "Nous n'avons pas vu qu'il a été frappé" to "Nous ne connaissons pas les vrais auteurs car ils étaient nombreux."

22. From "Je la connais seulement de visage" to "Je la connaissais déjà parce qu'elle était notre voisine dans le quartier."

23. Amadou repeatedly stated, "On abuse du droit de l'analphabèthe." On the interlinking of security, which gendarmes see as their moral mission and thus want to produce and trust, and which they realize that they are betraying, see Göpfert 2012, 68.

24. The gendarmes" argument was very similar to what Boaventura de Sousa Santos argues for the work of legal professionals: "In order to fulfill their function they inevitably distort reality. . . . However, the distortion of reality thus produced will not automatically involve the distortion of truth, if the mechanisms by which the distortion of reality is accomplished are known and can be controlled" (1987, 282).

25. According to an unpublished 2009 statistical report of the Gendarmerie Territorial de la Gendarmerie Nationale du Niger.

26. See, in this respect particularly, James C. Scott's *Seeing Like a State* (1998).

7. DRAMA WORK

1. This point is made by Beek 2012, 555; Baker 2003, 154; Blankenburg 1995, 13; Ignatieff 1979, 444.

2. Hausa: "Mu da ku, duka daia ne. C'est la même chose! Muna magana, muna gyara, shike nan!" (field notes).

3. A few days later, Chef Boubacar did almost the same thing when a conflict was about to escalate in the brigade's courtyard. And interestingly, weeks later somebody I did not know greeted me in a bar: "Monsieur le gendarme!" He had been waiting in the courtyard when I stepped between Chris and Pierre and thought I was some strange kind of white gendarmerie intern acting like a real gendarme.

4. This is very reminiscent of what Laura Nader (1969, 84) describes.

5. After seeing Pierre off, I went back to Souley and gave him the 5,000 francs CFA I had received from Pierre. "This is for you," I said, for all the phone calls he had made etc. He thanked me and said that he would give it to his men. We left his office together and Souley gave the 5,000 to Chef Boubacar, the second in command. He told him that Chaibou would get 1,000, Ali 1,000, Chef Tahirou 1,000, "and you, you eat 2,000," he said to Boubacar. Then another gendarme came around the corner and Souley laughed: "Okay, you eat only 1,000 after all."

6. French: "en cas de non-engagement je vais subir la rigueur de la loi."

8. REPAIR WORK

1. In this context, "fitina" can mean annoying behavior, disobedience, and cause of trouble.

2. By sending the negotiating parties away from the office building, the gendarmes tried to maintain a clear functional differentiation of spaces and thus their occupational image as strict law enforcers: the brigade is not a place for negotiations. The management and functional differentiation of spaces in and around police and gendarmerie stations anywhere can be understood as a means of the police officers' and gendarmes' face-work (see Ericson 1989, 211; Holdaway 1980, 82–84).

3. The prospect of being able to earn some extra money was, of course, another incentive for the gendarmes not to apply the law à la lettre. However, considering that the gendarmes worked in a blatantly underfunded institution and had to pay for most of the office materials, their uniforms, boots, handcuffs, fuel for the brigade's vehicle and so on out of "their own" pockets, the normative label "corruption" would not do justice to this complexity.

4. This understanding is also reflected in the global trend of "restorative justice" that institutionalizes the nonenforcement of the law in the form of specialized organizations charged—by the courts—with conflict resolution through mediation instead of criminal prosecution (Aubert 1969; Comaroff and Comaroff 2004, 189; Johnstone 2002; Roche 2006, 219; Steinberg 2010, 56; Wright and Galaway 1989). What is generally subsumed under "restorative justice" is, however, not limited to criminal justice programs but takes place in schools, welfare, health, and environment agencies (Roche 2006, 217–18), although, as Roche (ibid., 235) argues, "it works best when it is used in conjunction with the threat of tougher enforcement."

5. Jeffrey Martin (2007, 691) describes a similar principle at work in the Taiwanese police: "By contrast to the harsh cutting edge of law, reason is described as a circular, rounding, and smoothing quality that fits the law to context." For a critical discussion of Gluckman's concept of the reasonable man see Epstein (1973).

6. This would arguably be closer to Elizabeth Povinelli's (1998, 586) description of "repairing the law" in Australia as a legislative response against racial and cultural intolerances.

7. Really the "first" gatekeepers are, of course, the victims of a crime (see Gottfredson and Gottfredson 1988, 15–18).

9. TRAGIC WORK

1. Jean-Pierre Olivier de Sardan (1999, 47; 2004, 149; 2008) argues that, since bureaucrats in West Africa ostensibly do not follow the official norms, they must follow other "practical norms." He defines these as those norms "that regulate practices that are illegal but which are culturally legitimate or tolerated" (2009, 49n13). But he leaves open why even these are sometimes not followed. Rottenburg (1995) turns the issue upside down: he does not ask why bureaucrats do not draw on formal practices, but when and how they do draw on them.

2. For example by Blundo and Olivier de Sardan 2006a, 70; and Tidjani Alou 2006, 144.

3. This point has been made by Gupta 1995; 2012, 76; Leys 1965, 221; and Roitman 2006, 250.

4. In popular perceptions, bureaucrats seem to also represent a particular kind of liminality, as Colin Hoag argues colorfully: "Bureaucracies are Frankensteins: . . . Bureaucrats at such institutions embody the spirit of this unpredictable and liminal creature. They are at once inanimate—lazy automatons, blindly serving larger powers—and animate— nefarious, self-interested obstructionists" (2011, 82).

5. This was similar to what Markus Verne (2004, 179) describes as a typical way of showing the elderly respect in a Hausa community.

6. Hamani Oumarou (2011, 201–2) cites a prosecutor who makes this even more explicit: "En intervenant dans le règlement de litiges, en matières civiles, la police [and the gendarmerie] outrepasse ses attributions certes ; nous le savons tous, mais il faut reconnaître que cela nous arrange quelque part, parce qu'elle permet de régler un volume non négligeable de litiges. Ça permet de ne pas engorger les tribunaux."

7. Adjudant-Chef Souley explained this in an interview: "J'ai cinq postes reculés, il y a dix gendarmes. Mais je m'intéresse jamais à ce qu'ils font. C'est pas mon problème. Pourquoi? C'est des gendarmes, je dois avoir confiance en eux. Et jusqu'ici il y a pas de problème. Des petits problèmes qu'il y en a, c'est quand ça répercute. Mais quand ça n'a pas posé de problème . . . est-ce que je vais remuer le couteau dans la plaie? C'est pas possible! Ça m'intéresse pas de savoir tout ce qu'ils font sur les postes."

8. French: "On ne dit jamais 'non' à un supérieur. Mais si c'est gauche, tu vas trouver une autre manière" (field notes).

9. For the strategies gendarmes developed in the face of extreme career uncertainties, see Badou 2013.

10. Julia Eckert gave the talk "Empirie als Kritik: Die Geburt der Ethnologie aus dem Geist der Tragödie" in a plenary session on the Conference of the German Anthropological Association on October 3, 2013.

POSTSCRIPT: ON THE SIGNIFICANCE OF THE FRONTIER

1. On the state's embeddedness, see Benda-Beckmann and Benda-Beckmann 2006, 10. On its boundaries see Beek 2012; Bierschenk and Olivier de Sardan 2003, 146; Gupta 1995. On its margins see Das and Poole 2004; Kyed 2007.

Bibliography

Abadie, Maurice. 1927. *La Colonie du Niger*. Paris: Société d'éditions géographiques, maritimes et coloniales.

Abdoulkader, Aghali. 2013. "Le 'bien' sécurité dans trois communes (Guidan Roumdji, Balleyara et Say): des logiques de l'Etat aux logiques locales, ou la diversité d'acteurs." *Etudes et Travaux du LASDEL*, no. 105.

Abdourhamane, Boubacar I. 1999. "Alternances militaires au Niger." *Politique Africaine* 74: 85–94.

Abrahams, Ray. 2007. "Some Thoughts on the Comparative Study of Vigilantism." In *Global Vigilantes*, edited by David Pratten and Atreyee Sen, 419–42. London: Hurst.

Alpert, Geoffrey P., and Roger G. Dunham. 2004. *Understanding Police Use of Force: Officers, Suspects, and Reciprocity*. Cambridge: Cambridge University Press.

Alvarez, Robert. 1995. "The Mexican-US Border: The Making of an Anthropology of Borderlands." *Annual Review of Anthropology* 24: 447–70.

Amuwo, 'Kunle. 1986. "Military-Inspired Anti-Bureaucratic Corruption Campaigns: An Appraisal of Niger's Experience." *Journal of Modern African Studies* 24 (2): 285–301.

Anzaldúa, Gloria. 1987. *Borderlands. La Frontera. The New Mestiza*. San Francisco: Aunt Lute Books.

Aristotle. 1925. *Ethica Nicomachea*. Translated by R. C. Ross. Oxford: Clarendon Press.

Aubert, Vilhelm. 1969. "Law as a Way of Resolving Conflicts: The Case of a Small Industrialized Society." In *Law in Culture and Society*, edited by Laura Nader, 282–303. Chicago: Aldine.

Badou, Agnès. 2013. "Les parcours professionnels de policiers et gendarmes au Bénin: entrer et avancer dans les corps à l'épreuve des réformes et stratégies des acteurs (1960–2011)." Ph.D. diss., Johannes Gutenberg University, Mainz.

Baker, Bruce. 2002. "Living with Non-State Policing in South Africa: The Issues and Dilemmas." *Journal of Modern African Studies* 40 (1): 29–53.

——. 2003. "Policing and the Rule of Law in Mozambique." *Policing and Society* 13 (2): 139–58.

——. 2005. "Multi-Choice Policing in Uganda." *Policing and Society* 15 (1): 19–41.

——. 2007. "Conflict and African Police Culture: The Cases of Uganda, Rwanda, and Sierra Leone." In *Police Occupational Culture: New Debates and Directions*, edited by Megan O'Neill, Monique Marks, and Anne-Marie Singh, 321–47. Amsterdam: Elsevier JAI.

Bako-Arifari, Nassirou. 2001. "La corruption au port de Cotonou: douaniers et intermédiaires." *Politique Africaine* 83: 38–58.

——. 2006. "'We Don't Eat the Papers': Corruption in Transport, Customs and the Civil Forces." In *Everyday Corruption and the State: Citizens and Public Officials in Africa*, edited by Giorgio Blundo and Jean-Pierre Olivier de Sardan, 177–224. Cape Town: Philip.

Bat, Jean-Pierre, and Nicolas Courtin, eds. 2012a. *Maintenir l'ordre colonial. Afrique et Madagascar, XIXe-XXe siècles*. Rennes: Presses Universitaires de Rennes.

——. 2012b. "Postface." In *Maintenir l'ordre colonial. Afrique et Madagascar, XIXe-XXe siècles*, edited by Jean-Pierre Bat and Nicolas Courtin, 209–12. Rennes: Presses Universitaires de Rennes.

Bauer, Alain, and Émile Pérez. 2009. *Les 100 mots de la police et du crime*. Paris: Presses Universitaires de France.

Baulin, Jacques. 1986. *Conseiller du président Diori*. Paris: Éditions Eurafor-Press.

Bayart, Jean-François. 2010. "Le piège de la lutte antiterroriste en Afrique de l'Ouest." *Sociétés politiques comparées*, no. 26, accessed December 19, 2018, http://www. fasopo.org/sites/default/files/chro_n26.pdf.

Beek, Jan. 2011. "'Every Car Has an Offence on It': Register polizeilichen Handelns bei Verkehrskontrollen in Nordghana." *Sociologus* 61 (2): 197–222.

——. 2012. "'There Should Be No Open Doors in the Police': Criminal Investigations in Northern Ghana as Boundary Work." *Journal of Modern African Studies* 50 (4): 551–72.

Beek, Jan, and Mirco Göpfert. 2011. "'Ground Work' und 'Paper Work': Feldzugang bei Polizeiorganisationen in Westafrika." *Zeitschrift für Ethnologie* 136: 189–214.

——. 2013a. "Police Violence in West Africa: Perpetrators' and Ethnographers' Dilemmas." *Ethnography* 14 (4): 477–500.

——. 2013b. "State Violence Specialists in West Africa." *Sociologus* 63 (1/2): 103–24.

Beek, Jan, Mirco Göpfert, Olly Owen, and Jonny Steinberg, eds. 2017. "Introduction: Policing in Africa Reconsidered." In *Police in Africa: The Street Level View*, edited by Jan Beek, Mirco Göpfert, Olly Owen, and Jonny Steinberg, 1–18. London: Hurst & Company.

Beeman, William O. 1993. "The Anthropology of Theater and Spectacle." *Annual Review of Anthropology* 22: 369–93.

Behr, Rafael. 2003. "Polizeiforschung als Kontrolle der Kontrolleure?" In *Die Polizei als Organisation mit Gewaltlizenz: Möglichkeiten und Grenzen der Kontrolle*, edited by Martin Herrnkind and Sebastian Scheerer, 221–59. Münster: LIT.

Benda-Beckmann, Keebet von. 1981. "Forum Shopping and Shopping Forums: Dispute Settlement in a Minangkabau Village in West Sumatra." *Journal of Legal Pluralism* 19: 117–59.

Benda-Beckmann, Franz von, and Keebet von Benda-Beckmann. 2006. "The Dynamics of Change and Continuity in Plural Legal Orders." *Journal of Legal Pluralism* 53–54: 1–44.

Benda-Beckmann, Franz von, Keebet von Benda-Beckmann, and Julia Eckert. 2009. "Rules of Law and Laws of Ruling: Law and Governance between Past and Future." In *Rules of Law and Laws of Ruling: On the Governance of Law*, edited by Franz von Benda-Beckmann, Keebet von Benda-Beckmann, and Julia Eckert, 1–30. Farnham, UK: Ashgate.

Bensa, Alban, and Eric Fassin. 2002. "Les sciences sociales face à l'événement." *Terrain* 38: 5–20.

Bierschenk, Thomas. 2008. "The Everyday Functioning of an African Public Service: Informalization, Privatization, and Corruption in Benin's Legal System." *Journal of Legal Pluralism* 57: 101–39.

——. 2010. "States at Work in West Africa: Sedimentation, Fragmentation, and Normative Double-Binds." *Working Papers of the Department of Anthropology and African Studies of the Johannes Gutenberg University Mainz*, 113. Accessed December 3, 2013, http://www.ifeas.uni-mainz.de/Dateien/AP113.pdf.

Bierschenk, Thomas, Matthias Krings, and Carola Lentz. 2016. "World Anthropology with an Accent: The Discipline in Germany since the 1970s." *American Anthropologist* 118 (2): 364–75.

Bierschenk, Thomas, and Jean-Pierre de Olivier Sardan. 2003. "Powers in the Village: Rural Benin between Democratisation and Decentralisation." *Africa* 73 (2): 145–73.

———. 2014. *States at Work: Dynamics of African Bureaucracies*. Leiden: Brill.

Bittner, Egon. 1967. "The Police on Skid-Row: A Study of Peace Keeping." *American Sociological Review* 32 (5): 699–715.

———. 1974. "Florence Nightingale in Pursuit of Willie Sutton: A Theory of the Police." In *The Potential for Reform of Criminal Justice*, edited by Herberg Jacob, 17–44. Beverly Hills, CA: Sage.

Black, Donald J. 1970. "Production of Crime Rates." *American Sociological Review* 35: 733–48.

Blanchard, Emmanuel, and Joël Glasman. 2012. "Introduction générale: le maintien de l'ordre dans l'empire français: une historiographie émergente." In *Maintenir l'ordre colonial. Afrique et Madagascar, XIXe-XXe siècles*, edited by Jean-Pierre Bat and Nicolas Courtin, 11–41. Rennes: Presses Universitaires de Rennes.

Blankenburg, Erhard. 1980. "Recht als gradualisiertes Konzept: Begriffsdimensionen der Diskussion um Verrechtlichung und Entrechtlichung." In *Alternative Rechtsformen und Alternativen zum Recht*, edited by Erhard Blankenburg, Ekkehard Klausa, and Hubert Rottleuthner, 83–98. Opladen: Westdeutscher Verlag.

———. 1995. *Mobilisierung des Rechts: eine Einführung in die Rechtssoziologie*. Berlin: Springer.

Blundo, Giorgio. 2001. "Négocier l'État au quotidien: agents d'affaires, courtiers et rabatteurs dans les interstices de l'administration sénégalaise." *Autrepart* 20: 75–90.

———. 2006. "Dealing with the Local State: The Informal Privatization of Street-Level Bureaucrats in Senegal." *Development and Change* 37 (4): 799–819.

Blundo, Giorgio, and Joël Glasman. 2013. "Introduction: Bureaucrats in Uniform." *Sociologus* 63 (1/2): 1–9.

Blundo, Giorgio, and Jean-Pierre Olivier de Sardan. 2006a. "Everyday Corruption in West Africa." In *Everyday Corruption and the State: Citizens and Public Officials in Africa*, edited by Giorgio Blundo and Jean-Pierre Olivier de Sardan, 69–109. Cape Town: Philip.

———. 2006b. "The Popular Semiology of Corruption." In *Everyday Corruption and the State: Citizens and Public Officials in Africa*, edited by Giorgio Blundo and Jean-Pierre Olivier de Sardan, 110–34. Cape Town: Philip.

Bouchez. 1910. *Guide de l'Officier Méhariste au Territoire Militaire du Niger*. Paris: Émile Larose, Libraire-Éditeur.

Bourdieu, Pierre. 1984. *Distinction: A Social Critique of the Judgement of Taste*. Cambridge, MA: Harvard University Press.

Bozzini, David M. 2011. "Low-Tech Surveillance and the Despotic State in Eritrea." *Surveillance and Society* 9 (1/2): 93–113.

Brachet, Julien. 2009. *Migrations transsahariennes: Vers un désert cosmopolite et morcelé (Niger)*. Bellecombe-en-Bauges: Éditions du Croquant.

Brodeur, Jean-Paul, and Genevière Ouellet. 2005. "L'enquête criminelle." *Criminologie* 38 (2): 39–64.

Brunet-la-Ruche, Bénédicte. 2012. "'Discipliner les villes coloniales': la police et l'ordre urbain au Dahomey pendant l'entre-deux-guerres." *Criminocorpus, Revue Hypermédia*. Accessed January 17, 2013. http://criminocorpus.revues.org/1678.

Budniok, Jan. 2012. "The Politics of Integrity: Becoming and Being a Judge in Ghana." Ph.D. diss., Johannes Gutenberg University, Mainz.

Buur, Lars. 2006. "Reordering Society: Vigilantism and Expressions of Sovereignty in Port Elizabeth's Townships." *Development and Change* 37 (4): 735–57.

Buur, Lars, Steffen Jensen, and Finn Stepputat. 2007. "The Security-Development Nexus." In *The Security-Development Nexus: Expressions of Sovereignty and Securitization in Southern Africa*, edited by Lars Buur, Steffen Jensen, and Finn Stepputat, 9–33. Uppsala: HSRC Press.

Cabry, Gérard. 2009. *La Gendarmerie Outre-Mer*. Paris: Édition SPE-Barthélémy.

Callero, Peter L. 2003. "The Sociology of the Self." *Annual Review of Sociology* 29: 115–33.

Cast, Alicia D. 2003. "Power and the Ability to Define the Situation." *Social Psychology Quarterly* 66 (3): 185–201.

Chalfin, Brenda. 2010. *Neoliberal Frontiers. An Ethnography of Sovereignty in West Africa*. Chicago: University of Chicago Press.

Charlick, Robert B. 1991. *Niger: Personal Rule and Survival in the Sahel*. Boulder, CO: Westview Press.

Choongh, Satnam. 1998. *Policing as Social Discipline*. New York: Clarendon Press.

Clayton, Anthony. 1988. *France, Soldiers, and Africa*. London: Brassey's Defence Publishers.

Clifford, James. 1986. "Introduction: Partial Truths." In *Writing Culture: The Poetics and Politics of Ethnography*, edited by James Clifford and George E. Marcus, 1–26. Berkeley: University of California Press.

Cohen, David W. 1994. *The Combing of History*. Chicago: University of Chicago Press.

Cohen, William B. 1971. *Rulers of Empire: The French Colonial Service in Africa*. Stanford, CA: Hoover Institution Press.

Cole, John, and Eric Wolf. 1974. *The Hidden Frontier: Ecology and Ethnicity in an Alpine Valley*. New York: Academic Press.

Collins, Randall. 2008. *Violence: A Micro-Sociological Theory*. Princeton: Princeton University Press.

Comaroff, John L., and Jean Comaroff. 2004. "Criminal Justice, Cultural Justice: The Limits of Liberalism and the Pragmatics of Difference in the New South Africa." *American Ethnologist* 31 (2): 188–204.

——. 2009. "Reflections on the Anthropology of Law, Governance, and Sovereignty." In *Rules of Law and Laws of Ruling: On the Governance of Law*, edited by Franz von Benda-Beckmann, Keebet von Benda-Beckmann, and Julia Eckert, 31–59. Farnham, UK: Ashgate.

Conti, Norman. 2009. "A Visigoth System: Shame, Honor, and Police Socialization." *Journal of Contemporary Ethnography* 38 (3): 409–32.

Coote, Jeremy. 1992. "'Marvels of Everyday Vision': The Anthropology of Aesthetics and the Cattle-Keeping Nilotes." In *Anthropology, Art, and Aesthetics*, edited by Jeremy Coote and Anthony Shelton, 245–73. Oxford: Clarendon Press.

Corsianos, Marilyn. 2001. "Conceptualizing 'Justice' in Detectives' Decision Making." *International Journal of the Sociology of Law* 29: 113–25.

Czarniawska, Barbara, and Bernward Joerges. 1996. "Travels of Ideas." In *Translating Organizational Change*, edited by Barbara Czarniawska and Guje Sevón, 13–48. Berlin: de Gruyter.

Czarniawska, Barbara, and Carmelo Mazza. 2003. "Consulting as a Liminal Space." *Human Relations* 56 (3): 267–90.

Das, Veena. 2004. "The Signature of the State: The Paradox of Illegibility." In *Anthropology in the Margins of the State*, edited by Veena Das and Deborah Poole, 225–52. Santa Fe, NM: School of American Research Press.

Das, Veena, and Deborah Poole. 2004. "State and Its Margins: Comparative Ethnographies." In *Anthropology on the Margins of the State*, edited by Veena Das and Deborah Poole, 3–34. Santa Fe, NM: School of American Research Press.

Davis, John. 2007. "Introduction: Africa's Road to the War on Terror." In *Africa and the War on Terrorism*, edited by John Davis, 1–14. Aldershot, UK: Ashgate.

De Certeau, Michel. 1984. *The Practice of Everyday Life*. Berkeley: University of California Press.

Deleuze, Gilles. 1969. *Logique du sens*. Paris: Éditions de Minuit.

Deleuze, Gilles, and Félix Guattari. 1980. *Mille plateaux: capitalisme et schizophrénie*. Paris: Éditions de Minuit.

Deveneaux, Gus. 1978. "The Frontier in Recent African History." *International Journal of African Historical Studies* 11 (1): 63–85.

Deycard, Frédéric. 2007. "Le Niger entre deux feux: La nouvelle rébellion Touarègue face à Niamey." *Politique Africaine* 108: 127–44.

Dieu, François. 2002. *La gendarmerie, secrets d'un corps*. Bruxelles: Complexe.

———. 2008. *Sociologie de la gendarmerie*. Paris: L'Harmattan.

Dixon, David, Clive Coleman, and Keith Bottomley. 1990. "Consent and the Legal Regulation of Policing." *Journal of Law and Society* 17 (3): 345–62.

Djibo, Mamoudou. 2002. "Rébellion touarègue et question saharienne au Niger." *Autrepart* 23: 135–56.

Donovan, James M. 2008. *Legal Anthropology: An Introduction*. Plymouth: AltaMira Press.

Donovan, Kevin P., and Aaron K. Martin. 2014. "The Rise of African SIM Registration: The Emerging Dynamics of Regulatory Change." *FM (First Monday)* 19 (2).

Dramé, Patrick-Papa. 2007. *L'impérialisme colonial français en Afrique: enjeux et impacts de la défense de l'AOF, 1918–1940*. Paris: L'Harmattan.

Dubber, Markus D. 2006a. "The New Police Science and the Police Power Model of the Criminal Process." In *The New Police Science: The Police Power in Domestic and International Governance*, edited by Markus D. Dubber and Mariana Valverde, 107–44. Stanford, CA: Stanford University Press.

———. 2006b. *The Sense of Justice: Empathy in Law and Punishment*. New York: New York University Press.

Duboc, Albert. 1946. *Méharistes coloniaux*. Paris: L. Fournier & Compagnie.

Echenberg, Myron. 1991. *Colonial Conscripts: The Tirailleurs Senegalais in French West Africa, 1857–1960*. Portsmouth, NH: Heinemann.

Eckert, Julia. 2004. "Urban Governance and Emergent Forms of Legal Pluralism in Mumbai." *Journal of Legal Pluralism* 50: 29–60.

———. 2005. "The Politics of Security." Max Planck Institute for Social Anthropology Working Papers No. 76, accessed December 19, 2018, http://www.eth.mpg.de/pubs/wps/pdf/mpi-eth-working-paper-0076.pdf.

———. 2011. "Work in Progress: The State at Work in Urban India." In *Auf dem Boden der Tatsachen: Festschrift für Thomas Bierschenk*, edited by Nikolaus Schareika, Eva Spies, and Pierre-Yves Le Meur, 435–45. Köln: Köppe.

Eggen, Oyvind. 2012. "Performing Good Governance: The Aesthetics of Bureaucratic Practice in Malawi." *Ethnos: Journal of Anthropology* 77 (1): 1–23.

Ellis, Stephen. 2004. "Briefing: The Pan-Sahel Initiative." *African Affairs* 103 (412): 459–64.

———. 2007. "The Sahara and the 'War on Terror': A Response to Jeremy Keenan." *Anthropology Today* 23 (3): 21–22.

Emsley, Clive. 1999. *Gendarmes and the State in Nineteenth-Century Europe*. Oxford: Oxford University Press.

Epstein, A. L. 1967. "The Case Method in the Field of Law." In *The Craft of Social Anthropology*, edited by A. L. Epstein, 205–30. London: Tavistock.

———. 1973. "The Reasonable Man Revisited: Some Problems in the Anthropology of Law." *Law and Society Review* 7 (4): 643–66.

Ericson, Richard V. 1989. "Patrolling the Facts: Secrecy and Publicity in Police Work." *British Journal of Sociology* 40 (2): 205–26.

——. 1993. *Making Crime: A Study of Detective Work*. Toronto: University of Toronto Press.

——. 1994. "The Division of Expert Knowledge in Policing and Security." *British Journal of Sociology* 45 (2): 149–75.

Erlmann, Veit. 2004. "But What About the Ethnographic Ear? Anthropology, Sound, and the Senses." In *Hearing Cultures: Essays on Sound, Listening, and Modernity*, edited by Veit Erlmann, 1–20. Oxford: Berg.

Evrard, Camille. 2012a. "L'interprétation des éléments de maintien de l'ordre dans le Sahara mauritanien sous domination coloniale française (1920–1958)." In *Maintenir l'ordre colonial. Afrique et Madagascar, XIXe-XXe siècles*, edited by Jean-Pierre Bat and Nicolas Courtin, 111–24. Rennes: Presses Universitaires de Rennes.

——. 2012b. "Le Chef de bataillon François Beslay, un officier 'hors-cadres' des méharistes coloniaux à l'armée nationale mauritanienne." In *Maintenir l'ordre colonial. Afrique et Madagascar, XIXe-XXe siècles,* edited by Jean-Pierre Bat and Nicolas Courtin, 173–86. Rennes: Presses Universitaires de Rennes.

Farcy, Jean-Claude. 2001. "La gendarmerie, police judiciaire au XIXe siècle." *Histoire, Économie et Société* 20 (3): 385–403.

Fassin, Didier. 2011. *La force de l'ordre: une anthropologie de la police des quartiers*. Paris: Seuil.

Faulkingham, Ralph H. 1971. "Political Support in a Hausa Village." Ph.D. diss., Michigan State University.

Feest, Johannes, and Erhard Blankenburg. 1972. *Die Definitionsmacht der Polizei: Strategien der Strafverfolgung und soziale Selektion*. Düsseldorf: Bertelsmann.

Firth, Raymond. 1992. "Art and Anthropology." In *Anthropology, Art, and Aesthetics*, edited by Jeremy Coote and Anthony Shelton, 15–39. Oxford: Clarendon Press.

Fontaine, Jean-Yves. 2007. *Socioanthropologie du gendarme: gendarmerie et démocratie*. Paris: L'Harmattan.

Foucault, Michel. 1975. *Surveiller et punir. Naissance de la prison*. Paris: Éditions Gallimard.

——. 2004. *Sécurité, territoire, population: Cours au Collège de France, 1977–1978*. Paris: Seuil.

Fourchard, Laurent. 2003a. "Le contrôle de la rue en Afrique Occidentale Française et au Nigeria, fin 19ème siècle—1960." In *Sécurité, crime et ségrégation dans les villes d'Afrique de l'Ouest du XIXe siècle à nos jours*, edited by Laurent Fourchard and Isaac O. Albert, 101–17. Paris: Éditions Karthala.

——. 2003b. "Sécurité, crime et ségrégation: une perspective historique." In *Sécurité, crime et ségrégation dans les villes d'Afrique de l'Ouest du XIXe siècle à nos jours*, edited by Laurent Fourchard and Isaac O. Albert, 1–23. Paris: Éditions Karthala.

Fratto, Toni F. 1978. "Undefining Art: Irrelevant Categorization in the Anthropology of Aesthetics." *Dialectical Anthropology* 3: 129–38.

Frederickson, H. G. 2000. "Can Bureaucracy Be Beautiful?" *Public Administration Review* 60 (1): 47–53.

Fuchs, Martin. 2009. "Reaching Out; or, Nobody Exists in One Context Only: Society as Translation." *Translation Studies* 2 (1): 21–40.

Fuglestad, Finn. 1983. *A History of Niger 1850–1960*. Cambridge: Cambridge University Press.

Fyfe, Nicholas R. 1995. "Policing the City." *Urban Studies* 32 (4/5): 759–78.

Gadamer, Hans-Georg. 1975. *Truth and Method*. London: Continuum.

——. 1999 [1960]. *Hermeneutik 1. Wahrheit und Methode*. Tübingen: Mohr.

Gagliardi, Pasquale. 2003. "Exploring the Aesthetic Side of Organizational Life." In *Studying Organization: Theory and Method*, edited by Stewart R. Clegg and Cynthia Hardy, 311–26. London: Sage.

Garfinkel, Harold. 1967. *Studies in Ethnomethodology*. Englewood Cliffs, NJ: Prentice-Hall.

Gazibo, Mamoudou. 2005. "Foreign Aid and Democratization: Benin and Niger Compared." *African Studies Review* 48 (3): 67–87.

Geertz, Clifford. 1973. *The Interpretation of Cultures: Selected Essays*. New York: Basic Books.

——. 1983. *Local Knowledge: Further Essays in Interpretive Anthropology*. New York: Basic Books.

Gell, Alfred. 1992. "The Technology of Enchantment and the Enchantment of Technology." In *Anthropology, Art, and Aesthetics*, edited by Jeremy Coote and Anthony Shelton, 40–63. Oxford: Clarendon Press.

Gervais, Myriam. 1995. "Structural Adjustment in Niger: Implementations, Effects, and Determining Political Factors." *Review of African Political Economy* 22 (63): 27–42.

Gilliard Patrick, and Laurent Pédenon. 1996. "Rues de Niamey, espace et territoires de la mendicité." *Politique Africaine* 63: 51–60.

Ginsburg, Faye. 1994. "Embedded Aesthetics: Creating a Discursive Space for Indigenous Media." *Cultural Anthropology* 9 (3): 365–82.

Glasman, Joël. 2010. "Penser les intermédiaires coloniaux: note sur les dossiers de carrière de la police du Togo." *History in Africa* 37: 51–81.

——. 2014. *Les corps habillés au Togo: Genèse coloniale des métiers de police*. Paris: Éditions Karthala.

Gleizal, Jean-Jacques. 1993. *La Police en France*. Paris: Presses Universitaires de France.

Gluckman, Max. 1973 [1955]. *The Judicial Process among the Barotse of Northern Rhodesia*. Manchester, UK: Manchester University Press.

Goffman, Erving. 1956. *The Presentation of Self in Everyday Life*. Edinburgh: University of Edinburgh.

——. 1982 [1967]. *Interaction Ritual: Essays on Face-to-Face Behavior*. New York: Pantheon Books.

——. 1983. "The Interaction Order: American Sociological Association, 1982 Presidential Address." *American Sociological Review* 48 (1): 1–17.

Goldman, Alan. 2001. "The Aesthetic." In *The Routledge Companion to Aesthetics*, edited by Berys Gaut and Dominic McIver Lobes, 181–92. London: Routledge.

Goldstein, Joseph. 1960. "Police Discretion Not to Invoke the Criminal Process: Low-Visibility Decisions in the Administration of Justice." *Yale Law Journal* 69 (4): 543–94.

Goodsell, Charles T. 1992. "The Public Administrator as Artisan." *Public Administration Review* 52 (3): 246–53.

——. 1997. "Administration as Ritual." *International Journal of Public Administration* 20 (4/5): 939–61.

Goody, Jack. 1986. *The Logic of Writing and the Organization of Society*. Cambridge: Cambridge University Press.

Göpfert, Mirco. 2012. "Security in Niamey: An Anthropological Perspective on Policing and an Act of Terrorism in Niger." *Journal of Modern African Studies* 50 (1): 53–74.

——. 2013. "Bureaucratic Aesthetics: Report Writing in the Nigérien Gendarmerie." *American Ethnologist* 40 (2): 324–34.

——. 2016a. "Repairing the Law: The Search for Justice in the Nigerien Gendarmerie." *Theoretical Criminology* 20 (4): 446–61.

——. 2016b. "Surveillance in Niger: Gendarmes and the Problem of 'Seeing Things.'" *African Studies Review* 59 (2): 39–57.

Gottfredson, Michael R., and Don M. Gottfredson. 1988. *Decision Making in Criminal Justice: Toward the Rational Exercise of Discretion.* New York: Plenum Press.

Graeber, David. 2015. *The Utopia of Rules. On Technology, Stupidity, and the Secret Joys of Bureaucracy.* Brooklyn, NY: Melville House.

Graybeal N. Lynn, and Luis A. Picard. 1991. "Internal Capacity and Overload in Guinea and Niger." *Journal of Modern African Studies* 29 (2): 275–300.

Gupta, Akhil. 1995. "Blurred Boundaries: The Discourse of Corruption, the Culture of Politics, and the Imagined State." *American Ethnologist* 22 (2): 375–402.

——. 2012. *Red Tape: Bureaucracy, Structural Violence, and Poverty in India.* Durham, NC: Duke University Press.

Haberbusch, Benoît. 2003. "L'imaginaire colonial de la gendarmerie: à travers la revue de la gendarmerie, 1928–2000." *Sociétés and Représentations* 2 (16): 295–306.

Haberlandt, Karl, Claire Berian, and Jennifer Sandson. 1980. "The Episode Schema in Story Processing." *Journal of Verbal Learning and Verbal Behavior* 19: 635–50.

Haller, Mark H. 1970. "Urban Crime and Criminal Justice: The Chicago Case." *Journal of American History* 57 (3): 619–35.

Handelman, Don. 1998. *Models and Mirrors: Towards an Anthropology of Public Events.* New York: Berghahn Books.

Harper, Richard H. R. 1998. *Inside the IMF: An Ethnography of Documents, Technology, and Organisational Action.* San Diego, CA: Academic Press.

Harris, Norman D. 1911. "French Colonial Expansion in West Africa, the Sudan, and the Sahara." *American Political Science Review* 5 (3): 353–73.

Hastrup, Kirsten. 1997. "The Dynamics of Anthropological Theory." *Cultural Dynamics* 9 (3): 351–71.

Hauser-Schäublin, Brigitta. 1997. "Blick zurück im Zorn: Ethnologie als Kulturkritik." *Zeitschrift für Ethnologie* 122 (1): 3–17.

Heerey, Peter. 2003. "Aesthetics, Culture, and the Whole Damn Thing." *Law and Literature* 15 (3): 295–312.

Heisbourg, François. 2013. "A Surprising Little War: First Lessons of Mali." *Survival: Global Politics and Strategy* 55 (2): 7–18.

Herzfeld, Michael. 1992. *The Social Production of Indifference: Exploring the Symbolic Roots of Western Bureaucracy.* Chicago: University of Chicago Press.

Higgot, Richard, and Finn Fuglestad. 1975. "The 1974 Coup d'état in Niger: Towards an Explanation." *Journal of Modern African Studies* 13 (3): 383–98.

Hills, Alice. 2000. *Policing Africa: Internal Security and the Limits of Liberalization.* Boulder, CO: Lynne Rienner.

——. 2009. *Policing Post-conflict Cities.* London: Zed Books.

——. 2013. "On Being a Professional Police Officer in Kano." *Sociologus* 63 (1/2): 81–102.

Hoag, Colin. 2011. "Assembling Partial Perspectives: Thoughts on the Anthropology of Bureaucracy." *PoLAR: Political and Legal Anthropology Review* 34 (1): 81–94.

Hobart, Mark. 1987. "Summer's Day and Salad Days: The Coming of Age of Anthropology?" In *Comparative Anthropology*, edited by Ladislav Holy, 22–51. Oxford: Blackwell.

Hodgson, Jacqueline. 2002. "Hierarchy, Bureaucracy, and Ideology in French Criminal Justice: Some Empirical Observations." *Journal of Law and Society* 29 (2): 227–57.

Holdaway, Simon. 1980. "The Police Station." *Journal of Contemporary Ethnography* 9 (1): 79–100.

Hornberger, Julia. 2004. "'My Police—Your Police': The Informal Privatization of the Police in the Inner City of Johannesburg." *African Studies Review* 63 (2): 213–30.

Houte, Arnaud. 2008. "Nul n'est policier en son pays? Le dépaysement des gendarmes français au XIXe siècle." In *Métiers de police: être policier en Europe, XVIIIe-XXe siècle*, edited by Jean-Marc Berlière, Cathrine Denys, Dominique Kalifa, and Vincent Milliot, 427–38. Rennes: Presses Universitaires de Rennes.

——. 2009. "La fabrique du procès-verbal dans la France du XIXe siècle: contribution à l'histoire de l'écrit administratif." *L'Atelier du Centre de recherches historiques*, no. 5. Accessed May 18, 2010. http://acrh.revues.org/index1488.html.

Hull, Elizabeth. 2012. "Paperwork and the Contradictions of Accountability in a South African Hospital." *Journal of the Royal Anthropological Institute* 18: 613–32.

Hull, Matthew S. 2003. "The File: Agency, Authority, and Autography in an Islamabad Bureaucracy." *Language and Communication* 23: 287–314.

——. 2008. "Ruled by Records: The Expropriation of Land and the Misappropriation of Lists in Islamabad." *American Ethnologist* 35 (4): 501–18.

Idrissa, Kimba. 2008. "Les régimes militaires entre 1974 et 1999 au Niger." In *Armée et politique au Niger*, edited by Kimba Idrissa, 165–206. Dakar: CODESRIA.

Ignatieff, Michael. 1979. "Police and the People: The birth of Mr. Peel's 'Blue Locusts.'" *New Society* 49: 443–45.

Innes, Martin. 2002. "Organizational Communication and the Symbolic Construction of Murder Investigations." *British Journal of Sociology* 53 (1): 67–87.

Issa, Mahaman Malam. 2008. "Le régime militaire de Seyni Kountché (1974–1987)." In *Armée et politique au Niger*, edited by Kimba Idrissa, 125–61. Dakar: CODESRIA.

Jacobs, Bruce A. 1992. "Undercover Deception: Reconsidering Representations of Self." *Journal of Contemporary Ethnography* 21 (2): 200–225.

Jeanjean, Marc. 1991. "La 'culture policière' et l''affaire': une approche ethnographique de la police." *Ethnologie française* 21 (1): 79–87.

Jensen, Steffen. 2007. "Policing Nkomazi: Crime, Masculinity, and Generational Conflicts." In *Global Vigilantes*, edited by David Pratten and Atreyee Sen, 47–68. London: Hurst.

Johnston, Les. 1992. *The Rebirth of Private Policing*. London: Routledge.

Johnstone, Gerry. 2002. *Restorative Justice: Ideas, Values, Debates*. Cullompton, UK: Willan.

Karlström, Mikael. 2003. "On the Aesthetics and Dialogics of Power in the Postcolony." *Africa* 73 (1): 57–76.

Kashani-Sabet. 1999. *Frontier Fictions: Shaping the Iranian Nation, 1804–1946*. Princeton, NJ: Princeton University Press.

Katovich, Michael A., and William A. Reese. 1993. "Postmodern Thought in Symbolic Interaction: Reconstructing Social Inquiry in Light of Late-Modern Concerns." *Sociological Quarterly* 34 (3): 391–411.

Keenan, Jeremy. 2004. "Political Destabilisation and 'Blowback' in the Sahel." *Review of African Political Economy* 31 (102): 691–98.

——. 2006a. "Conspiracy Theories and 'Terrorists': How the 'War on Terror' Is Placing New Responsibilities on Anthropology." *Anthropology Today* 22 (6): 4–9.

——. 2006b. "Security and Insecurity in North Africa." *Review of African Political Economy* 33 (108): 269–96.

——. 2007. "The Banana Theory of Terrorism: Alternative Truths and the Collapse of the 'Second' (Saharan) Front in the War on Terror." *Journal of Contemporary African Studies* 25 (1): 31–58.

——. 2008. "US Militarization in Africa: What Anthropologists Should Know about AFRICOM." *Anthropology Today* 24 (5): 16–20.

——. 2009a. "Al-Qaeda Terrorism in the Sahara? Edwin Dyer's Murder and the Role of Intelligence Agencies." *Anthropology Today* 25 (4): 14–18.

——. 2009b. *The Dark Sahara: America's War on Terror in Africa*. London: Pluto Press.

Kemp, Charles, Clive Norris, and Nigel G. Fielding. 1992. *Negotiating Nothing: Police Decision-Making in Disputes*. Aldershot: Avebury.

Kirsch, Thomas G. 2010. "Violence in the Name of Democracy: Community Policing, Vigilante Action, and Nation-Building in South Africa." In *Domesticating Vigilantism in Africa*, edited by Thomas G. Kirsch and Tilo Grätz, 139–62. Oxford: Currey.

Kirsch, Thomas G., and Tilo Grätz. 2010. "Vigilantism, State Ontologies, and Encompassment: An Introductory Essay." In *Domesticating Vigilantism in Africa*, edited by Thomas G. Kirsch and Tilo Grätz, 1–25. Oxford: Currey.

Knorr Cetina, Karin. 2002. *Die Fabrikation von Erkenntnis: zur Anthropologie der Naturwissenschaft*. Frankfurt am Main: Suhrkamp.

Kopytoff, Igor. 1987. "The Internal Frontier: The Making of African Political Culture." In *The African Frontier: The Reproduction of Traditional African Societies*, edited by Igor Kopytoff, 3–84. Indianapolis: Indiana University Press.

Körling, Gabriella. 2011. *In Search of the State: An Ethnography of Public Service Provision in Urban Niger*. Uppsala: Uppsala University.

Kravel-Tovi, Michal. 2012. "Rite of Passing: Bureaucratic Encounters, Dramaturgy, and Jewish Conversion in Israel." *American Ethnologist* 39 (2): 371–88.

Kristeva, Julia. 1982. *Powers of Horror: An Essay on Abjection*. New York: Columbia University Press.

Kyed, Helene M. 2007. "State Vigilantism and Political Community on the Margins in Post-War Mozambique." In *Global Vigilantes*, edited by David Pratten and Atreyee Sen, 393–415. London: Hurst.

Lasslett, Kristian. 2010. "Crime or Social Harm? A Dialectical Perspective." *Crime, Law, and Social Change* 54: 1–19.

Latour, Bruno. 1994. "On Technical Mediation: Philosophy, Sociology, Genealogy." *Common Knowledge* 3 (2): 29–64.

——. 1996. *Der Berliner Schlüssel: Erkundungen eines Liebhabers der Wissenschaften*. Berlin: Akademie Verlag.

——. 2000. "When Things Strike Back: A Possible Contribution of 'Science Studies' to the Social Sciences." *British Journal of Sociology* 51 (1): 107–23.

——. 2002. *La fabrique du droit: une ethnographie du Conseil d'État*. Paris: La Découverte.

——. 2010. *The Making of Law: An Ethnography of the Conseil d'Etat*. Cambridge: Polity.

Latour, Bruno, and Steve Woolgar. 1986. *Laboratory Life: The Construction of Scientific Facts*. Princeton, NJ: Princeton University Press.

Laurent, Samuel. 2013. *Sahelistan: de la Libye au Mali au cœur du nouveau jihad*. Paris: Seuil.

Lentz, Carola. 2006. *Ethnicity and the Making of History in Northern Ghana*. Edinburgh: Edinburgh University Press.

——. 2010. "'I take an oath to the state, not the government': Career Trajectories and Professional Ethics of Ghanaian Public Servants." Working Papers of the Department of Anthropology and African Studies of the Johannes Gutenberg University Mainz, no. 119. Accessed May 20, 2012, http://www.ifeas.uni-mainz.de/workingpapers/AP119.pdf.

——. 2013. *Land, Mobility, and Belonging in West Africa*. Bloomington: Indiana University Press.

Le Rouvreur, Albert. 1997. *Teski Timmi. Carnets d'un méhariste au Niger et au Tchad: 1942–1958.* Paris: L'Harmattan.

Leys, Colin. 1965. "What Is the Problem about Corruption?" *Journal of Modern African Studies* 3 (2): 215–30.

Lignereux, Aurélien. 2008. "Être ou ne pas être gendarme: l'usage du déguisement dans la gendarmerie française au premier XIXe siècle." In *Métiers de police: être policier en Europe, XVIIIe-XXe siècle,* edited by Jean-Marc Berlière, Cathrine Denys, Dominique Kalifa, and Vincent Milliot, 403–14. Rennes: Presses Universitaires de Rennes.

Lipsky, Michael. 1980. *Street-Level Bureaucracy: Dilemmas of the Individual in Public Services.* New York: Russell Sage Foundation.

Lizurey, Richard. 2006. *Gendarmerie Nationale: les soldats de la loi.* Paris: Presses Universitaires de France.

Loader, Ian. 2000. "Plural Policing and Democratic Governance." *Social and Legal Studies* 9 (3): 323–45.

López, Laurent. 2007. "'Faire du chiffre' pour exister." *Histoire et Mesure* 12 (2): 75–101.

Luc, Jean-Noël. 2005. "Pour une histoire de la gendarmerie." In *Histoire de la maréchaussée et de la gendarmerie: guide de recherche,* edited by Jean-Noël Luc, 19–36. Maisons-Alfort: Service Historique de la Gendarmerie Nationale.

Luhmann, Niklas. 2013 [1983]. *Legitimation durch Verfahren.* Frankfurt am Main: Suhrkamp.

Lund, Christian. 1998. *Law, Power and Politics in Niger: Land Struggles and the Rural Code.* Hamburg: LIT.

——. 2001. "Precarious Democratization and Local Dynamics in Niger: Micro-Politics in Zinder." *Development and Change* 32: 845–69.

Lyon, David. 2006. "The Search for Surveillance Theories." In *Theorizing Surveillance: The Panopticon and Beyond,* edited by David Lyon, 3–10. London: Routledge.

Maguire, Mike. 2008 [2003]. "Criminal Investigation and Crime Control." In *Handbook of Policing,* edited by Tim Newburn, 430–63. Cullompton, UK: Willan.

Mahamane, Addo. 2008. "L'État et le contrôle des chefs militaires en Afrique précoloniale: l'apparition des chefs de guerre au Katsina à la fin du XIXe siècle." In *Armée et politique au Niger,* edited by Kimba Idrissa, 19–44. Dakar: CODESRIA.

Mahamane, Aliou. 2008. "La naissance de l'armée nationale au Niger: 1961–1974." In *Armée et politique au Niger,* edited by Kimba Idrissa, 45–92. Dakar: CODESRIA.

Mandoki, Katya. 2007. *Everyday Aesthetics: Prosaics, the Play of Culture, and Social Identities.* Aldershot, UK: Ashgate.

Mann, Gregory. 2009. "What Was the *Indigénat?* The 'Empire of Law' in French West Africa." *Journal of African History* 50: 331–53.

Manning, Peter K. 1977. *Police Work: The Social Organization of Policing.* Cambridge, MA: MIT Press.

——. 1982. "Producing Drama: Symbolic Communication and the Police." *Symbolic Interaction* 5 (2): 223–42.

——. 1986. "Texts as Organizational Echoes." *Human Studies* 9 (2/3): 287–302.

——. 1992. "Information Technologies and the Police." *Crime and Justice* 15: 349–98.

——. 2001. "Technology's Ways: Information Technology, Crime Analysis, and the Rationalizing of Policing." *Criminology and Criminal Justice* 1 (1): 83–103.

Marenin, Otwin. 1982. "Policing African States: Toward a Critique." *Comparative Politics* 14 (4): 379–96.

Martin, Jeffrey. 2007. "A Reasonable Balance of Law and Sentiment: Social Order in Democratic Taiwan from the Policeman's Point of View." *Law and Society Review* 41 (3): 665–98.

Mbembe, Achille. 1992. "Provisional Notes on the Postcolony." *Africa* 62 (1): 3–37.

McGregor, JoAnn. 2013. "Surveillance and the City: Patronage, Power-Sharing and the Politics of Urban Control in Zimbabwe." *Journal of Southern African Studies* 39 (4): 783–805.

McKay, Ramah. 2012. "Documentary Disorders: Managing Medical Multiplicity in Maputo, Mozambique." *American Ethnologist* 39 (3): 545–61.

Meehan, Albert J. 1986. "Record-Keeping Practices in the Policing of Juveniles." *Journal of Contemporary Ethnography* 15 (1): 70–102.

Merry, Sally E. 1979. "Going to Court: Strategies of Dispute Management in an American Urban Neighbourhood." *Law and Society Review* 14 (4): 891–925.

——. 2006. "Transnational Human Rights and Local Activism: Mapping the Middle." *American Anthropologist* 108 (1): 38–51.

Migdal, Joel S., and Klaus Schlichte. 2005. "Rethinking the State." In *The Dynamics of States: The Formation and Crises of State Domination*, edited by Klaus Schlichte, 1–40. Aldershot, UK: Ashgate.

Mignon, Jean-Marie. 1989. "Les mouvements de jeunesse dans l'Afrique de l'Ouest francophone, de 1958 aux années 1970–1975." In *Le mouvement associatif des jeunes en Afrique noire francophone au XXe siècle*, edited by Hélène Almeida-Topor and Odile Georg, 107–28. Paris: L'Harmattan.

Miles, William F. 1987. "Partitioned Royalty: The Evolution of Hausa Chiefs in Nigeria and Niger." *Journal of Modern African Studies* 25 (2): 233–58.

——. 1993. "Colonial Hausa Idioms: Toward a West African Ethno-Ethnohistory." *African Studies Review* 36 (2): 11–30.

Misztal, Barbara A. 2001. "Normality and Trust in Goffman's Theory of Interaction Order." *Sociological Theory* 19 (3): 312–24.

Mitchell, Timothy. 1991a [1988]. *Colonising Egypt*. Cambridge: Cambridge University Press.

——. 1991b. "The Limits of the State: Beyond Statist Approaches and Their Critics." *American Political Science Review* 85 (1): 77–96.

Monjardet, Dominique. 1994. "La culture professionnelle des policiers." *Revue Française de Sociologie* 35 (3): 393–411.

——. 1996. *Ce que fait la police: sociologie de la force publique*. Paris: La Découverte.

——. 2005. "Gibier de recherche: la police et le projet de connaître." *Criminologie* 38 (2): 13–37.

Moore, David C. 1994. "Anthropology Is Dead, Long Live Anthro(a)pology: Poststructuralism, Literary Studies, and Anthropology's 'Nervous Present.'" *Journal of Anthropological Research* 50 (4): 345–65.

Moore, Sally F. 2000 [1978]. *Law as Process: An Anthropological Approach*. Hamburg: LIT.

Moore, Sally Falk, and Barbara G. Myerhoff. 1977. "Secular Ritual: Forms and Meanings." In *Secular Ritual*, edited by Sally Falk Moore and Barbara G. Myerhoff, 3–24. Assen: Van Gorcum.

Moraga, Cherríe, and Gloria Anzaldúa, eds. 2001. *This Bridge Called My Back: Writings by Radical Women of Color*. 3rd ed. Berkeley, CA: Third Woman Press.

Mosse, David, and David Lewis. 2006. "Theoretical Approaches to Brokerage and Translation in Development." In *Development Brokers and Translators: The Ethnography of Aid and Agencies*, edited by David Lewis and David Mosse, 1–26. Bloomfield, CT: Kumarian Press.

Mouhanna, Christian. 2001. "Faire le gendarme: de la souplesse informelle à la rigueur bureaucratique." *Revue Française de Sociologie* 42 (1): 31–55.

Mouzelis, Nicos. 1992. "The Interaction Order and the Micro-Macro Distinction." *Sociological Theory* 10 (1): 122–28.

Nader, Laura. 1969. "Styles of Court Procedure: To Make the Balance." In *Law in Culture and Society*, edited by Laura Nader, 69–91. Chicago: Aldine.

———. 1990. *Harmony Ideology: Justice and Control in a Zapotec Mountain Village*. Stanford, CA: Stanford University Press.

———. 2003. "Crime as a Category: Domestic and Globalized." In *Crime's Power: Anthropologists and the Ethnography of Crime*, edited by Philip C. Parnell and Stephanie C. Kane, 55–76. New York: Palgrave Macmillan.

Nader, Laura, and Harry F. Todd Jr. 1978. "Introduction." In *The Disputing Process: Law in Ten Societies*, edited by Laura Nader and Harry F. Todd Jr., 1–40. New York: Columbia University Press.

Navaro-Yashin, Yael. 2006. "Affect in the Civil Service: A Study of a Modern State-System." *Postcolonial Studies* 9 (3): 281–94.

———. 2007. "Make-Believe Papers, Legal Forms, and the Counterfeit: Affective Interactions between Documents and People in Britain and Cyprus." *Anthropological Theory* 7 (1): 79–98.

Nelken, David. 2009. "Corruption as Governance? Law, Transparency, and Appointment Procedures in Italian Universities." In *Rules of Law and Laws of Ruling: On the Governance of Law*, edited by Franz von Benda-Beckmann, Keebet von Benda-Beckmann, and Julia Eckert, 257–77. Farnham, UK: Ashgate.

Novitz, David. 2001. "Postmodernism: Barthes and Derrida." In *The Routledge Companion to Aesthetics*, edited by Berys Gaut and Dominic McIver Lobes, 155–65. London: Routledge.

Nuijten, Monique, and David Lorenzo. 2009. "Ritual and Rule in the Periphery: State Violence and Local Governance in a Peruvian *Comunidad*." In *Rules of Law and Laws of Ruling: On the Governance of Law*, edited by Franz von Benda-Beckmann, Keebet von Benda-Beckmann, and Julia Eckert, 101–23. Farnham, UK: Ashgate.

Olivier de Sardan, Jean-Pierre. 1984. *Les sociétés Songhay-Zarma (Niger—Mali): chefs, guerriers, esclaves, paysans*. Paris: Karthala.

———. 1999. "A Moral Economy of Corruption in Africa?" *Journal of Modern African Studies* 37 (1): 25–52.

———. 2001. "La sage-femme et le douanier: cultures professionnelles locales et culture bureaucratique privatisée en Afrique de l'Ouest." *Autrepart* 20: 61–73.

———. 2004. "État, bureaucratie et gouvernance en Afrique de l'Ouest francophone: un diagnostique empirique, une perspective historique." *Politique Africaine* 96: 139–62.

———. 2008. "À la recherche des normes pratiques de la gouvernance réelle en Afrique." Discussion Paper no. 5. London: Africa Power and Politics Programme, accessed December 19, 2018, http://www.institutions-africa.org/filestream/20090109-discussion-paper-5-la-recherche-des-norms-pratiques-de-la-gouvernance-r-elle-en-afrique-jean-pierre-olivier-de-sardan-d-c-2008.

———. 2015. "Practical Norms: Informal Regulations within Public Bureaucracies (in Africa and Beyond)." In *Real Governance and Practical Norms in Sub-Saharan Africa: The Game of the Rules*, edited by Tom de Herdt and Jean-Pierre Olivier de Sardan, 19–62. London: Routledge.

Oumarou, Hamani. 2011. "Les modes de régulation de l'appareil judiciaire nigérien." Ph.D. diss., Ecole des Hautes Etudes en Sciences Sociales, Marseille.

Owen, Oliver. 2013. "The Police and the Public: Risk as Preoccupation." *Sociologus* 63 (1/2): 59–80.

Palmer, Ronald D. 2007. "Political Terrorism in West Africa." In *Africa and the War on Terrorism*, edited by John Davis, 103–12. Aldershot, UK: Ashgate.

Paperman, Patricia. 2003. "Surveillance Underground: The Uniform as Interaction Device." *Ethnography* 4 (3): 397–419.

Pérouse de Montclos, Marc-Antoine. 2008. *États faibles et sécurité privée en Afrique noire: de l'ordre dans les coulisses de la périphérie mondiale*. Paris: L'Harmattan.

Peterson, Abby. 2008. "Who 'Owns' the Streets? Ritual Performances of Respect and Authority in Interactions between Young Men and Police Officers." *Journal of Scandinavian Studies in Criminology and Crime Prevention* 9: 97–118.

Pinheiro, Paulo S. 2003. "Die Polizei: ein Risiko?" In *Die Polizei als Organisation mit Gewaltlizenz: Möglichkeiten und Grenzen der Kontrolle*, edited by Martin Herrnkind and Sebastian Scheerer, 24–31. Münster: LIT.

Poole, Deborah. 2004. "Between Threat and Guarantee: Justice and Community in the Margins of the Peruvian State." In *Anthropology in the Margins of the State*, edited by Veena Das and Deborah Poole, 35–65. Santa Fe, NM: School of American Research Press.

Povinelli, Elisabeth A. 1998. "The State of Shame: Australian Multiculturalism and the Crisis of Indigenous Citizenship." *Critical Inquiry* 24 (2): 575–610.

Pratten, David. 2008. "Introduction. The Politics of Protection: Perspectives on Vigilantism in Nigeria." *Africa* 78 (1): 1–15.

——. 2010. "Bodies of Power: Narratives of Selfhood and Security in Nigeria." In *Domesticating Vigilantism in Africa*, edited by Thomas G. Kirsch and Tilo Grätz, 118–38. Oxford: Currey.

Punch, Maurice. 1989. "Researching Police Deviance: A Personal Encounter with the Limitations and Liabilities of Field-Work." *British Journal of Sociology* 40 (2): 177–204.

Purdeková, Andrea. 2011. "'Even if I am not here, there are so many eyes': Surveillance and State Reach in Rwanda." *Journal of Modern African Studies* 49 (3), 475–97.

Raison-Jourde, Françoise, and Gérard Roy. 2010. *Paysans, intellectuels et populisme à Madagascar: de Monja Jaona à Ratsimandrava (1960–1975)*. Paris: Karthala.

Rash, Yehoshua Janvier. 1972. "Un établissement colonial sans histoires: les premières années françaises au Niger, 1897–1906." Ph.D. diss., Abdou-Moumouni University, Niamey.

Rawls, Anne. 1987. "The Interaction Order Sui Generis. Goffman's Contribution to Social Theory." *Sociological Theory* 5 (2): 136–49.

Reemtsma, Jan Philipp. 2003. "Organisationen mit Gewaltlizenz: ein zivilisatorisches Grundproblem." In *Die Polizei als Organisation mit Gewaltlizenz: Möglichkeiten und Grenzen der Kontrolle*, edited by Martin Herrnkind and Sebastian Scheerer, 7–23. Münster: LIT.

Reiner, Robert. 2000. *The Politics of the Police*. Oxford: Oxford University Press.

République du Niger. 2003. *Code Pénal* (last modification). Niamey: République du Niger.

——. 2007. *Code de Procédure Pénale* (last modification). Niamey: République du Niger.

Riles, Annelise. 1998. "Infinity within Brackets." *American Ethnologist* 25 (3): 378–98.

Roberts, Richard. 2005. *Litigants and Households: African Disputes and Colonial Courts in the French Soudan, 1895–1912*. Portsmouth, NH: Heinemann.

Roche, Declan. 2006. "Dimensions of Restorative Justice." *Journal of Social Issues* 62 (2): 217–38.

Roitman, Janet. 2006. "The Ethics of Illegality in the Chad Basin." In *Law and Disorder in the Postcolony*, edited by Jean Comaroff and John L. Comaroff, 247–72. Chicago: University of Chicago Press.

Rosas, Gilberto. 2007. "The Fragile Ends of War. Forging the United States—Mexico Border and Borderlands Consciousness." *Social Text* 91 (2): 81–102.

——. 2010. "Chulos, Chúntaros, and the 'Criminal' Abandonments of the New Frontier." *Identities* 6: 695–713.

——. 2016. "The Thickening Borderlands." *Cultural Dynamics* 3: 335–49.

Rothiot, Jean-Paul. 1988. *L'ascension d'un chef Africain au début de la colonisation: Aouta, le conquérant (Dosso—Niger)*. Paris: L'Harmattan.

——. 2001. "Une chefferie précoloniale au Niger face aux représentants coloniaux, naissance et essor d'une dynastie." *Cahiers d'histoire. Revue d'histiore critique* 85: 67–83.

Rottenburg, Richard. 1995. "Formale und informelle Beziehungen in Organisationen." In *Organisationswandel in Afrika: kollektive Praxis und kulturelle Aneignung; Erträge eines Symposiums in Petzow bei Potsdam 10. bis 13. Februar 1994*, edited by Achim von Oppen, 19–34. Berlin: Verlag Das Arabische Buch.

——. 2003. "Crossing the Gaps of Indeterminacy." In *Translation and Ethnography: The Anthropological Challenge of Intercultural Understanding*, edited by Tullio Maranhão and Bernhard Streck, 30–43. Tucson: University of Arizona Press.

——. 2009. *Far-fetched Facts: A Parable of Development Aid*. Cambridge, MA: MIT Press.

Ruteere, Mutuma, and Marie-Emmanuelle Pommerolle. 2003. "Democratizing Security or Decentralizing Repression? The Ambiguities of Community Policing in Kenya." *African Affairs* 102: 587–604.

Sanders, Andrew, and Richard Young. 2002. "From Suspect to Trial." In *The Oxford Handbook of Criminology*, edited by Mike Maguire, Rod Morgan, and Robert Reiner, 953–89. Oxford: Oxford University Press.

Sanders, William B. 1979. *Detective Work: A Study of Criminal Investigations*. New York: Free Press.

Santos, Boaventura de Sousa. 1987. "Law: A Map of Misreading: Toward a Postmodern Conception of Law." *Journal of Law and Society* 14 (3): 279–302.

Schapera, Isaac. 1972. "Some Anthropological Concepts of 'Crime': The Hobhouse Memorial Lecture." *British Journal of Sociology* 23 (4): 381–94.

Schröer, Norbert. 2003. "Zur Handlungslogik polizeilichen Vernehmens." In *Hermeneutische Polizeiforschung*, edited by Jo Reichertz and Norbert Schröer, 62–77. Opladen: Leske + Budrich.

Scott, James C. 1969. "The Analysis of Corruption in Developing Nations." *Comparative Studies in Society and History* 11 (3): 315–41.

——. 1998. *Seeing Like a State: How Certain Schemes to Improve the Human Condition Have Failed*. London: Yale University Press.

Searle, John R. 1969. *Speech Acts: An Essay in the Philosophy of Language*. Cambridge: Cambridge University Press.

——. 1979. *Expression and Meaning: Studies in the Theory of Speech Acts*. Cambridge: Cambridge University Press.

Serres, Michel. 1974. *Hermès*. Vol. 3. *La traduction*. Paris: Éditions de Minuit.

Shapland, Joanna, and Jon Vagg. 1988. *Policing by the Public*. London: Routledge.

Shiner, Roger A. 1994. "Aristotle's Theory of Equity." *Loyola of Los Angeles Law Review* 27: 1245–64.

Simon, David. 2009 [1991]. *Homicide: A Year on the Killing Streets*. Edinburgh: Canongate.

Singy, Pascal, and Fabrice Rouillet. 2001. "Les francophones face à leur langue: le cas des Nigériens." *Cahier d'Études Africaines* 41 (163/164): 649–65.

Skogan, Wesley, and Kathleen Frydl. 2003. *Fairness and Effectiveness in Policing: The Evidence*. Washington, DC: National Academies Press.

Skolnick, Jerome Herbert. 1966. *Justice without Trial: Law Enforcement in Democratic Society*. New York: John Wiley & Sons.

Smith, Daniel W. 2004. "'Knowledge of Pure Events': A Note on Deleuze's Analytics of Concepts." In *Ereignis auf Französisch: von Bergson bis Deleuze*, edited by Marc Rölli, 363–74. München: Wilhelm Fink Verlag.

Smith, Douglas A., and Jody R. Klein. 1984. "Police Control of Interpersonal Disputes." *Social Problems* 31 (4): 468–81.

Spiro, Rand J. 1980. "Prior Knowledge and Story Processing: Integration, Selection, and Variation." *Poetics* 9: 313–27.

Spittler, Gerd. 1978. *Herrschaft über Bauern: die Ausbreitung staatlicher Herrschaft und einer islamisch-urbanen Kultur in Gobir (Niger)*. Frankfurt/Main: Campus-Verlag.

———. 1980. "Konfliktaustragung in akephalen Gesellschaften: Selbsthilfe und Verhandlung." In *Alternative Rechtsformen und Alternativen zum Recht*, edited by Erhard Blankenburg, Ekkehard Klausa, and Hubert Rottleuthner, 142–64. Opladen: Westdeutscher Verlag.

———. 1982. *Verwaltung in einem afrikanischen Bauernstaat: das koloniale Französisch-Westafrika 1919–1939*. Wiesbaden: Steiner.

Star, Susan L., and James R. Griesemer. 1989. "Institutional Ecology, 'Translations' and Boundary Objects: Amateurs and Professionals in Berkeley's Museum of Vertebrate Zoology, 1907–39." *Social Studies of Science* 19: 387–420.

Steinberg, Jonny. 2010. *Thin Blue: The Unwritten Rules of Policing South Africa*. Johannesburg: Jonathan Ball.

Stirrat, R. L. 2000. "Cultures of Consultancy." *Critique of Anthropology* 20 (1): 31–46.

Strathern, Marilyn. 1996. "Cutting the Network." *Journal of the Royal Anthropological Institute* 2 (3): 517–35.

Strati, Antonio. 1992. "Aesthetic Understanding of Organizational Life." *Academy of Management Review* 17 (3): 568–81.

Szreter, Simon, and Keith Breckenridge. 2012. "Editors' Introduction: Recognition and Registration: The Infrastructure of Personhood in World History." In *Registration and Recognition: Documenting the Person in World History*, edited by Keith Breckenridge and Simon Szreter, 1–36. Oxford: Oxford University Press.

Tamari, Tal. 2006. "Joking Pacts in Sudanic West Africa: A Political and Historical Perspective." *Zeitschrift für Ethnologie* 131 (2): 215–43.

Taussig, Michael. 1996. "The Injustice of Policing: Prehistory and Rectitude." In *Justice and Injustice in Law and Legal Theory*, edited by Austin Sarat and Thomas R. Kearns, 19–34. Ann Arbor: University of Michigan Press.

Taylor, Charles. 1985. *Philosophy and the Human Sciences: Philosophical Papers 2*. Cambridge: Cambridge University Press.

Taylor, Steven S., and Hans Hansen. 2005. "Finding Form: Looking at the Field of Organizational Aesthetics." *Journal of Management Studies* 42 (6): 1211–31.

Tidjani Alou, Mahamane. 2001. "La dynamique de l'État post colonial au Niger." In *Le Niger: État et démocratie*, edited by Kimba Idrissa, 85–126. Paris: L'Harmattan.

———. 2006. "Corruption in the Legal System." In *Everyday Corruption and the State: Citizens and Public Officials in Africa*, edited by Giorgio Blundo and Jean-Pierre Olivier de Sardan, 137–76. Cape Town: Philip.

———. 2008. "Les militaires politiciens." In *Armée et politique au Niger*, edited by Kimba Idrissa, 93–124. Dakar: CODESRIA.

———. 2009. "La chefferie au Niger et ses transformations: de la chefferie coloniale à la chefferie post coloniale." *Etudes et Travaux du LASDEL*, no. 76, accessed December 19, 2018, http://www.lasdel.net/images/etudes_et_travaux/La_chefferie_au_Niger_et_ses_transformations.pdf.

Tonkin, Elizabeth. 2000. "Autonomous Judges: African Ordeals as Dramas of Power." *Ethnos: Journal of Anthropology* 65 (3): 366–86.

Touchard, Théodore, and Charles Lacoste. 1860. *Histoire de la Gendarmerie d'Afrique et de la Colonie: d'après les documents de l'arme, de 1830 à 1860*. Alger: Librairie Algérienne de Dubos.

Turner, Frederick Jackson. 1921. *The Frontier in American History*. New York: Henry Holt and Company.

Turner, Victor W. 1979. "Dramatic Ritual/Ritual Drama: Performative and Reflexive Anthropology." *Kenyon Review* n.s. 1 (3): 80–93.

——. 1980. "Social Dramas and Stories about Them." *Critical Inquiry* 7 (1): 141–68.

——. 1985. *On the Edge of the Bush: Anthropology as Experience*. Tucson: University of Arizona Press.

——. 1986. "Dewey, Dilthey, and Drama: An Essay in the Anthropology of Experience." In *The Anthropology of Experience*, edited by Victor W. Turner and Edward M. Bruner, 33–44. Urbana: University of Illinois Press.

——. 1989 [1969]. *The Ritual Process: Structure and Anti-Structure*. New York: Aldine.

Valier, Claire. 2002. "Punishment, Border Crossings, and the Powers of Horror." *Theoretical Criminology* 6 (3): 319–37.

van Dijk, Rijk. 2001. "'Voodoo' on the Doorstep: Young Nigerian Prostitutes and Magic Policing in the Netherlands." *Africa* 71 (4): 558–86.

Van Maanen, John. 1981. "The Informant Game: Selected Aspects of Ethnographic Research in Police Organizations." *Journal of Contemporary Ethnography* 9 (4): 469–94.

Verne, Markus. 2004. "Das provozierte Geschenk: Rhetoriken des Schnorrens in einem nigrischen Hausadorf: Formen, Folgen und theoretische Implikationen." In *Blick nach vorn: Festgabe für Gerd Spittler zum 65. Geburtstag*, edited by Kurt Beck, 171–85. Köln: Köppe.

Võsu, Ester. 2010. "Metaphorical Analogies in Approaches of Victor Turner and Erving Goffman: Dramaturgy in Social Interaction and Dramas of Social Life." *Sign Systems Studies* 38 (1): 130–66.

Waddington, P. A. J. 1999. *Policing Citizens: Authority and Rights*. London: UCL Press.

Weber, Eugen. 1976. *Peasants into Frenchmen: The Modernization of Rural France, 1870–1914*. Stanford, CA: Stanford University Press.

Weber, Max. 1980 [1921]. *Wirtschaft und Gesellschaft: Grundriss der verstehenden Soziologie*. Tübingen: Mohr-Siebeck.

Weick, Karl E. 1995. *Sensemaking in Organizations*. Thousand Oaks, CA: Sage.

Weller, Jean-Marc. 1999. *L'État au guichet: sociologie cognitive du travail et modernisation administrative des services publics*. Paris: Éditions Desclée de Brouwer.

Wender, Jonathan M. 2008. *Policing and the Poetics of Everyday Life*. Urbana, IL: University of Illinois Press.

Wiseman, Boris. 2007. *Lévi-Strauss, Anthropology, and Aesthetics*. Cambridge: Cambridge University Press.

Witte, Annika. 2011. "Grey Areas: How Beninese Policemen Conduct Their Work and Shape the Police's Image." Paper presented in the panel Bureaucrats in Uniform: Historical and Anthropological Explorations of an African Professional Field, Fourth European Conference on African Studies in Uppsala, June 2011.

Wright, Martin, and Burt Galaway, eds. 1989. *Mediation and Criminal Justice: Victims, Offenders, and Community*. London: Sage.

Zangaou, Moussa. 2008. "Femmes en uniforme dans les secteurs militaire et para-militaire au Niger." In *Armée et politique au Niger*, edited by Kimba Idrissa, 255–88. Dakar: CODESRIA.

Zauberman, Renée. 2001. "The French Gendarmerie: Crossing Sociological and Historical Perspectives." *Crime, Histoire and Sociétés / Crime, History and Societies* 5 (2): 149–56.

Index

CPSIA information can be obtained
at www.ICGtesting.com
Printed in the USA
LVHW091354260220
648271LV00001BA/277